JUNG AND THE JUNGIANS ON MYTH

An Introduction

Steven F. Walker

GARLAND PUBLISHING, Inc.
New York & London / 1995

Library of Congress Cataloging-in-Publication Data

Walker, Steven F.
Jung and the Jungians on myth : an introduction / Steven F. Walker
p. cm. — (Theorists of myth ; vol. 4)
(Garland reference library of the humanities ; vol. 1163)
Includes bibliographical references.
ISBN 0-8240-3443-0 (alk. paper)
1. Myth—Psychological aspects. 2. Jung, C.G. (Carl Gustav),
1875–1961. I. Title. II. Series.
III. Series: Garland reference library of the humanities ; vol. 1163.
BF175.5.M95W35 1994
291.1'3'019—dc20   94-15753

Printed on acid-free, 250-year-life paper
Manufactured in the United States of America

For Swami Sarvagatananda

Contents

Series Editor's Foreword   ix

Introduction   xi

Chapter One—Mythology and the Archetypes of the
   Collective Unconscious   3
      Instinct and Archetype   5
      Archetype and Archetypal Image   12
      Archetypal Image and Myth   15
      Myth as Compensation   19
Chapter Two—The Strange Mythology of the Psyche: The
   Shadow, Anima, and Animus   29
      The Shadow   33
      The Anima and the Animus   45
Chapter Three—The Strange Mythology of the Psyche: The
   Hero, Wise Old Man, Great Mother, Divine Child, and
   Self   63
      The Wise Old Man   72
      The Great Mother   76
      The Divine Child: *Puer Aeternus*   81
      The Self   83
Chapter Four—The Jungian Analysis of Myth   91
      The Role of Myth in Culture: Myth as Compensation   96
      Myth and Inflation   102
      Myth and Politics   104
      Neumann and Myths of the Great Mother   109
      "The Purest Expression": Von Franz on Fairy Tales   113
      Alchemy and Psychology   116
      The Holy Grail   119

Chapter Five—New Orientations and Developments   125
    Archetypal Dimensions of Daily Life   125
    Gods and Goddesses in Everyone   128
    Symbolic Interpretation and the Remythologization
      of Religion   132
    Jungian Primitivism   136
    Jungian (Archetypal) Criticism   143
    Recent Controversies and Debates   150
Selected Bibliography   165

Series Editor's Foreword

Theories of myth are always derivative. They are theories of something underlying—for example, society, culture, literature, and the mind—of which myth is a manifestation. Some theorists of the underlying domain themselves apply their theories to myth. Others leave the application to disciples. While Sigmund Freud, for instance, briefly analyzes the myth of Oedipus in his *Interpretation of Dreams*, the pioneering psychoanalytic interpretation of myth was left largely to followers like Karl Abraham, Otto Rank, and Géza Róheim. By contrast, Carl Jung did much of his own pioneering application, and his writings brim with invocations of myths worldwide.

While, then, no introduction to Jung's psychology can avoid the topic of myth, Steven F. Walker's book is distinctive because it focuses on myth. Writing as a sympathetic yet not uncritical devotee, Walker presents the Jungian view of both the origin and the function of myth, and he considers the function of myth for not only the individual but also society. In both cases, the chief function is compensatory: myth serves to raise to consciousness heretofore untended aspects of the societal and individual personality and thereby to promote balance or wholeness. The achievement of that aim requires a middle ground between wholesale identification with myth and outright rejection of it. Walker spells out the fateful consequences of overidentification for society and the individual alike.

Walker's book is distinctive not only in its concentration on myth but also in its extensive reliance on Jung's letters and seminar notes rather than on the Collected Works alone. He relies as well on Jung's autobiography, *Memories, Dreams, Reflections*, since he wishes to connect Jungian theory to Jung's internal life—his dreams and visions—as well as to his external life—his contacts, his relationships, his analysands, his studies, and his travels. Walker also ties Jung's views to cultural and political events of the time.

The author carefully disentangles various concepts that Jungians themselves sometimes blur. Instinct gets distinguished from archetype, archetype gets distinguished from archetypal image, and image gets distinguished from symbol. Walker explicates such commonly bandied terms as constellation, projection, inflation, and individuation. He explains the differences between myth on the one hand and dream and fantasy on the other. He gives special attention to Jung's particular fascination with alchemy, though not, it might be noted, to his almost equal fascination with Gnosticism.

Attention is also given to the work of Jung's disciples and successors, especially the work of Erich Neumann, who was particularly concerned with myths of the Great Mother archetype, and of Marie-Louise von Franz, who has been especially interested in fairy tales as expressions of the self archetype. Walker details the contemporary Jungian emphasis on the mythological nature of ordinary, daily experience and not just of extraordinary, "peak" experience. At the same time he describes the spur by the New Age movement, by feminism, and by the men's movement toward the quest for divinity within human beings—a quest which for traditional Jungian psychology would veer on inflation. Finally, Walker outlines the radical, archetypal psychology of James Hillman and David Miller, with its stress on Greco-Roman polytheism rather than on biblical monotheism.

Drawing frequently on Western myths of various kinds to illustrate his insights, Walker, whose professional field is comparative literature, provides a lucid, comprehensive, and exciting overview of the emergence and development of the Jungian approach to mythology.

Robert A. Segal

Introduction

This book constitutes a concise and sympathetic presentation of Carl Gustav Jung and of some of his outstanding followers as theoreticians of myth. C.G. Jung was never more insightful and intriguing and at the same time more baffling and outrageous than when he discussed mythology. The remarks he made concerning it in the course of his long life (1875–1961) resist facile summary and reduction. The reader encountering for the first time Jungian ideas concerning myths and their unsuspected presence in modern psychology and culture may need to work at keeping an open mind and to accept provisionally a number of hypotheses that seem to run counter to common sense, especially Jung's theory of the collective unconscious as the wellspring of the imagery of mythology. Yet the reader who perseveres in the quest will discover that Jung and his followers open up theoretical perspectives that provide further new insights into the psychological significance of mythology.

To set out on this quest for meaning requires, however, that the student of mythology understand beforehand a fair amount of Jungian psychology—"analytical psychology," as it is commonly designated by Jungians. Thus a large portion of this book will be taken up with a systematic presentation of what the reader needs to know in order to begin to make use of Jungian ideas in the study of mythological texts. The work of pioneering thinkers has often suffered from well-meaning attempts to simplify the complexities of their thought. Narrow reductionism and the uncritical glossing over of difficulties have been the frequent result. I hope that my own attempt at clear exposition and systematic elaboration will not lead to a misleading simplification of Jungian ideas but rather will serve to encourage the reader to deal more actively and critically with the theoretical bases of Jungian thought.

Since Jung discusses myth haphazardly and unsystematically for the most part, the second service this book will perform for its readers will be to present a short account of Jung's theoretical approaches to the study of mythology, along with suggestions on how to apply these theoretical perspectives to myths and to cultural texts in which myths are present and play a major role. My own training in comparative literature no doubt leads me to favor the application of Jungian theory to myths taken primarily as narrative texts, but I hope to highlight at least some of the potential interest that Jungian perspectives on mythology can have for other fields such as anthropology, art, folklore, history, political science, and religion.

For purposes of illustration and quotation I will draw not only on Jung's major writings published during his lifetime but also on his more informal utterances in letters, interviews, and seminars. These texts frequently have the advantage of presenting in plain language what Jung's formal writings in academic German sometimes fail to state as clearly or as engagingly. The slow growth in Jung's reputation, as compared with Freud's, must be at least partially due to Jung's reluctance to express himself in easily comprehensible terms. Unlike Freud, Jung did not have the popular polemicist's touch, and much of his writing is hard going for the casual reader. Only in the last years of his life did Jung succeed in reaching a wider audience, with *Answer to Job* (1952), *The Undiscovered Self* (1957), his posthumously published autobiography *Memories, Dreams, Reflections* (1961–2), and the essay "Approaching the Unconscious," which was written in English shortly before his death as the keynote chapter for *Man and His Symbols*, a popular introduction to his psychology which he edited himself. No doubt there are real treasures of insightful aphorism to be found at every turn in the forest of Jung's academic German writings, but the value of his more informal pronouncements—lively, frequently humorous, and delightfully unstuffy—should not be neglected or underestimated. The letters of his old age are especially valuable, since by then Jung had a perspective on his own life and work that only the passage of time could have provided. The frequent occasions when Jung was obliged to speak or write in English— even when his English was slightly incorrect or unidiomatic— may have helped him attain greater simplicity and clarity in his formulations. The translations of Jung's German works into English (mainly by his devoted translator R.F.C. Hull) are uniformly excellent; still, Jung's "plain English" sometimes reaches the American reader more directly. These English quotations, in texts published for the most part in the last ten or twenty years, also have the advantage of not having been endlessly cited or anthologized in standard introductions to Jung's psychology; consequently they may be of unexpected value even to seasoned Jungians.

My editor, Robert A. Segal, has been consistently kind, supportive, and constructively critical. This book owes much to his friendly encouragement as well as to his dedication to high standards as an editor. On a somewhat outrageously mytho-poetic note, I would also like to thank the three Graces who have presided over the birth of this little book. My humble offerings thus go to the nymph of the spring Arethusa, whose waters have done much to wash the *puer* out of me; to Janet, for many lively and productive discussions about Jung and Jungian psychology over the years; and finally, with some trepidation, to the ever youthful Fr. S.W., Jungian muse and *anima extraordinaire*.

This book is dedicated to Swami Sarvagatananda, head of the Ramakrishna Vedanta Society of Massachusetts. His sense of the psyche as a gateway to the spirit is something I have only begun to assimilate.

Jung and the Jungians on Myth

CHAPTER ONE

Mythology and the Archetypes of the Collective Unconscious

The road leading from C.G. Jung's concept of the archetypal world of the collective unconscious to the world of mythology is a rocky one, theoretically speaking. Jung was not a philosopher, and his thought proceeded through intuitive leaps, not logical progressions. His terminology is vague enough to create misunderstandings on a purely formal level, not to speak of the natural difficulties involved in communicating the intellectual system resulting from a highly introspective probing of the human mind.

The key to understanding the Jungian approach to mythology lies, in my opinion, in the concept of *image*. By emphasizing the image over the word, Jungian psychology differentiates itself radically from Freudian, Lacanian, and other psychologies that stress the task of interpreting the *language* of the unconscious. The term first used by Jung to designate what he would later call an *archetype* of the collective unconscious was *urtümliches Bild* ("primordial image"), a phrase Jung borrowed from the great nineteenth-century historian Jacob Burckhardt.[1] Late in his life Jung gave what was probably the most vivid illustration of his theory of the archetypes as containing latent images of instinct in humans and animals alike when he wrote that the form of an instinct,

> when represented to the mind, appears as an *image* which expresses the nature of the instinctive impulse visually and concretely, like a picture. If we could look inside the psyche of the yucca moth, for instance, we would find in it a pattern of ideas, of a numinous or fascinating character, which not only compel the moth to carry out its fertilizing

3

activity on the yucca plant, but help it "recognize" the total situation.[2]

Since the term *archetype* designates an unconscious and unrepresentable element of the instinctual structure of the human psyche, the more proper term to use for one of the pictures of an archetype that the human mind is capable of representing is *archetypal image*. However, even though the term archetypal image proves useful in differentiating an unconscious archetype from an image or representation of it in human consciousness, both Jung and his followers frequently, though incorrectly, use archetype and archetypal image interchangeably.

From the treasure house of archetypal images are drawn the elements, the *archetypal motifs*, of mythology. Whether represented visually, dramatically, musically, or verbally, these motifs are usually found linked in a sequence, which we call a *myth*. Myths are thus not purely spontaneous products of the psyche; they are *culturally elaborated*. Over the centuries innumerable cultures have created a bewildering variety of myths out of the common human fund of the archetypal images of the collective unconscious. Mythology as a whole therefore constitutes a mirror for the collective unconscious, which is the common psychological basis for all human life.

From the Jungian perspective, then, *myths* are essentially culturally elaborated representations of the contents of the deepest recesses of the human psyche: the world of the archetypes. Myths represent the unconscious archetypal, instinctual structures of the mind. They represent these structures not in an historical and cultural vacuum but rather as they are culturally elaborated and expressed in terms of the world view of a particular age and culture. Just as human instincts are the same universally, so the collective unconscious is the same for all human beings. If myths present such astonishing diversity, it is because of the various ways of representing them culturally as images of the psyche. The vast diversity of myths and symbolic images point, not to some universal message or monomyth (as Joseph Campbell seems to have concluded) valid for all human beings, but rather to a common human instinctual organization which Jungian psychology theorizes as the collective unconscious. Since the collective unconscious is the same for all, Jungians assume that, in spite of the bewilderingly rich diversity one finds in the full spectrum of world mythology, nothing in mythology is ever alien to us as modern human beings, nothing is ever totally culture-bound. Every myth, however peculiar or exotic, contains the potential for revealing indirectly some unforeseen or neglected aspect of the human psyche.

Instinct and Archetype

In Jungian terminology, myths are ultimately expressions of archetypes. But what is an *archetype*?

At various times and in various ways Jung attempted to define this key term. For example, in 1959 a zoology student in Zurich, who apparently considered the aged Jung a Wise Old Man or "guru" (the word used by Jung in his friendly reply to the student's letter), had sent him some offprints of his scientific publications. In reply, Jung reformulated his definition of "archetype" in terms of the student's own biological interests. Jung wrote, "for me the archetype means: an image of a probable sequence of events, an habitual current of psychic energy. To this extent it can be equated with the biological pattern of behaviour."[3] Now Jung had frequently speculated over the years about the relationship between archetype and pattern of behavior, but this late reformulation underlines the biological dimension of the archetypes of the collective unconscious with particular clarity. It is also completely in line with his earlier definitions, which had asserted that archetypes represent different aspects of the human instinctual structure, inasmuch as human beings, like animals, are creatures of instinct.

Later that same year Jung, in a letter written in English, defined archetypes as "instinctual forms of mental functioning." He then underlined most of the following sentence: "*they are not inherited ideas, but mentally expressed instincts, forms and not con-*tents."[4]

In another letter in English written a few months later, Jung seems close to equating archetypes and instincts, stating that "our instincts (i.e., archetypes) are biological facts." He goes on to explain the archetype's "spontaneity" as well as its "functional relation to the actual situation," with special reference to the archetype of the "helpful divine being." When people feel themselves to be in danger, he writes, "even people who can boast of no particular religious belief find themselves compelled by fear to utter a fervent prayer." As a result of this prayer, he explains, the archetype of a "helpful divine being" "is constellated by their submission and may eventually intervene with an unexpected influx of strength, or an unforeseen saving impulse, producing at the last moment a turn in the threatening situation which is felt to be miraculous."[5] In this way at the end of his career Jung continues to insist on the close connection between the biological sphere and the psychological, between instinctually based behavior patterns and the archetypes of the collective unconscious.

Let us examine more closely the association in Jung's thought between instinct and archetype. In the last essay he wrote for publication, the 1961 essay "Approaching the Unconscious," written in English for the volume *Man and His Symbols*, Jung made his final attempt to clarify the "relation between instincts and archetypes" in the following terms: "what we properly call instincts are physiological urges, and are perceived by the senses. But at the same time they also manifest themselves in fantasies and often reveal their presence only by symbolic images. These manifestations are what I call archetypes."[6] Jung uses, as he and other Jungians do frequently, the term "archetype" for "archetypal image," but there is no need for us to quibble. What is clear is that once again the term *image* is the key to understanding archetypes. While the archetypes are in and of themselves unknowable, they are known indirectly through their effects, that is, through the images they produce in the mind. These images are their psychological "effects" in the same way that actions are the natural effects of instinctual, physiological urges.

But archetypes express themselves not only through images passively reflected in the mirror of the conscious mind but also through a kind of "suggestive effect" that, like that of the instincts, tends to stimulate action. In 1957 Jung was interviewed and filmed in his home at Küsnacht near Zurich by the psychologist Richard I. Evans of the University of Houston. In the first of these interviews Jung was asked to elaborate on his concept of the archetype. He brought up the "behavior pattern" of animals, citing his favorite example of the way in which the weaver bird builds its nest. He qualified the analogy by saying that the weaver bird may or may not be conscious of a mental image while it weaves its nest. That is, the archetypal image may not be present in animals' response to instinctual behavior patterns, as tends to be the case with humans.[7] The relevance of such animal behavior patterns to human life may be seen, he said, in situations when "you are seized by an emotion or by a spell, and you behave in a certain way you have not foreseen at all."[8] This kind of unpremeditated act stems from the "suggestive effect" of an archetype.

Jung illustrates such an act by referring to a well-known event in Swiss history, the assassination of Albrecht I by his nephew Johannes and his cohorts in 1308. Albrecht's would-be assassins were riding with him on a journey, and they remained plagued by doubt and indecision, unable to bring themselves to murder him; but the moment Albrecht rode into the ford of the river Reuss near Zurich, they set upon him immediately and spontaneously. This change of heart, for Jung, demonstrated the strength of the "suggestive effect" of the archetype of "the passage of the ford"[9] that had been "constellated" (activated or stimulated) in their unconscious. The sight of Albrecht riding into the river had suggested to Johannes and his men the metaphorical need to "cross the Rubicon," to take decisive action, to kill the king. Jung commented elsewhere on this event:

> the ford is the natural ambush, the place where the hero
> slays the dragon. Then suddenly Johannes found it in him
> to do the deed; the archetype was constellated.[10]

What proof is there, however, that archetypes actually exist? Jung seems satisfied with the argument that the only scientific proof for a scientific hypothesis lies in its *applicability*: "the idea of the archetype explains more than any other theory."[11] But others may not be so easily contented, since any argument for the existence of archetypes and instincts can only be based on the existence of their concrete manifestations. Falling in love and other "archetypal situations" may be alleged to derive from *a priori* conditioning factors of the human mind, whether one calls these factors archetypes or instincts. But the existence of these situations does not in and of itself provide any definitive proof for the existence of the archetypes of the collective unconscious; ultimately, the existence of archetypes may be only a useful, if very useful, hypothesis.

The idea of the biological basis of the archetypes was well anchored in Jung's mind in his later years. Does he thereby consider that the archetypes, those "living dispositions . . . that preform and continually influence our thoughts and feelings and actions,"[12] are *inherited* genetically? In 1958, writing to his British colleague Michael Fordham, Jung emphasizes that "we follow patterns as the weaver-bird does." He goes on to add that "the assumption . . . that the . . . archetypes are inherited is for many reasons far more probable than that they are handed down by tradition." Nevertheless, in the final analysis, "it is an entirely secondary question"[13] whether archetypes are inherited; the *fact* of their existence, and not the *cause* of their existence, is the primary question for Jung.

Still, Jung seems comfortable with the idea of "inherited archetypes."[14] But it is the form (for example, the instinctual capacity to experience sexual desire) and not the content (for example, the particular way the individual actually experiences or imagines sexual desire) that is inherited. In a foreword written in 1948 for the third edition of his early (1909) essay "The Significance of the Father in the Destiny of the Individual,"[15] Jung refers several times to the "inherited structure" of the human personality on which has been "imprinted" all the varieties of normal human situations. He accounts for this imprinting by the fact that these situations have occurred over and over again in the long history of the human race.

Jung's earlier position was much influenced by Freud. Jung initially believed that the obstacles to psychological health were constituted by "the long-forgotten psychic contents of childhood."[16] Now he believes that the parameters of human life—the limits placed on spontaneous activity—are the result of patterns established not only in childhood but also and more fundamentally in the course of human evolution. These patterns are presumably present at birth in every individual as part of the general human "instinctual substrate." In his introduction to the first of his contributions to a work coauthored with Carl Kerényi, the 1941–2 *Essays on a Science of Mythology*, Jung had already speculated that the collective structural elements of the psyche were inherited in the same way as the physical aspects of the body.[17] Yet in his essay for *Man and His Symbols* written just before his death, Jung states that the archetypes are "of unknown origin."[18]

Perhaps the easiest way to negotiate this rough stretch of a rocky theoretical road is not to require of Jung the logical rigor of the systematic thinker that he is not, but rather to appreciate the *tentativeness* of his formulations. As an empiricist, he remained open to the possibility of new conclusions based on new data and developments. It may be wisest to conclude that for Jung the archetypes *may* be inherited, but their direct as well as their ultimate origins, whether biological or psychoid, remain somewhat of a mystery.

The *collective unconscious* (*das kollektive Unbewusste*) is a term that most centrally captures Jung's particular contribution to the study of myth. Appropriately enough, when he was asked in his last years what myth or central idea had made his life meaningful, Jung had answered without hesitation that it was the collective unconscious.[19]

The collective unconscious belongs to a category of ideas that posit a universal human nature—one that, if not eternal, is at least very slow in changing. The concept of a universal human nature was one of the great democratic ideas of the Enlightenment, whether expressed by Rousseau's evocation of humanity in a state of nature or as developed later by Romantics such as Henry David Thoreau, who uses the same biological analogy as Jung in *Walden*: "the improvements of ages have had but little influence on the essential laws of man's existence; as our skeletons, probably, are not to be distinguished from those of our ancestors."[20]

In his essay "The Archetypes of the Collective Unconscious," Jung provides a succinct description of the collective unconscious as the *image* of the results of humanity's long psychological evolution:

The collective unconscious, being the repository of man's experience and at the same time the prior condition of this experience, is an image of the world which has taken aeons to form. In this image certain features, the archetypes or dominants, have crystallized out in the course of time. They are the ruling powers, the gods, images of the dominant laws and principles, and of typical, regularly occurring events in the soul's cycle of experience.[21]

The archetypes, as inherited structures, belong to the collective unconscious of the human race and may be said to constitute the images as well as the essential laws of human nature as humanity has slowly evolved over the ages. There are as many archetypes as there are "normal human situations" and relationships over which they preside, from getting into a fight (the "throat-grappling instinct" that Stephen Crane anatomizes in *The Red Badge of Courage*) to falling in love like Romeo and Juliet. We have already cited Jung's evocation of two of them: the archetype of the *helpful divine being*, and the archetype of the *ford*. Jung would later say that it was Freud who discovered the first archetype—the incest problem or Oedipus complex—but that unfortunately Freud interpreted it along purely personalistic lines.[22] Other leading archetypes discussed by Jung include the archetypes of the *mother*, the *father*, the *child*, the *anima* and the *animus*, the *hero*, the *trickster*, and the *Self*.

The list of archetypes is nearly endless, since each archetype is said to correspond to some variety of human situation. Archetypes prepare and prompt human beings to react instinctively and spontaneously to the presence of parents, of children, of male or female lovers, and so on. For Jung, one does not discover through experience alone what a mother is. The mother archetype predisposes one to discover in the world a "mother." The actual experience of the flesh and blood parenting mother merely "constellates" or "stimulates"[23] the mother archetype. Human beings are naturally inclined to seek something resembling a mother in the outside world, because the behavioral pattern of "being mothered" is already imprinted on our unconscious by the mother archetype.

In similar fashion the presence of a sexually attractive person of the opposite sex constellates the *anima* or the *animus*.

Especially after Michel Foucault's *History of Sexuality*, it is clear that human sexuality is far more of a social construction than previously thought. Nevertheless, sexual desire does not originate *only* in our experience of the world, nor does it manifest itself *only* along the lines laid down by our culture and society. And, however important reason, experience, and custom as well as conscious individual ethical decisions may be in determining how we channel and express our desire, we respond *spontaneously* to someone whose presence excites us sexually, without knowing exactly why. This is because the unconscious *anima/animus* contrasexual archetypes are already present in us from birth, and when these archetypes become *constellated* or stimulated by the presence of someone attractive, they put pressure on us to respond, as lovers have traditionally insisted, "in spite of ourselves."

The question might still be raised, of course, whether the archetypal basis is the same for all humanity, or whether it varies from racial group to racial group, and from culture to culture. In the 1930s Jung had made some tactless remarks which purported to distinguish the Jewish from the Aryan psyche, and the European from the Asian psyche. Although it is clear in retrospect that Jung was neither a racist nor a Nazi sympathizer and that in the 1930s he could be called at worst politically naive concerning the dangers presented by the Nazi regime,[24] nevertheless his remarks raised the specter of psychological distinctions based on race, and the possibility of justifying racial discrimination by pointing to alleged racial differences and disparities in archetypal psychic inheritance.[25]

Fortunately, except for a few brief lapses in the 1930s, Jung was consistent in his references to the archetypes of the collective unconscious as the common psychic inheritance of all humanity. One example will illustrate his position particularly well. From 1934 to 1939 Jung gave a seminar to a small circle of students and colleagues at the Zurich Psychological Club on Nietzsche's *Thus Spake Zarathustra*. A student in the seminar called the figure of the ancient Persian sage Zarathustra an "archetype . . . of a foreign race" in the course of a question concerning the effect of such a powerful figure on Nietzsche's own psychology, and asked Jung whether he felt that "the fact that this power, this unconscious force in him, does belong to another race," was of any importance. Jung replied, in somewhat incorrect English, that "there are no strange [i.e., "foreign"] archetypes. They are generally human, everybody practically contains the basic psyche and therefore the same archetypes as other races."[26]

If the archetypes constitute the common instinctual substratum of all humanity, why do myths, which owe their existence to the archetypes of the collective unconscious, present such a bewildering variety? To respond to this possible objection to the theory of a single human archetypal inheritance it is necessary to distinguish between an *archetype* and an *archetypal image*.

Archetype and Archetypal Image

An archetype is *not* the same thing as an archetypal image or representation, although Jungians, and Jung himself, frequently and misleadingly use the term "archetype" when they actually mean "archetypal image." Needless misunderstandings could have been avoided if the two terms had been more consistently distinguished. Jung was occasionally moved to clarify this distinction: "the perceptible archetypal image is not identical with the inherited thought-form [i.e., archetype], which allows an indefinite number of empirical expressions,"[27] he wrote to his English translator R.F.C. Hull after what had amounted to half a lifetime of misunderstandings. The interchangeable use of the term *archetype* and the term *archetypal image*, however sanctioned by Jungian tradition, is confusing and unjustifiable, since the archetypal image, as Jung himself made clear on a number of occasions, is "not identical with the archetype itself," which remains unknowable by the conscious mind. In fact, the image, since it is "the symbolic formulation of the instinct itself," is "our only means of recognizing the manifestation of an instinctual [i.e., archetypal] situation."[28]

The differences between archetype and archetypal image include the following:

(1) An *archetype* is probably inherited; the *archetypal image* is not. Jung frequently puts forward the analogy of the archetype with the invisible axial system of a crystal, which "preforms the crystalline structure in the mother liquid, although it has no material existence of its own." The *form* (the archetype), like the axial system of a crystal, is "a possibility of representation which is given *a priori*" and so it is determined and inherited. But the *content* (the archetypal image) is the result of the archetype's becoming conscious and being "filled out with the material of conscious experience."[29]

(2) An *archetype* is, on account of its transcendence in the Kantian sense, irrepresentable.[30] It cannot be known directly; its existence can only be inferred from its effects. When, for example, one falls in love, an archetype (the *anima* or the *animus*) has been constellated or stimulated. One does not perceive the archetype itself; one only experiences its effect. One falls in love without knowing why. The instinctual pattern/archetype itself remains hidden from consciousness. For that reason the effect of the archetype (falling in love) seems spontaneous, without any significant apparent cause.

An *archetypal image*, by contrast, can be perceived, as in dreams, visions and fantasies. A vague but dazzling image of the beloved, owing more to the effect of constellated anima or animus than to any realistic perception of the person of the beloved, obsesses the lover's imagination. This archetypal image can also be represented in terms of the cultural codes presiding over the depiction of symbols. For instance, the picture of a heart struck by an arrow chalked on a wall or depicted on the Valentine sent to the beloved would be our culture's artistic representation of one perceivable archetypal image associated with love. An *archetype*, of course, can no more be directly represented than an atom or the axial system of a crystal.

(3) There is a single *archetype* for each human situation, but there is "an indefinite number of empirical expressions" for each archetype. That is, there are not only many

activities and patterns of thought associated with each archetype, but also many *archetypal images*. Thus one *archetype* can produce an indefinite number of *archetypal images*, which may be said to be "visualizations" or "personifications" of that archetype.[31] Images of gods and goddesses are cultural representations of archetypal images, not archetypes.

(4) *Archetypes* are conditions (*Bedingungen*) rather than pure causes. They condition our experience of life situations, but they are far from determining our experience completely. They express themselves in a variety of *archetypal images*, which can become culturally elaborated into myths and symbols. If archetypes were sufficient causes—if they could determine our actions and mental representations completely—they would presumably impose specific predetermined images of themselves on our consciousness. But they do not. Archetypal images vary not only across cultures but also within a particular culture.

Despite these differences between *archetypes* and *archetypal images*, the term *archetype* as actually employed by Jung and Jungians may refer to either. In such cases only the context allows one to make the distinction. Worse, *symbol*, which is a culturally elaborated representation in mythology, art, and ritual, is frequently used for *archetypal image*, which is a spontaneous representation in dreams, fantasies, and visions.

Jung was not a professional philosopher. When faced with philosophical objections to his theory of the archetypes, he frequently took refuge in scientific empiricism, the philosophy of his youth and early medical training. When challenged, he could seek to avoid argument by protesting that he was only interested as a scientist in "verifiable phenomena." As he wrote to the Swiss existential psychoanalyst Medard Boss, who had questioned the validity of his theoretical assumptions, "I have no philosophy regarding the archetype, only the experience of it."[32] As someone who early in his life had read Kant with profit, he would also protest that, since the archetypal realm was transcendent, it was for all practical purposes unknowable: "transcendence is simply that which is unconscious to us," he wrote, although he added "it cannot be established whether this is permanently inaccessible or only at present."[33] Time and time again Jung would insist that he was making no metaphysical statements about things that are ultimately unknowable, but simply describing psychological phenomena.

Nevertheless, Jung was always willing to rethink his assumptions, often in response to some correspondent's query. As he says in reply to someone who asked him to clarify the distinction between archetype and archetypal image:

> The "Christ archetype" is a false concept, as you say. Christ is not an archetype but a personification of the archetype. This is reflected in the idea [=archetype] of the Anthropos. . . . The spiritual (as contrasted with the worldly) Messiah, Christ, Mithras, Osiris, Dionysos, Buddha are all visualizations or personifications [=archetypal images] of the irrepresentable archetype which, borrowing from Ezechiel and Daniel, I call the Anthropos.[34]

We must now go on to examine how the archetypal image constitutes the bridge between archetypes and myths. It remains to be seen exactly how archetypes as "unconscious *a priori* determinants of imagination and behaviour" reach "conscious apperception in the human mind chiefly in the form of so-called mythological images."[35]

Archetypal Image and Myth

In a letter to Miguel Serrano, a Chilean diplomat and poet who spoke with Jung on several significant occasions during the last two years of his life, Jung writes cryptically about the archetypes not only as *a priori* determinants abstractly defined as "the psychic manifestations of the instincts," but also as "autonomous *animalia* gifted with a sort of consciousness and psychic life of their own." He adds that "whether we call them gods, demons, or illusions, they exist and function and are born anew with every generation."[36]

One might at first imagine that Jung is carelessly speaking of archetypal images under the guise of speaking of archetypes, since one could could conceivably attribute "a sort of consciousness" to a mythic *personification* of an archetype, be it Venus or Cupid or Wotan. But such is not the case. In the same letter Jung carefully distinguishes these strange animated beings (*animalia*), which are "curiously non-human"—these "living" archetypes—from the various and changing archetypal images that might represent them. "They are basic forms," he writes, "but not the manifest, personified, or otherwise concretized images. They have a high degree of autonomy, which does not disappear when the manifest images change."

In order to illustrate the relationship between "basic form" and "manifest image," Jung offers the example of the old Germanic god Wotan. The name "Wotan," as applied to the deity, refers to a "manifest image"—to a particular archetypal image that, through a process of cultural elaboration, became represented as the protagonist of a number of mythic tales. Underlying the various manifest images is the "basic form": the Wotan "phenomenon." Jung saw this Wotan phenomenon at work behind what he called the "spiritual catastrophe" of National Socialism. In a March 1936 article in the *Neue Schweizer Rundschau* he maintained that in the Hitler movement "Wotan the wanderer was on the move,"[37] and that Nazi Germany, the "land of spiritual catastrophes,"[38] had appealed to an archetypal force and had recklessly put itself in the hands of the god of storm and frenzy.

Jung's willingness to *personify* the archetypes of the unconscious is perhaps the most controversial dimension of his theory. It is one thing to describe archetypes as mental expressions of instincts. It is something else to describe them as animated beings with a consciousness of their own. At times Jung seems to have substituted a poetic and polytheistic view of the archetypes for a more soberly scientific, biological model.

As Anthony Storr has pointed out, the "tendency to personify" was a characteristic of Jung's thought throughout his life.[39] There is indeed a poet in Jung who, as he himself admits, disdains "rational, scientific language," and who, "in describing the living processes of the psyche, . . . deliberately and consciously" gives "preference to a dramatic, mythological way of thinking."[40] In so doing Jung operates as a mythological thinker, and demonstrates his unusual capacity not only to empathize with the archaic mythological world view, but also to actually operate within it and adopt it as his own.

Jung's empathic relationship with archaic mythological world views derives partly from a deeply fatalistic streak in his character. With some justified pessimism, after a lifetime during which two world wars, the Holocaust, and the creation of nuclear weapons had dashed many rational hopes concerning the future of humanity, Jung describes the modern human being to Serrano as "a being operated and manoeuvered by archetypal forces instead of his 'free will,' that is, his arbitrary egoism and his limited consciousness." The modern human being has been given signs that he is not entirely in control of his own destiny; like his primitive forebear, he needs to honor the divinities that shape his ends. "He should learn," wrote Jung, "that he is not master in his own house and that he should carefully study the other side of his psychic world which seems to be the true ruler of his fate."[41]

For the study of the "other side" of the psyche, the world of the archetypes of the collective unconscious, Jung finds mythology of inestimable value: "there are numbers of archetypal situations and the whole of them make up the world of mythology." He calls mythology "the textbook of the archetypes," adding that in mythology the unconscious psyche "is not rationally elucidated and explained, but simply represented like a picture or a story book."[42] As narrative, myth may even be said to be superior to conceptual modes of thought, in that its lively stories reflect a more faithful image of the archetypal realm, of the "living processes of the psyche." Thus Jung says that

> myth is the primordial language natural to these psychic processes, and no intellectual formulation comes anywhere near the richness and expressiveness of mythological imagery. Such processes are concerned with the primordial images [*Urbilder* = archetypes], and these are best and most succinctly reproduced by figurative language.[43]

Jung is wary of the use of overly abstract language or conceptual discourse in the area of depth psychology. For him, psychology is an empirical science concerned with experiences and facts, not with the construction of abstract systems of thought unrooted in the experience of the psyche—a project which he stigmatized as "metaphysical." Much that is rich, provocative, and rewarding in Jung's comments on myth derives from his colorful and poetic use of mythological language, which aims at conveying some of the uncanny and emotionally unsettling quality of the experience associated with the twilight zone of archetypal reality. As he wrote in 1942,

> The protean mythologem and the shimmering symbol express the processes of the psyche far more trenchantly and, in the end, far more clearly than the clearest concept; for the symbol not only conveys a visualization of the process but—and this is perhaps just as important—it also brings a re-experiencing of it, of that twilight which we can learn to understand only through inoffensive empathy, but which too much clarity only dispels.[44]

That myths can be considered as narrative elaborations of archetypal images (the conscious representations of the unconscious instincts) makes sense, once one accepts the proposition that archetypes were originally "situations," that they are imprinted patterns of behavior left behind by untold ages of human evolution. Seen from this perspective, myths are culturally elaborated "representations of situations." They enable us to re-experience consciously the unconscious instinctual processes of the psyche.

In fact, the transition from archetypal image to myth, from spontaneous representation of instinct to culturally elaborated verbal narrative, is not clearly delineated in Jung's writings. If the archetypes have not only a basis in instinct but also a psychic dimension (revealed, for example, when he refers to archetypes as "*animalia* gifted with a sort of consciousness and psychic life of their own"), then it is no wonder that an archetype can be represented by "a figure—be it daemon, a human being, or a process—that constantly . . . appears whenever creative fantasy is freely expressed. Essentially, therefore, it is a mythological figure."[45]

It is thus "creative fantasy"—the human imagination—that creates myths out of archetypal images. It is through a process of conscious, imaginative elaboration that spontaneously generated archetypal images become the specific culturally determined figures of mythology.

To summarize the process through which archetypal images become the basis for mythmaking: the conscious mind reflecting on the psyche may become aware of an *archetypal image*—put in Jung's own terms, there may occur in the mind an "unconscious activation of an archetypal image."[46] So far we are describing a passive process of perception, not an active process of creation. When, however, the creative imagination manufactures a myth out of elements (archetypal motifs) taken from the storehouse of the archetypal images, something more dynamic is at work. Mythmaking thus has to be viewed as an archaic form of artistic activity. As the active and conscious elaboration of an archetypal image, mythmaking brings what is relatively timeless (the archetypal image as a representation of the instinctual world of the archetypes) into the world of human history; mythmaking brings what is pre-cultural into the world of human culture. Since the *archetypal image* as *archetypal motif* becomes represented in a *myth* in the terms of a particular culture and of a particular moment in history, it is improper to consider a myth as ageless or as universal as an archetype, since it bears the particular stamp of the specific age and culture that produces it.

What is the function of myth in culture? To answer this question one must turn to Jung's concept of *compensation*.

Myth as Compensation

In Jungian theory, dreams are said to play a *compensatory* role in the psychological life of the individual. As manifestations of the activity of the unconscious part of the mind, dreams balance the one-sided activities and attitudes of ego-consciousness. The psyche, as a self-regulating system, thereby maintains a state of psychological homeostasis. In a similar fashion, myths, in the collective life of cultures, compensate for "the inadequacy and one-sidedness of the present."[47]

For Jung, society is essentially the individual psyche writ large. Just as the individual's conscious mind needs to be brought into greater harmony and balance with the countervailing tendencies of the unconscious, so a particular culture needs to readjust its collective perspectives through the agency of myth and symbol. It is the mythmaking artist, says Jung, who discovers the compensatory archetypal image that the age and the culture require for greater balance: "the artist seizes on this image, and in raising it from deepest unconsciousness he brings it into relation with conscious values, thereby trans-forming it until it can be accepted by the minds of his contemporaries according to their powers."[48]

For example, Ovid's *Metamorphoses*, the source for much of later Western culture's knowledge of Greco-Roman mythology, originally provided the power-oriented culture of the early Roman Empire with a multitude of compensatory myths of love and erotic adventure. While reading Ovid's gracefully amoral tales of love and frustrated desire, the modern reader easily forgets the military might and social moralism that characterized the age of Augustus. Ovid's poetry was in many ways an antidote to the Augustan spirit of seriousness. Unfortunately, an age is not always grateful for an artist's efforts to provide compensation, and Ovid ended his life in exile, possibly because he had come to be identified with a playful hedonistic spirit that was seen as subverting Augustan moralism and the consolidation of imperial power.

Another example might be the poets and artists of the Renaissance, whose elaboration of the myth of the Golden Age— the image of a simple but happy life enjoyed by the earliest human beings—may be seen as a effort at compensating for the growing complexity and disorientation of Renaissance life, increasingly cut loose from the stability of its medieval moorings and faced with the breakdown of feudal society. The Florentine artist Piero di Cosimo, for instance, was fascinated by the primitive dimensions of what he imagined to be the life of early humanity. He evoked this primeval mythic dimension of life in the wilds of nature in some of his most original paintings, and even his own lifestyle was deliberately and provocatively primitive. Yet the city of Florence, where he spent his life, was by 1500 the center of Renaissance sophistication and was by all accounts the least primitive urban civilization imaginable. Thus Piero di Cosimo's existential and artistic primitivism may be viewed as compensatory, both for himself as a sophisticated Renaissance artist and for his complex urban society.

Jung himself provides another example of the compensatory function of myth in his 1932 essay on James Joyce's *Ulysses*. Jung contrasts the compensatory "lack of feeling" in *Ulysses* with the "hideous sentimentality in the age that produced it."[49] Joyce wrote *Ulysses* during and just after World War I, and it is perspicacious of Jung to contrast the idealistic glorification of war and the patriotic enthusiasms of the period— all false feeling, in Jung's opinion—with the cool, unsentimental approach Joyce takes to his subject matter. Jung believes that in *Ulysses* Joyce's ironic distance and emotional disengagement compensate for the hideous sentimentality that had led to the massacre of millions during the First World War; better than false feeling is no feeling at all. (Many readers of *Ulysses* find much in the way of feeling in the novel, and a comic exuberance Jung seems to have missed completely; but Jung's theoretical point is well taken.)

Goethe's representation of the Faust myth was a constant source of fascination for Jung, much as the myth of Oedipus was for Freud. Goethe altered the traditional Faust myth radically by having his Renaissance scholar and magician fall in love with the innocent young girl Gretchen. Jung sees in Gretchen one of the archetypal images of the Eternal Feminine which compensates for the unbridled search for knowledge and experience of modern industrial civilization symbolized by Faust. Faust's quest is unchecked by ethical scruples or psychological misgivings. In Goethe's poetic drama the figure of Gretchen thus provides a "compensation for Faust's inhumanity," a female erotic compensation for male dreams of knowledge and power. In the wake of World War II Jung came to see the myth of Faust as having particular relevance to Germans. Faust, whose "avowed and unavowed worship of success stands in the way of any moral reflection," "remains the German idea of a human being, and therefore an image—somewhat overdone and distorted—of the average German."[50] The myth of Faust had the potential to bring to German cultural awareness that dangerous and unacknowledged propensity to seek success at any cost.

Jung intends his theory of compensation to apply specifically to the art and literature of modern European civilizations, but his theory applies to other societies as well. Jung, while undertaking journeys in the 1920s to Africa and America that brought him in contact with archaic cultures, remained fairly Eurocentric in his attitudes. But on more than one occasion Jung found it possible to enter completely into the spirit of an archaic culture and to understand it from the inner empathetic psychological standpoint he adopted toward his own modern European culture.

For example, his visit to the Taos Pueblo in New Mexico in January 1925 gave him the feeling that he had entered into a strangely congenial archaic culture. As he tells the story in *Memories, Dreams, Reflections,* he met a kindred spirit ("I was able to talk with him as I have rarely been able to talk with a European")[51] in the form of a Pueblo Indian chief by the name of Ochwiay Biano (Mountain Lake), with whom he would stay in correspondence for several years. Ochwiay Biano insisted vehemently, in the course of a discussion during which he protested America's hostility to his traditional religion, that, living on the roof of the world as the children of Father Sun, the Pueblo Indians helped the sun across the sky every day, and [were] therefore of benefit to all human beings. "I then realized," wrote Jung, "on what the 'dignity,' the tranquil composure of the individual Indian, was founded":

> It springs from his being a son of the sun; his life is cosmologically meaningful, for he helps the father and preserver of all life in his daily rise and descent. If we set against this our own self-justifications, the meaning of our own lives as it is formulated by our reason, we cannot help but see our poverty. . . . Knowledge does not enrich us; it removes us more and more from the mythic world in which we were once at home by right of birth.[52]

Without using the term "compensation" in his remarks, Jung has presented the mythic world as a potential means of compensation for the sense of meaninglessness that plagues modern culture, proud of its rationality but at the same time a prey to doubts and existential anguish. One can thus envy Ochwiay Biano, as one might envy any "true believer" in a mythic vision, for the sense of security that feeling at home in a myth can give.

But one might analyze the text further. Perhaps Jung's status as an affluent and fairly apolitical upper-middle class Swiss professional blinded him to the immediate context of the Pueblo chief's impassioned defense of his native religion: the white man's constant attempts to stamp it out. "Why can they not let us alone? What we do, we do not only for ourselves but for the Americans also."[53] For the myth that Ochwiay Biano puts forward—that the Pueblo Indians through the practice of their particular religion guarantee that the sun will continue to shine on all human beings, including the Americans who wish to stamp out their religion—may also be seen as a myth *compensating* for the Pueblo Indians' feelings of fear and worthlessness in the face of severe religious and cultural persecution. In fact, it may have constituted part of their cultural defense against such attacks on their traditional beliefs. An oppressed culture may well find in a myth that designates them as the Chosen People a compensatory vision that uplifts and inspires them in the midst of persecution. This reaction may have been that of the ancient Hebrews and of the early Christians. Such a myth inspires a sense of lofty superiority and spiritual strength that compensates for feelings of inferiority and helplessness in the face of materially and militarily superior forces. This reaction may even stimulate effective resistance to further cultural oppression.

As we have seen, Jung's theory of myth's compensatory role in a culture is based on the analogy with the role that, in the psychology of the individual, unconscious factors play in relationship to the conscious mind, when an archetype "is activated, independently of the will, in a psychic situation that needs compensating by an archetype."[54] Dreams, the royal road to the unconscious for Jungian no less than for Freudian psychology, are thus part of the general efforts of the psyche toward self-regulation. As Jung writes in his last essay "Approaching the Unconscious":

The general function of dreams is to try to restore our psychological balance by producing dream material that re-establishes, in a subtle way, the total psychic equilibrium. That is what I have called the complementary (or compensatory) role of dreams in our psychic make-up.[55]

In order to proceed further in the analysis of Jungian approaches to mythology, it is necessary to examine how Jung discovered in dreams and fantasies unexpected analogies to myths. This "strange mythology of the psyche" will be the topic of the next chapter.

NOTES

1.   See Richard C. Lewis, "The Historical Development of the Concept of the Archetype," *Quadrant*, 22 (1989), 47.

2.   Jung, *The Undiscovered Self*, trans. R.F.C. Hull (New York: New American Library, 1959), p. 81.

3.   Jung, *Letters, II, 1951–1961*, ed. Gerhard Adler in collaboration with Aniela Jaffé, trans. R.F.C. Hull (Princeton, N.J.: Princeton University Press, 1975), p. 505.

4.   Jung, letter dated November 16, 1959; in *Letters*, II, p. 521.

5.   Jung, letter dated February 9, 1960; in *Letters*, II, p. 541.

6.   In Jung et al., *Man and His Symbols* (New York: Dell Laurel Editions, 1968), p. 58.

7.   Jung, letter in English dated February 13, 1954; in *Letters*, II, pp. 151–2.

8.   William McGuire and R.F.C. Hull, eds., *C.G. Jung Speaking: Interviews and Encounters* (Princeton, N.J.: Princeton University Press, 1977), p. 293.

9.   For a more detailed discussion of the passage of the ford, see Jung, *Nietzsche's Zarathustra: Notes of the Seminar Given in 1934–1939*, ed. James L. Jarrett (Princeton, N.J.: Princeton University Press, 1988), I, pp. 22–4.

10. C.G. *Jung Speaking*, p. 213. This quotation comes from notes taken by Ximena de Angulo in 1952 during a session in which Jung commented orally on a doctoral thesis of Ira Progoff.

11. Jung, letter to E.A. Bennet dated May 22, 1960; in *Letters*, II, p. 558.

12. Jung, "Psychological Aspects of the Mother Archetype," in *Four Archetypes*, trans. R.F.C. Hull (Princeton, N.J.: Princeton University Press, 1970), p. 13.

13. Jung, letter dated June 14, 1958; in *Letters*, II, pp. 450–1.

14. Ibid., p. 451.

15. Jung, *The Psychoanalytic Years*, trans. R.F.C. Hull (Princeton, N.J.: Princeton University Press, 1974), p. 95.

16. Ibid., p. 96.

17. Jung and C. Kerényi, *Essays on a Science of Mythology*, trans. R.F.C. Hull (Princeton, N.J.: Princeton University Press, 1963), p. 74.

18. Jung et al., *Man and His Symbols*, p. 58.

19. E.A. Bennet, *Meetings with Jung: Conversations recorded during the years 1946–1961* (Zurich: Daimon, 1985), p. 101.

20. Henry David Thoreau, *Walden; or, Life in the Woods* (New York: New American Library, 1980), p. 13 (chapter on "Economy").

21. Jung, *Two Essays on Analytical Psychology*, trans. R.F.C. Hull (New York: Meridian Books, 1956), p. 105.

22. Bennet, p. 62.

23. In a letter in English to Father Victor White dated February 13, 1946, Jung gives "stimulate" as a near synonym for the Jungian term "constellate" (Jung, *Letters*, I, p. 414).

24. See Aniela Jaffé, "C.G. Jung and National Socialism" in her book *Jung's Last Years* (Dallas: Spring, 1984), pp. 78–98. The final word is probably to be found in the preface Andrew Samuels wrote to a recent paperback edition of Jung's *Essays on Contemporary Events: Reflections on Nazi Germany* (London: Routledge, 1988). According to Samuels, Jung "really did slip up, realized that, and tried to make amends."

25. For more detail, see the chapter "National Socialism: 'Yes, I Slipped Up'" in Gerhard Wehr, *Jung: A Biography*, trans. David M. Weeks (Boston: Shambhala, 1987), pp. 304–30. The phrase quoted by Samuels and Wehr, "Yes, I slipped up" (concerning Jung's initial failure to recognize the Nazis for the evil force they were), was allegedly said by Jung to the Berlin Rabbi Leo Baeck (who had accompanied his congregation to the concentration camp, where he was one of the few to

survive), during a long conversation after the War, after which the two were reconciled (Wehr, pp. 325–6, based on an account given in a letter by Gershom Scholem to Aniela Jaffé). Marie-Louise von Franz, however, disagrees with Jaffé; in her *C.G. Jung: His Myth in Our Time* (Boston: Little, Brown, 1977) she concludes that Jung's "therapeutic optimism," and not any unresolved shadow contents, led him to underestimate the evil tendencies of Nazism (pp. 63–4).

26. Jung, *Nietzsche's Zarathustra*, pp. 648–9.

27. Jung, letter in English dated August 15, 1958; in *Letters*, II, p. 461.

28. Jung, letter in English dated March 5, 1959; in *Letters*, II, p. 491.

29. Jung, *Four Archetypes*, p. 13.

30. See Jung's letter dated August 30, 1951; in *Letters*, II, p. 23.

31. See Jung's letter dated May 30, 1960; in *Letters*, II, p. 560.

32. Jung, letter dated June 27, 1947; in *Letters*, II, p. xl.

33. Jung, letter dated June 1957; in *Letters*, II, pp. 378–9.

34. Jung, letter dated June 1, 1956; in *Letters*, II, pp. 304–5.

35. Jung, letter in English dated February 9, 1956; in *Letters*, II, p. 289.

36. Jung, letter in English dated September 14, 1960; *Letters*, II, p. 563. This letter was published for the first time in Miguel Serrano's book *Jung and Hesse: A Record of Two Friendships* (New York: Schocken Books, 1966).

37. Jung, "Wotan," in *Essays on Contemporary Events*, trans. R.F.C. Hull (Princeton, N.J.: Princeton University Press, 1989), p. 11.

38. Ibid., p. 18.

39. Anthony Storr, *Jung* (London: Fontana/Collins, 1973), p. 13.

40. Jung, *Aion: Researches into the Phenomenology of the Self*, 2nd ed., trans. R.F.C. Hull (Princeton, N.J.: Princeton University Press, 1968), p. 13.

41. Jung, *Letters*, II, pp. 594–5.

42. Jung, *Nietzsche's Zarathustra*, I, p. 24.

43. Jung, *Psychology and Alchemy*, 2nd ed., trans. R.F.C. Hull (Princeton, N.J.: Princeton University Press, 1968), p. 25.

44. Jung, "Paracelsus as a Spiritual Phenomenon," in *Alchemical Studies*, trans. R.F.C. Hull (Princeton, NJ: Princeton University Press, 1968), p. 199.

45. Jung, "On the Relation of Analytical Psychology to Poetry," in *The Spirit in Man, Art, and Literature* (Princeton, N.J.: Princeton University Press, 1971), p. 81.

46. Ibid., p. 82.

47. Ibid., p. 83.

48. Ibid.

49. Jung, "*Ulysses*: a Monologue," in *The Spirit in Man, Art and Literature*, p. 122.

50. Jung, "After the Catastrophe" (1945), in *Essays on Contemporary Events*, p. 63.

51. Jung, *Memories, Dreams, Reflections*, ed. Aniela Jaffé, trans. Richard and Clara Winston (New York: Vintage Books, 1963), p. 247.

52. Ibid., p. 252.

53. Ibid., pp. 251–2.

54. Jung, letter in English dated February 9, 1960; in *Letters*, II, p. 541.

55. Jung et al., *Man and His Symbols*, p. 34.

CHAPTER TWO

The Strange Mythology of the Psyche: The Shadow, Anima, and Animus

C.G. Jung's foremost contribution as a theoretician of myth lies in his discovery of the presence of mythological motifs in dreams and fantasies. Not all dreams and fantasies have a mythological side, for some are interpretable on a wholly personal level. But many dreams and fantasies carry the weight of *collective* meaning. They are vehicles for what Jung labels the "strange myths of the psyche" (*wunderlichen Mythen der Seele*).[1] Following Jung's example, Jungians interpret such archetypal dreams with the help of analogies and parallels from mythology.

In a letter dated November 2, 1960, Jung interprets one of his own dreams in this manner. The dream revolves around the difficulties of carrying a giant boar's carcass back to camp, where a ritual feast is about to be celebrated. In order to elucidate the background of the dream, Jung points to two myths concerning the ending of one cosmic age and the beginning of another: the Hindu myth of the god Vishnu incarnating himself as a boar, and the Jewish Kabbalistic myth of Yahweh serving up Leviathan as a meal for the righteous.

This kind of dream interpretation is both original and disconcerting. It presumes that the study of dreams and myths can be mutually illuminating. But for many the Jungian approach to mythology may seem too subjective in its nature and origin. The study of mythology as traditionally practiced by folklorists, classicists, anthropologists, historians of religion and so forth has been heavily influenced by the paradigm of scientific objectivity. The subjective nature of the experience of the psyche has tended to put it off limits to what many would consider objective, fact-finding, scientific inquiry. Jungian psychology in particular has had to constantly defend itself against charges of irrationalism. But slowly opinion has shifted, and Jungian psychology in the late twentieth century has begun to enjoy the kind of respect that Freudian psychology had gained earlier in the century. It can thus be taken as a sign of the times when even Alan Dundes, one of the foremost American folklorists of our time, who has major objections to Jungian theory (he finds it "mystical" and "anti-intellectual," for starters), can bring himself to write that, "despite the theoretical problems with the Jungian approach to myth, students of mythology should be familiar with it."[2]

It is true that Jungian psychology is primarily concerned with the inner psychological world, the realm of subjectivity *par excellence*, and that it values the data of the objective world mainly as a support for the investigation of this inner world. Other fields have emphasized traditionally the study of the external world more or less as an end in itself, and have slighted the importance of subjective factors. Thus the potential impact of the Jungian approach to mythology has been dampened by a cultural bias in favor of objective over subjective material. Whereas Jungians parallel myths with dreams, others contrast them: a myth is out there, *in the world*; a dream is in here, *in the psyche*.

Furthermore, the primary focus of the Jungian approach to mythology is the study of the modern psyche, and only secondarily the study of past cultures. This point is well illustrated by the Canadian Jungian Ginette Paris, who distinguishes her approach to classical mythology from that of the French classicist Jean-Pierre Vernant:

> his [Vernant's] work in psychological history is intended to contribute to our understanding of the psychological history of ancient Greece, while we wish to contribute to the comprehension of contemporary psychology . . . [for example] how the myth of Hestia may be useful in symbolizing our daily lives. [3]

Because, unlike other fields, literary criticism has traditionally been attuned to the problems and benefits of subjective interpretation, it is probably no coincidence that, outside of the immediate realm of psychology and psychotherapy, it is literary criticism that has most fully employed Jungian theory. A flourishing school of Jungian literary criticism—often called "archetypal criticism"—has demonstrated the fruitfulness of Jung's theory in the realm of literary study, and continues to do so. Jungian analysts themselves have often been drawn to examine the rich archetypal dimension manifested in the mythic subtexts of literature.

In spite of the fact that Jung, faithful to the medical training of his youth and to the philosophy of scientific empiricism that presided over it, adhered throughout his life to the belief that the archetypes were "biological facts and not arbitrary opinions,"[4] there is much to be gained by frankly facing the subjective origin of the concept of archetypal images—its origin in Jung's own mind. Jungian psychology is first of all the psychology of C.G. Jung. For it was primarily Jung's own experience of the unconscious, and his own long self-analysis, that led to the creation of such major categories of archetypal images and their corresponding myths as the *shadow*, the *anima* and the *animus*, the *hero*, the *Wise Old Man*, the *Great Mother*, the *self*, and the *puer* and *puella*. Having examined in both this chapter and the next how Jung theorized his own experiences of the unconscious, as well as how he drew general conclusions from his self-analysis and his extensive study of the dreams and problems of his analysands, we will be in a better position to examine in the fourth chapter some of the ways in which Jungians have analyzed myths and, in the fifth chapter, some of the recent directions Jungian theory has taken.

The individual's relationship with the inner mythology of the mind, according to Jungian psychology, is a complicated affair. It is especially complicated once the individual is no longer blithely *unconscious* of the other side of the mind. The experiential coming to terms with the archetypes of the collective unconscious is a heroic journey that few should undertake unless they are ready for it or are forced into it by fate and by the pressure of the unconscious.[5] By contrast, secondhand knowledge about the journey is useful as a means of understanding the archetypal basis for human consciousness. Understanding mythology and understanding the unconscious go hand in hand, since the "patterns [that] are the precondition for the inner affinity of all races of men" "express themselves chiefly in mythological motifs" and "reappear spontaneously again and again in the unconscious products of modern individuals."[6]

Jungians use certain key terms in describing the individual's relationship with the collective unconscious. Once an archetype has been *constellated* (activated, stimulated), it becomes numinous (divine or diabolical) for the person under its spell. In the face of numinosity, the ideal procedure is to *realize* the archetype by establishing a relationship with it in which the ego is neither unconscious of the power of the archetype nor overwhelmed by it. Even so, there is a fine line between being *possessed* by an archetype—identifying oneself with it too much (the state of *inflation*)—and *projecting* its unconscious effect onto others—identifying with it too little. Jung was fond of saying that it is not possible to realize an archetype without first identifying oneself with it to some degree; otherwise no real contact between ego and archetype can occur. One can presumably say the same of projection, in that perceiving the archetypal negative or positive power of fascination in another is at least one step toward greater consciousness of the archetype's effect. Falling passionately in love is one step toward realizing the anima or the animus—the archetypes presiding over passionately sexual bonding.

Inflation involves too little conscious relating and selection. It is a major source of illusion about ourselves. We forget our common humanity, identify ourselves with a numinous archetypal image, and take ourselves for sages, prophets, witches, angels, or demons. But, as Pascal said, a human being is neither an angel nor a beast. In the end we must come down to earth and through a process of *deflation* ("disidentification") accept our personal limitations. We are not mythical beings. Our ego-consciousness, small as it is, is our most precious possession and the key to our maintaining a balanced psychological relationship with the numinous world of the collective unconsciousness. The Delphic oracle's famous injunction "Know thyself," interpreted as meaning "Know that you are a mortal human being, not a god," is the ancient world's warning against what in Jungian terms is the danger of psychological inflation.

Projection is a major source of illusions about others and the world, for by projecting unconscious archetypal images—our inner gods and demons—outward onto the world, we overcomplicate the world and oversimplify ourselves. "Because projections are unconscious," wrote Jung, "they appear on persons in the immediate environment, mostly in the form of abnormal over- or undervaluations which provoke misunderstandings, quarrels, fanaticisms, and follies of every description."[7] To *withdraw* projections is to take back consciously what we originally cast out unconsciously onto the outside world, and to accept responsibility for our own inner turmoil— no easy task! *Integration* is the process of relating the ego carefully and cautiously to the archetypal material put forward by the unconscious, and of changing conscious attitudes through selective assimilation of what will benefit the development of the total personality.

The study of myths, the "textbook of the archetypes," can be helpful in the task of recognizing and then withdrawing projections, a process that helps a person attain greater self-knowledge. Given the importance of dreams for the knowledge of the collective unconscious, and given the importance of mythology for the Jungian interpretation of dreams, it is clear that Jungians value the study of mythology primarily as a means of furthering *individuation*. In individuation the individual integrates, at least to some degree, the inner world of split-off personalities based on unconscious identifications, withdraws projections, and realizes to some extent the archetype of the Self, the foundation for the secure sense of self-identity. Individuation is the ultimate goal of human life, although Jungians are quick to admit that it is rare for anyone to realize it completely.

The Shadow

Jung was the son of a Swiss Protestant clergyman, and the general problem of good and evil exercised him keenly throughout his life. The *collective shadow*, viewed as a component of the collective unconscious, is the archetype of collective evil and can be represented by such archetypal images as the Devil, the Enemy, the Bad Guys, and the Evil Empire. In wartime or in any other situation of political confrontation the shadow is likely to be *projected* onto the enemy side, which is consequently viewed as hopelessly depraved, vicious, cruel, and inhuman. (Sam Keen's recent book *Faces of the Enemy* constitutes a good popular introduction to this collective dimension of shadow projection.)[8] At the same time our side, having projected its shadow contents onto the enemy, appears to be all good and thoroughly justified in bombing the enemy back into the Stone Age, if necessary! The myth of the combat between Good and Evil often covers up a situation of moral unconsciousness, with inflation with the Good and projection of Evil the usual result. Fifty years after the first use of nuclear weapons, the tragic irony of this moral blindness has perhaps begun to dawn on thoughtful people and on some political thinkers here and there. Jung, who could hardly be labeled a communist sympathizer, was nevertheless quoted as having said at the height of the Cold War in 1955,

> I am not afraid of communism; I am afraid of unconsciousness and of modern science. . . . You see, that is our real problem: the collective shadow. The atom bomb is in the hands of unconscious people. It is like giving a baby a kilo of gelignite, it eventually blows itself up.[9]

The *personal shadow*, as opposed to the archetypal shadow, may be said to correspond roughly to the Freudian unconscious, the repressed side of the individual psyche. Jung considers the confrontation with the shadow, with one's own evil, to be of the greatest psychological value. Understanding something about one's shadow side is the beginning of self-knowledge: "There is no point in trying to make a patient understand archetypal material as long as he has not gained some insight into his personal complexes, and particularly into the nature of his shadow."[10] Without the realization of the shadow all real further psychological progress is blocked, and Jung near the end of his life castigated "those foolish Jungians, who . . . avoid the shadow and make for the archetypes."[11] For this reason, Jung feels that depth psychology, with its ambition of coming to terms with the archetypes of the collective unconscious, usually has little to offer to young people or infantile adults. For them, sidestepping the distasteful problem of the shadow in favor of focusing on the romantic adventure of allegedly archetypal psychology would be equivalent to resisting self-knowledge. The neurotic failure to deal with one's own personal repressions and weaknesses can make the archetypes into an "escape camouflage" for one's own shortcomings. Jung's warning near the end of his life was clear: *"One cannot avoid the shadow* [Jung's emphasis] unless one remains neurotic, and as long as one is neurotic one has omitted the shadow."[12]

The personal shadow contains elements repressed from an individual's ordinary consciousness. Jung personifies it in a dramatic and quasi-mythological way as "your brother, your shadow, the imperfect being in you that follows after and does everything which you are loath to do, all the things you are too cowardly or too decent to do."[13] For that reason becoming aware of one's own shadow, even just catching sight of it out of the corner of one's eye, so to speak, is often a cause of alarm and of embarrassment. Acknowledging one's shadow and learning to deal with it honestly is one of life's great, if usually distasteful, psychological tasks. But in spite of the unpleasantness of the process, one must come to be able to say of one's shadow, as Prospero says of the monster Caliban at the end of Shakespeare's *Tempest*, "this thing of darkness I acknowledge mine."

Jung does not minimize the difficulty of getting to know the personal shadow. Of his own shadow he said late in his life: "The shadow is something very evasive. I don't know mine. I study it by the reaction of those around me."[14] People are so frequently blind to their shadow sides that sometimes only the expressions of fear, shock, and alarm on others' faces can give them a clue to its presence. But Jung himself never forgot that he had a shadow, and he could demonstrate that fact vividly to people who liked to take him for a saint. Two German ladies protested after a lecture of Jung's in Munich in 1930 that a great artist like Bach could not have had a shadow:

> Jung answered, "Be glad that you were not married to Johann Sebastian Bach!" Thereupon the other said: "But *you*, Herr Professor, you are, after all, an exception!" Jung

said nothing. The subject of conversation changed. A few
minutes later, Jung leaned back in his chair and stared at
two strange ladies who stood in the foyer very modishly
got up and said with tiny narrowed eyes: "Now *those*
ladies would interest me a lot!"[15]

Jung's personal shadow contained, as he demonstrated for
the benefit of the two idealistic German ladies, less than
eminently respectable sexual components. And in fact, Jung's
sexual life was complicated. His lifelong affair with Toni Wolff
was well known both to his wife Emma and to some members of
his inner circle. In addition, the discovery of a passionate affair
between Jung and an analysand of his by the name of Sabina
Spielrein has recently created somewhat of a scandal.[16] Since
Jung felt obliged to tell his mentor Freud about the affair, this
breach of professional ethics on his part (sexual contact between
psychoanalyst and analysand is considered taboo) must have
been both ethically problematic and professionally embarrassing
for him.

A rather intriguing representation of Jung's personal
shadow greeted his guests in the waiting room to his home office
at Küsnacht: a reproduction of Houdon's famous bust of
Voltaire. To one colleague who wrote that it was as though Jung
had "left his shadow in the waiting-room," and commented on
the opposition between Jung, "the benevolent, warmly human
doctor," and Voltaire's "cynical-superior smile," Jung wrote:

> I like to look at the mocking visage of the old cynic, who
> reminds me of the futility of my idealistic aspirations, the
> dubiousness of my morals, the baseness of my motives, of
> the human—alas!—all too human. That is why Monsieur
> Arouet de Voltaire still stands in the waiting room, lest my
> patients let themselves be deceived by the amiable doctor.
> My shadow is indeed so huge that I could not possibly
> overlook it in the plan of my life, in fact I had to see it as
> an essential part of my personality, accept the con-
> sequences of this realization, and take responsibility for
> them.[17]

Literature, art, popular culture, and mythology are full of
vivid representations of the shadow. Since in ordinary psychological life the conventionally adapted social personality and its

shadow play a constant game of hide-and-seek with each other, literary or mythic representations are often organized around the presence of a deformed, inferior, or evil alter ego, which acts the part of a kind of splinter personality in relation to the hero.

One of the most striking literary representations of the shadow, a representation that has become a modern myth in its own right, is Robert Louis Stevenson's *The Strange Case of Dr. Jekyll and Mr Hyde* (1886).[18] We know that the initial idea for the story came to Stevenson in a frightening dream. The thirty-six-year-old author had been in poor health and was unable to sleep soundly. During one of his welcome moments of sleep he had a nightmare. Alarmed by his "cries of horror," his wife woke him up, only to be told indignantly that he had been dreaming a "fine bogey tale."[19] The first draft of this tale, which he wrote at a feverish speed, stayed close to the experience of the dream, but it was almost at once rewritten as a moral allegory and as such was delivered to the press within a week. The work immediately captured the imagination of a wide reading audience and was even used as a text for sermons.

What is most astonishing about the genesis of *Dr. Jekyll and Mr. Hyde* was the fact that its sickly and bedridden author wrote a total of about sixty thousand words (the first and then the second, final version) while he was suffering from continual hemorrhages and was hardly allowed to speak.[20] Obviously some strong source of archetypal energy had enabled the physically debilitated Stevenson to write like a fiend, at a rate of ten thousand words per day, as opposed to the usual respectable quota for a writer of about one thousand or so. It was as though once an archetypal image of the shadow (which became in the text the diabolical and deformed Mr. Hyde) had presented itself to Stevenson's unconscious mind in a dream, the elaboration of the mythic tale had been taken in hand by the author's "creative fancy," which was extraordinarily energized by the constellation of the archetype.

According to Stevenson's wife, Fanny, the first version of the tale was too hastily written and required rewriting in order to bring out its latent moral allegory, which, Mrs. Stevenson surmised, was initially overlooked partly because of the compelling influence of the dream. But the account of Stevenson's stepson, Lloyd Osbourne, was quite different. According to Osbourne, Stevenson was in fact quite happy with the first version. It was Mrs. Stevenson's moral revulsion in the face of what she considered to be "a magnificent bit of sensationalism" that caused the author, after a furious fit of resentment at his wife's lack of appreciation, to throw the first version into the fire.[21]

If Osbourne's version of the genesis of the tale is correct, it is hard not to regret that the first draft of the story has not been preserved, since it may well have contained more psychological truth and less conventional Victorian moralizing. But perhaps this is a vain regret. Although it is true that Stevenson may well have toned down a shockingly vivid myth of the shadow in order to fend off his wife's moral disapproval, Fanny Stevenson, in her spontaneous recoil from the naked power of the original version, no doubt wound up playing the advocate for Victorian public standards that her husband would have had to come to terms with anyhow, if he wished to publish the story without creating a scandal. The story as published is typically Victorian in its mixture of horror and moralism. Generally speaking, myths need to be clothed in dress that the age and culture find presentable. And the age of Queen Victoria required of art and literature that moral allegory clothe the nakedness of psychological truth.

Still, even as it stands, allegorical figleaf and all, Stevenson's tale is a magnificent example of a narrative with mythic resonance. The horror of evil is dramatized mythologically in terms of Dr. Jekyll's agonized struggle with his monstrous double, Mr. Hyde, whose uncontrolled manifestations begin to fill him with panic, as during this scene where Dr. Jekyll is speaking from his balcony with a lawyer friend:

> "Why, then," said the lawyer good-naturedly, "the best thing we can do is to stay down here and speak with you from where we are."
> "That is just what I was about to venture to propose," returned the doctor with a smile. But the words were hardly uttered before the smile was struck out of his face and succeeded by an expression of such abject terror and

> despair as froze the very blood of the two gentlemen
> below. They saw it but for a glimpse, but the window was
> instantly thrust down; but that glimpse had been
> sufficient, and they turned and left the court without a
> word.[22]

The initial experience of the shadow is baffling; neither the lawyer nor the doctor can make heads or tails of it.

The following passage might be taken as a masterly portrayal of the shadow's disturbing aura as well as of its "evasive" nature and its curiously imprecise ("shadowy") outlines:

> He [the unidentified Mr. Hyde] is not easy to describe.
> There is something wrong with his appearance; something
> displeasing, something downright detestable. I never saw
> a man I so disliked, and yet I scarcely know why. He must
> be deformed somewhere; he gives a strong feeling of
> deformity, although I couldn't specify the point. He's an
> extraordinary-looking man, and yet I really can name
> nothing out of the way. No, sir; I can make no hand of it; I
> can't describe him. And it's not want of memory; for I
> declare I can see him this moment.[23]

The tragic ending of Stevenson's mythic tale fulfills the best intentions of Victorian moralism: the good doctor decides to bid "a resolute farewell to the liberty, the light step, leaping impulses and secret pleasures, that I had enjoyed in the disguise of Hyde."[24] But this separation turns out to be impossible to maintain. The hidden killer shadow represented by Mr. Hyde is inseparable from the respectable doctor selflessly dedicated to saving lives, on whom it casts a *shadow* of murderous self-assertion. Becoming conscious of his violent shadow side leads Dr. Jekyll to suicidal despair. Since he overidentifies himself with Mr. Hyde—an overidentification that results in a tragic *inflation*—he is unable to integrate "his brother, his shadow." For Jekyll, his evil side is so inextricably intertwined with his good side that he believes that, if his evil side is to be eliminated, he has no alternative but to have good and evil perish together in a suicide that eliminates both himself and Hyde.

Stevenson's published version of the myth of Dr. Jekyll and Mr. Hyde thus seems to lend support to a harsh and idealistic Victorian moral position which sees good and evil as tragically irreconcilable principles and can only envisage the triumph of good through the total suppression of evil. But the reader may also choose to see in the tale a *reductio ad absurdum* of that same position. For myths do not convey a single message; they are *polysemous*—they suggest a variety of meanings.

When interpreting the story from a Jungian standpoint, it is important to notice that, for Stevenson's Dr. Jekyll, the figure of Mr. Hyde contains not only evil tendencies but also a kind of repressed *vitality* ("the liberty, the light step," etc.). This vitality in some ways is potentially life-enhancing and, if properly integrated, could have been a valuable addition to Jekyll's conscious personality. For the shadow is not all evil. For Jung, "the shadow is merely somewhat inferior, primitive, unadapted and awkward; not wholly bad. It even contains childish or primitive qualities which would in a way vitalize and embellish human existence, but convention forbids!"[25]

A reading of the tale that takes Jung's concept of the shadow into account, while not slighting its morally disturbing aspects, points beyond the tragic ending of Stevenson's Victorian moral allegory. To become conscious of the shadow is a constant ethical imperative for Jungian psychology. But there is no hope of eliminating the shadow. As Jung wrote in 1949, "Noone stands beyond good and evil, otherwise he would be out of this world. Life is a continual balancing of opposites, like every other energic process. The abolition of opposites would be equivalent to death."[26]

Thus the shadow, like other aspects of the unconscious, has a "compensatory significance."[27] Dealing with the shadow is for Jung a highly individual matter, a process that raises questions that conventional morality often cannot answer. Dr. Jekyll's solution—to kill off his own shadow by killing himself— is a tragic error due to overidentification with the shadow. A more Jungian version of Stevenson's mythic tale would call for a representation of some degree of *integration* of the shadow: Dr. Jekyll would have to find some means of acquiring the youthful *vitality* of Hyde without taking on his murderously aggressive propensities as well.

The Israeli Jungian Erich Neumann, who wrote his provocative book *Depth Psychology and a New Ethic* in the wake of the Holocaust and World War II, cites Stevenson's Hyde as one of "the endless series of shadow and Doppelgänger [double] figures in mythology, fairy tales and literature."[28] He also points out the difficulty of this process of integration of the shadow, which may well involve a certain amount of unrespectable living out of shadow contents as well as of practicing moral self-examination:

> The share of evil "allotted" to an individual by his constitution or personal fate should be worked through and deliberately endured by him. In the process, to an extent which varies with the individual, part of the negative side must be consciously lived. And it is no small part of the task of depth psychology to enable the individual to become capable of living in this world by acquiring the moral courage not to want to be either worse *or better* than he actually is.[29]

It is clear that becoming conscious of the shadow not only is a moral duty in its own right (since what we are unconscious of in ourselves is likely to be unjustly projected onto others), but that it also entails the ethical obligation to "'work through' our own evil in an independent and responsible way."[30]

Like Stevenson's creation of a modern myth of man's dual personality, C.G. Jung's discovery of a figure personifying the unconscious shadow seems to owe its immediate origin to a frightening vision full of mythological resonances. On December 12, 1913, having broken with his mentor, Sigmund Freud, a year before after six years of close collaboration, thirty-eight years old and nearly overwhelmed by fantasies from the unconscious he could not control (Anthony Storr calls this period a mid-life crisis "of psychotic intensity"),[31] Jung sat at his desk determined to undertake his personal descent into the infernal world of the frightening fantasies that plagued him by *voluntarily* letting these fantasies unroll inside his mind. The vision he allowed to materialize was a descent into the underworld (*katabasis*) of mythological proportions, which he later described as follows:

Before me was the entrance to a dark cave, in which stood
a dwarf with a leathery skin, as if he were mummified. I
squeezed past him through the narrow entrance and
waded deep through icy water to the other end of the cave
where, on a projecting rock, I saw a glowing red crystal. I
grasped the stone, lifted it, and discovered a hollow
underneath. At first I could make out nothing, but then I
saw that there was running water. In it a corpse floated by,
a youth with blond hair and a wound in the head. He was
followed by a gigantic black scarab and then by a red,
newborn sun, rising out of the depths of the water. [32]

The linked mythological motifs of the shadow (the dwarf)
and the death of the hero (the youth with blond hair) manifested
themselves even more clearly a week later at a moment which
Jung later felt had been the turning point of his life. On
December 18, 1913, he had the following dream:

I was with an unknown, brown-skinned man, a savage, in
a lonely, rocky mountain landscape. It was before dawn;
the eastern sky was already bright, and the stars fading.
Then I heard Siegfried's horn sounding over the
mountains and I knew that we had to kill him. We were
armed with rifles and lay in wait for him on a narrow path
over the rocks.

Then Siegfried appeared high up on the crest of the
mountain, in the first ray of the rising sun. On a chariot
made of the bones of the dead he drove at furious speed
down the precipitous slope. When he turned a corner, we
shot at him, and he plunged down, struck dead.

Filled with disgust and remorse for having destroyed
something so great and beautiful, I turned to flee, impelled
by the fear that the murder might be discovered. But a
tremendous downfall of rain began, and I knew that it
would wipe out all traces of the dead. I had escaped the
danger of discovery; life could go on, but an unbearable
feeling of guilt remained. [33]

The "small, brown-skinned savage who accompanied me
and had actually taken the initiative in the killing was an
embodiment of the primitive shadow," wrote Jung almost fifty
years later in his autobiography. "The rain showed that the
tension between consciousness and unconsciousness was being

resolved."[34] Jung felt that the dream had both collective and personal significance. On the one hand it constituted a strong criticism of the militaristic spirit threatening Europe just before the outbreak of World War I, during which Jung's native Switzerland was to maintain its tradition of neutrality. The sinister image of Siegfried represented the ruthless Germanic power drive, a peculiarly German form of bullying heroism. On the other hand, in terms of its personal relevance to him, Jung felt that the dream's message was that "the attitude embodied by Siegfried, the hero, no longer suited me."[35] The mythic dimension of the dream—the slaying of the Germanic hero Siegfried—could be equally well explicated along personal and collective lines. The dream shed a critical light on both a personal dilemma and a collective one.

The small brown-skinned savage of Jung's 1913 dream, together with the dwarf of the earlier vision (leathery-skinned "as if he were mummified"), presents a striking analogy with Mr. Hyde, whom Stevenson had described as "a little man,"[36] "small and very plainly dressed, "pale and dwarfish," who laughs with a "savage laugh"[37] and who leaves behind "the haunting sense of unexpressed deformity."[38] Jung does not, however, appear to have been familiar with Stevenson's story at that time.[39] Both Hyde and the dwarf/savage may be taken as shadow figures. These figures appeared vividly to both of them first in a dream. For both Jung and Stevenson, the constellation of the archetype of the shadow, once they came to terms with it through literary composition or psychological introspection, released a flood of creative energy. For Stevenson, ailing and confined to his room, a burst of unexpected strength enabled him to write over ten thousand words per day for a six-day stretch. For Jung, coming to terms with the dream also proved psychologically invigorating: "although at the time I was not able to understand the meaning of the dream beyond these few hints, new forces were released in me which helped me to carry the experiment with the unconscious to a conclusion."[40]

This influx of new energy was especially important since Jung was at midlife, a transition period Jungians consider to be fraught with difficulty, when the natural flow of energy in life begins to change direction. As Jung was to write several years later:

> Our life is like the course of the sun. In the morning it gains continually in strength until it reaches the zenith-heat of high noon. Then comes the enantiodromia: the steady forward movement no longer denotes an increase, but a decrease, in strength. . . . The transition from morning to afternoon means a revaluation of earlier values. There comes the urgent need to appreciate the value of the opposite of our former ideals, to perceive the error in our former truth, and to feel how much antagonism and even hatred lay in what, until now, had passed for love.[41]

Since the hero myth (the blond youth, Siegfried) in both the vision and the dream is linked with a figure representing the shadow as well as with a solar myth (the rising sun), it is tempting to see the origin of Jung's later comparison of life to the course of the sun in the two visions of December 1913. In terms of *enantiodromia* ("things running into their opposites"—a change in the direction of psychic energies and in the orientation of values), the *hero* may be interpreted as representing the force of youth symbolized in the solar myth by the rising sun. Consequently, the *murder of the hero* represents the need for a change, for a "revaluation of earlier values," at midlife. The *shadow figures* of savage and dwarf represent the murderous energy as well as the insight, the shadow wisdom,[42] needed to kill the hero and to transcend a youthful heroic attitude toward life. For Jung, "to perceive the error in [his] former truth" perhaps meant seeing the shadow side (ambitious and ruthless striving for recognition) of the intellectual heroism that had led him to great success as a psychotherapist and as the Crown Prince of the Freudian school. His crisis-ridden "revaluation of earlier values" led to a greater turning inward of his already intensely introspective mind and to his discovery of the archetypes of the collective unconscious.

Jung's encounter with archetypal images of the shadow, however painful and unsettling initially, became the basis for his recognition of evil as a necessary part of life, one of the *pairs of opposites* that provide psychic life with its energy. The basis for this discovery lay in his struggle and break with Freud (is Freud possibly the Siegfried of the dream, the murdered hero of the vision?)[43] and in the midlife crisis that precipitated Jung into his descent into the underworld of the collective unconscious.

The Anima and the Animus

The *anima*, the archetype of the feminine, and the *animus*, the archetype of the masculine, are psychic representations of the sexual instinct. In Jungian theory their role is primarily one of *compensation*. The *animus*, the unconscious masculine element in a woman, compensates for her conscious femininity—the female elements of her *persona*—and the *anima*, the unconscious female element in a man, compensates for his conscious masculinity—the male elements of his *persona*. Typically, Jung *personifies* these contrasexual archetypal images. Thus the most macho male perhaps will harbor the figure of a shy little girl inside him; the most feminine woman may be cohabiting psychologically with the figure of a violent hoodlum. Whatever the conscious sexual persona, the figure inside will tend to compensate for its one-sidedness.

Biologically, the anima, the inner woman, expresses the presence of a minority of female genes in a man, just as the animus, the inner man, expresses the presence of a minority of male genes in a woman. At the same time, the figures of anima and animus are also influenced by an individual's actual experiences with members of the opposite sex from an early age onwards. Such a simple theoretical definition would be adequate for understanding anima and animus, if only the psychology of sexuality were a simple phenomenon![44]

Although it is true that almost everybody falls in love or at least experiences sexual desire, few people are capable of realizing the *projecting factor* (anima/animus) that has made the object of their desire desirable in the first place. From the outside, love looks simple: the subjective factor is clearly the key; people fall in love with someone who seems beautiful to *them*, whether others agree or not. The old truism applies: beauty is in the eye of the beholder. The Greek poet Sappho puts it well when she defines beauty in the following terms: "whatever one loves, *that* is the most beautiful thing on earth." In *Remembrance of Things Past* Proust has a servant put the same idea bluntly and humorously in her peasant French: *"Qui du cul d'un chien s'amourose, il lui paraît une rose"* ("Whoever falls in love with a dog's asshole, it looks like a rose to him"). Jung puts the same idea just as laconically, if more technically: "The projection of anima and animus causes mutual fascination."[45]

Perhaps the best way to shed light on this particularly difficult and murky area of psychology is to examine how Jung came to experience what he later called the anima. As with the shadow, Jung's description of this archetype has its roots partially in his own self-analysis and experience of the unconscious. He first detected the existence of what he was to call the anima when he was consciously yielding to the flood of fantasies that nearly overwhelmed him near the outbreak of World War I:

> In order to seize hold of these fantasies, I frequently imagined a steep descent. . . . I found myself at the edge of a cosmic abyss. It was like a voyage to the moon, or a descent into empty space. First came the image of a crater, and I had the feeling that I was in the land of the dead. The atmosphere was that of the other world. Near the steep slope of a rock I caught sight of two figures, an old man with a white beard and a beautiful young girl. . . . [S]he called herself Salome! She was blind.[46]

Jung adds that he was "distinctly suspicious" of Salome and felt that she was blind because she did not see the meaning of things.

As he was writing down his fantasies in order to come to terms with them, Jung began to wonder just what it was that he was creating with the accounts of these experiences. A moment later, "A voice within me said, 'It is art.' I was astonished. It had never entered my head that what I was writing had any connection with art. Then I thought, 'Perhaps my unconscious is forming a personality that is not me. . . .'"[47] He identified the voice within him as the voice of a psychopathic patient of his, a talented woman who, he wrote, "had become a living figure within my mind." (Jung typically underplays the importance of the outer relationship with the actual woman, though he does mention later that breaking off relations with her was a significant step for him.) He proceeded to argue with the figure mentally, insisting that what he was writing was *not* art. Eventually these conversations with the anima,[48] for all Jung's initial misgivings—"at first it was the negative aspect of the anima that most impressed me"[49]—enabled him to differentiate himself from the anima by personifying her and then by conversing with her as if she were a real female presence.

Jung finds in a male's irrational *moods* the most common sign of the presence of the anima, of whose power over his emotional life he usually remains unconscious. Resentment, testiness, touchiness, and sentimentality are typical manifestations of the anima. Ironically, women generally are quite put off by these moods in men, which are really expressions of a man's inferior female side, of his unconscious and therefore undeveloped femininity. In modern American culture, at least, so much genuine male feeling is locked up in the unconscious that what men express verbally is often only sentimental or irritated anima feelings rather than their true feelings, which they may have great difficulty recognizing and expressing.

For Jung, the anima also contains *eros*, "the function of relationship,"[50] but an undeveloped, unrealistic, and strangely unrelated kind of *eros*: "a certain inferior kind of relatedness to the surroundings, and particularly to women, which is kept carefully concealed from others as well as from oneself."[51] It is this unintegrated *eros* of the anima that accounts for the unrelated quality of the romantic intensity of men who are—or think they are—in love, or the unrealistic sentimentality that possesses them when they believe their lives are fatally and inextricably intertwined with those of others, even others who care little for them or exploit them. That is why Jung wrote that "it is absolutely essential for a certain type of modern man to recognize his distinction . . . from the anima."[52]

For a man who is unaware of his feminine side, the anima can easily play the negative role of archetypal temptress and deceiver—a Lorelei, a Belle Dame Sans Merci, a Calypso—subtly luring him into confusion and despair. Representations of the anima are legion in art, folklore, literature, mythology, and popular culture. Every female figure who enters the tale to cast a

spell on a hero, or to lead him into and then perhaps out of the
labyrinthine perils of life, is the figure of the anima in another
mythological incarnation: Ariadne, Melusine, Circe, a naked
nymph vanishing into the woods, a dangerous *femme fatale*. Or
she may be represented as a group: sirens, Rhinemaidens,
dancing fairies, swan maidens, or water nymphs who lure young
men to an early death. One of Jung's first students, M. Esther
Harding, observed the pluralistic representation of the anima in
her work with male analysands and concluded that the anima
figure in immature men tends to be multiple, "represented by
rather indefinite groups of nymphs, the sirens of Ulysses'
temptation, or the flower-girls of Tannhauser's."[53] Only as a man
grows more mature psychologically does his image of the anima
become represented by a single figure.

Jung first discovered images of the anima in literature in
such mythical figures as Rider Haggard's "She-who-must-be-
obeyed" and Pierre Benoit's Saharan Queen Antinea—women
whose power to fascinate and seduce is nearly irresistible and
before whose august majesty masculine concerns and ambitions
seem futile and irrelevant. As a wonderful evocation of the
anima as a peculiarly evasive figure of the psychic world he later
recommended the portrayal of Lara in Boris Pasternak's *Doctor
Zhivago*: "You don't know who she is, she's not quite real, too
good to be true; and there's something wrong somewhere. . . . If
you want to know what the anima is you must read that book!"[54]

Virginia Woolf, writing about the time that Jung was
discovering the anima, also sensed that many memorable female
figures in literature were not wholly convincing as portraits of
actual women. She hypothesized that male authors were
portraying images of their own inner compensatory idea of
femininity, in both its negative and its positive dimensions,
under the guise of creating fictional female characters:

> It is becoming daily more evident that Lady Macbeth,
> Cordelia, Ophelia, Clarissa, Dora, Diana, Helen and the
> rest are by no means what they pretend to be. Some are
> plainly men in disguise; others represent *what men would
> like to be, or are conscious of not being* . . . [my emphasis]. To
> cast out and incorporate in a person of the opposite sex all
> that we miss in ourselves and desire in the universe and

detest in humanity is a deep and universal instinct on the part both of men and of women. But though it affords relief, it does not lead to understanding. Rochester [the demon lover in *Jane Eyre*] is as great a travesty of the truth about men as Cordelia [the saintly self-sacrificing daughter in *King Lear*] is of the truth about women.[55]

In distinguishing between the "truth" about the sexes and the "travesty of the truth" one finds in gender stereotypes, whether in the positive terms of idealizing images or in the negative terms of sexual scapegoating, Woolf was expressing in ordinary language what Jung as a psychologist was struggling to express in his descriptions of animus and anima.

Still, one might argue that what is a travesty of the truth about women for Woolf may prove to be a truthful representation of the anima for Jung. One might argue that it is the truth of the portrayal of the anima that accounts for the fascination that fictional heroines have exercised on readers' minds. Consider, for example, Flaubert's Emma Bovary, not only as a figure in a nineteenth-century novel but also as the quasi-mythical figure she has become for the modern imagination. Jung never seems to have mentioned her as an example of an anima figure (perhaps because his own wife's name was Emma?), but she surely epitomizes the primitive and unrelated *eros* characteristic of the anima along with an evocation of a broad spectrum of anima moods. Flaubert was alleged to have said at one point: "Madame Bovary, c'est moi!" ("*I* am Madame Bovary!"). Whether or not the statement was actually made, it certainly expresses the feeling of fascination and identity with the heroine that many of Flaubert's male readers have experienced.[56] By contrast, it seems that some female readers at least have found Emma Bovary to be rather stupid and unalluring.[57]

As a remarkably ambiguous figure, the anima manifests both negative and positive qualities. She can be the delusion-making and fatal factor in a man's life, but she can also be a helpful figure, his companion in his exploration of the psyche. Like Circe in the *Odyssey*, she can send a man on a journey into the depths of the unknown. Like Dante's Beatrice, she may become the inspiration for a great spiritual quest. Projected unconsciously onto a woman, the anima causes a man to feel passionately attracted, in both positive and negative ways. Or again, like a jealous mistress, she may pull him away from all relationships with the opposite sex and, like Calypso, keep him imprisoned on her island, cut off from the world and from life. As long as a man remains unconscious of his anima, he also remains—whether blissfully or painfully—a fool in relation to the opposite sex.

Nevertheless, bringing the anima to some degree of consciousness—through dreams, through what Jung called "conversations with the anima," through the study of her mythological representations—is not a task for everyone, especially in the first half of life. But there is this advantage to greater consciousness: to *realize* one's anima is to begin to integrate the power of *eros* into one's life and to gain some glimpse of the secret of "the love that moves the sun and other stars," as Dante exclaims at the end of the *Divine Comedy*.

Jung wrote in his autobiography that he had the first clear impression of his anima in a strange dream he had had at Christmastime 1912, when he was thirty-seven years old:

> I found myself in a magnificent Italian loggia with pillars, a marble floor, and a marble balustrade. I was sitting on a gold Renaissance chair; in front of me was a table of rare beauty. It was made of green stone, like emerald. There I sat, looking out into the distance, for the loggia was set high up on the tower of a castle. My children were sitting at the table too.
>
> Suddenly *a white bird* [my emphasis] descended, a small sea gull or dove. Gracefully it came to rest on the table, and I signed to the children to be still so that they would not frighten away the pretty white bird. Immediately, the dove was was *transformed into a little girl* [my emphasis], about eight years of age, with golden blond hair. She ran off with the children and played with them among the colonnades of the castle.
>
> I remained lost in thought, musing about what I had just experienced. The little girl returned and tenderly placed her arms around my neck. Then she suddenly vanished; the dove was back and spoke slowly in a human voice. "Only in the first hours of the night can I transform myself into a human being, while the male dove is busy with the

twelve dead." Then she flew off into the blue air, and I
awoke.[58]

When a colleague, E.A. Bennet, asked him about his first
impressions of the anima, this is the dream he mentioned. In his
reply to Bennet's question, Jung mentioned something not
specified in his autobiography: that the little girl with the golden
hair reminded him of his eldest daughter.[59] Since the image of
the anima, in its personal dimension, is formed out of impressions of significant members of the female sex in a man's life, it
makes sense for Jung's eldest daughter to have suggested a
component of the anima figure in his dream. But the anima is
composed also of childhood impressions of the opposite sex. In
his autobiography Jung also tells of a black-haired, olive-skinned
maid who took care of him for a while when he was three, whose
image became a component of his anima.[60] In a late letter he calls
this his first anima experience.[61]

According to Bennet, Jung linked another aspect of his
anima with the spiritual element represented by the white bird
in whose form she initially appears and into which she is
apparently metamorphosed at the end of the dream. The word
"anima" means "soul" in Latin, and in the Christian tradition the
soul is frequently represented as a bird, as in Andrew Marvell's
poem "The Garden:"

> Here at the Fountains sliding foot,
> Or at some Fruit-trees mossy root,
> Casting the Bodies Vest aside,
> My Soul into the boughs does glide:
> There like a bird it sits, and sings,
> Then whets, and combs its silver Wings;
> And, till prepar'd for longer flight,
> Waves in its Plumes the various Light.

Thus far we have examined Jung's discovery of the strange
mythology of his own psyche. But Jung, like Freud, was certain
that in studying his own psyche he had discovered things about
the human psyche in general. When Jung *personified* (by
preferring concrete figures over abstract concepts) and then
mythologized (by linking these figures of the unconscious to
myths) the contents of his own unconscious, he succeeded in

presenting in a mythological mode some of his insights concerning dreams and fantasies.

But as we move to a discussion of the *animus*, the archetypal masculine compensatory figure for a woman's psychology, it will be necessary to supplement Jung's naturally less direct knowledge of this archetypal image of masculinity in women. As a male, Jung could not discover images of the animus in his own psyche directly; he had to rely on accounts which his female analysands gave him of the images of *their* dreams and fantasies. Some of his female colleagues later enriched Jung's description of the animus with observations based on their own direct experience of it. We will draw on some of their insights to supplement those of Jung himself, which, it should be noted, have frequently come under attack in recent feminist criticism of his theory.

In classical Jungian theory, a male cannot have any direct experience of the animus, since it is not a component of his own masculine psychological make-up. But a male can experience the force of a woman's animus indirectly through a woman's envenomed attacks on him and his work. For Jung, a woman's animus—which, like the anima, is partly personal and partly archetypal in origin—is a source of stubbornly held and unquestioned *opinions* and results in an exasperating know-it-all attitude, carping criticism, and a tendency to argue at the drop of a hat. "Animus opinions irritate a man to death," Jung writes.[62] A woman's ruthless criticism is one form of animus attack that men resent greatly. A woman identified with (possessed by) her animus is "always right," and Jung believes that "in intellectual women the animus encourages a critical disputatiousness and would-be high-browism."[63]

In order to illustrate the effects on him of a woman's animus, Jung tells the story of his hostess at a social gathering who had talked to him for an hour and a half straight, without letting him get a word in edgewise. But her talk, though "in a way, intelligent and highly intellectual talk," was all parroting of collective opinions and textbook definitions. In the end Jung told her that he wanted to know what she herself thought about these highly abstruse matters: "I really want to know what *you* think, and not what the books say." And his hostess replied "quite naively," "If you want to know that, I must think about it first!"[64] It was thus not the woman herself so much as her animus which had been spouting opinions; her own thoughts, like the feelings of a man under the domination of his anima, hardly entered the picture.

It is clear from the previous anecdote that Jung's description of the animus can seem hostile, as he generally points out only its negative and untrustworthy side. Jung's distrust of the animus may have stemmed from his fear of an aspect of female psychology that he liked to call "the natural mind"—something I believe his colleague Marie-Louise von Franz more accurately called the *undeveloped* animus, which even in its undeveloped aspect can have a certain down-to-earth, no-nonsense, positive dimension to it.[65] Jung's fear of the power of his mother's animus in particular may have inspired his rather vivid assertion that "many men remain nice spectres painted on the wall, the devils in them are all killed; the mother has eaten them with her natural mind."[66] Jung's experience of his own mother's "natural mind" was problematic for him well into his adulthood. In one of his seminars Jung spoke of an episode from his early years as a psychologist:

> At a very critical moment in my life, when I was working very hard, my mother came to see me. My mother loved me very much and tried to help me, but she could undermine me with her natural mind. I had been working very hard on my association tests and my walls were covered with charts, when my mother came unexpectedly to visit me. She looked all around my walls and said, "Do those things really mean anything?" What she said was thin as air but it fell on me heavier than tons of lead. I did not touch a pen for three days. If I had been a weak boy I would have been crushed and said, "Of course, it is no good," and given up. My mother would have said that she loved me and meant nothing by it, but man is a civilized being and his greatest danger is nature. . . . Well, I had a terrific fit of anger and then I could work again.[67]

One aspect of the animus as Jung experienced it was thus the subtle undermining of a man's confidence in himself and in his work, the "discouraging word" that provokes moodiness and resentment. The reader might compare to this the unsettling effect on Robert Louis Stevenson of his wife's scathing criticism of his first version of *Dr. Jekyll and Mr. Hyde*. Like Jung, Stevenson regained his creative energy by getting furiously angry—thereby clearing the air and allowing him to judge what his wife had been saying more objectively. For Jung, what happens when a woman nags and a man gets moody and resentful is more a battle between animus and anima than a dialogue between human beings, which explains why such arguments frequently produce more smoke than light.

Possession by the animus in the psychological context of a woman's life has been depicted in the following terms by von Franz:

> She is suddenly entered by a mood of cold male determination, taken over by abstract opinionated thinking, and driven by an impulse toward rash, brutal, determined action—none of which is at all her feminine nature. When a woman gets possessed by the animus, the feminine character of her face changes, her eyes and the expression of her mouth become hard. I notice that when I get in the animus I pull up my shoulders like somebody who is preparing for battle. When I do that, I say to myself, "Oh, oh, stop and relax."[68]

Jung believed that the animus contains the masculine power of *logos*, the capacity to see things not in terms of relationship (*eros*) but more coolly and objectively—in terms of logic, not emotion. The blindly opinionated aspect of the animus, its powerfully primitive dimension, can be dealt with by a woman who develops her own mind, who puts aside animus opinions and makes the effort to discover what she *really* thinks about things: "The animus of a woman is always powerful at the expense of the extension of her mind. As her mind expands, the animus grows less powerful. . . ."[69] As for the irritating effect of animus attacks on close relationships, Jung thinks that a woman needs to stay true to her feelings since "the unpleasant power-complex of the female animus is encountered only when a woman does not allow her feeling to express itself naturally."[70]

Animus issues provide a psychological focus to the problem of women's oppression by men and by patriarchal norms; they may be said to constitute the internal psychological dimension of an external social and cultural problem. The problem of the animus is linked to the general problem of the status of women. Since the animus is such a source of irritation to men (and to their animas!), perhaps it is true that only women can be sufficiently aware of the complexities of the issue to treat them positively yet without sentimentality. For instance, in the following statement Jung's wife, Emma, deals sympathetically as a woman with the problem of the negative animus in a way that one cannot readily imagine her husband doing:

> What we women have to overcome in our relationship to the animus is . . . lack of self-confidence and the resistance of inertia. . . . It seems to us a presumption to oppose our own unauthoritative conviction to those judgments of the animus, or the man, which claim a general validity . . . . But without this sort of revolt . . . she will never be free from the power of the tyrant, never come to find herself.[71]

As an ambiguous figure of the psyche, the animus has positive as well as negative roles to play in a woman's life. When projected, the animus serves as a bridge to the opposite sex. It triggers romance when it leads a woman to find a particular man outrageously attractive. It enables bonding to take place, love to blossom, and the world to keep on going round. For all his emphasis on the inner psychic dimension, Jung thinks that, like the anima, the animus can only be *realized* through the presence of a partner of the opposite sex, because "only in such a relationship do . . . projections become operative."[72] When, as in a love relationship, projections are there to deal with in another person, there is the eventual possibility of slowly *withdrawing* the projections—that is, of coming to know a man as something other than as a source of animus fascination, and of coming to know the animus as an intrapsychic figure distinct from the man on whom this archetypal image of maleness has been projected. The same is, of course, true of the man's relation to the woman and to his anima.

The comments on the animus by one of Jung's earliest students, M. Esther Harding, like those of Emma Jung, have special value, inasmuch as they confirm, qualify, or extend Jung's original findings from a woman's perspective. For

instance, like Jung, Harding was of the opinion that the image of
the animus

> is not so clearly marked in a woman [as the image of the
> anima is in a man], partly because, being impersonal, it is
> more diffused, and indeed may be represented by a group
> of masculine figures, as, for instance, a council of men, the
> Fathers of the Church or State, but there are in literature
> several excellent examples of him, notably Heathcliff in
> *Wuthering Heights.* . . .[73]

One can question whether, as Harding thinks is true for the
anima, the undeveloped rather than the developed animus is
more likely to appear as a group. If so, the more developed
animus may be represented by a single figure such as Heathcliff,
the animus as imagined by a highly sophisticated woman writer.

In Emily Brontë's *Wuthering Heights* the foundling
Heathcliff is a dark, demonic figure of extraordinary mythological resonance, and as such he may be said to represent the
demon lover aspect of the animus who, when unconsciously
projected onto a man, arouses the deepest passion in a woman's
soul but who also may seem too wild and undependable for
marriage. In the novel the heroine Catherine rejects Heathcliff
and accepts the "safe" Edgar Linton as her husband, only to
spend the rest of her short life regretting the decision. Since
Heathcliff has grown up with Catherine, he is like a twin brother
to her, and in the end Catherine's love for him goes so far as to
assimilate him into herself: "He's more myself than I am.
Whatever our souls are made of, his and mine are the same . . . I
am Heathcliff—he's always, always in my mind—not as a
pleasure, anymore than I am always a pleasure to myself—but,
as my own being. . . ."[74]

In Jungian terms, Catherine has unconsciously projected
her animus onto Heathcliff. Indeed, since he has been with her
since childhood, he had already added significant elements to
her image of the animus. Her tragedy will be that, unable to
accept him as a husband because of her desire for the social
status that marriage with Edgar Linton can give her, she will
miss the opportunity of *realizing* and *integrating* her animus by
living with the man who has received its projection. Con-

sequently, she remains *possessed* by the animus, and this spoils her marriage with Linton and nearly drives her mad.

Only at the end of her short life, when Heathcliff returns to see her on her death bed and proves to be all too human in his self-centered demands and resentments, does Catherine begin to distinguish between Heathcliff as a man of flesh and blood and the animus image she has projected onto him: "He would not relent a moment to keep me out of the grave! *That* is how I'm loved! Well, never mind! That is not *my* Heathcliff. I shall love mine yet; and take him with me—he's in my soul."[75]

It is Catherine's fate to fail to recognize the need to come to terms with her animus until it is too late. But her daughter, to whom she gives birth just before she dies, eventually chooses a husband more passionately and more wisely, and the second half of *Wuthering Heights* does *not* replicate the theme of her mother's tragic split between passion and respectability. Thus Emily Brontë does not show animus issues only in a tragic light. It is part of the strength of her novel that the somewhat neglected second volume establishes a more hopeful perspective.

Wuthering Heights is a masterpiece of psychological introspection, especially when viewed from a Jungian vantage point. For a discussion of animus issues it is invaluable. For example, a remark of Emma Jung's, without specific reference to *Wuthering Heights*, may be taken as pointing out one thing that was conspicuously lacking in Catherine's life: significant female relationships. Catherine's mother had died when she was a child, and the orphaned child lacked female friends of her own age. Such relationships with other women, writes Emma Jung,

> establish a human bulwark and orientation point over against the supra- or non-human character of the animus. The relationship of a woman to other women has great meaning in this connection. I have had occasion to observe that as the animus problem became acute, many women began to show interest in other women, the relationship to women being felt as an ever-growing need, even a necessity. Perhaps this may be the beginning of a feminine solidarity, heretofore wanting, which becomes possible now only through our growing awareness of a danger threatening us all. Learning to cherish and emphasize feminine values is the primary condition of holding our

own against the masculine principle which is mighty in a double sense—both within the psyche and without.[76]

But for Emma Jung the relationship with the animus is not only a question of "holding one's own" against an alien principle. Like Emily Brontë, she also presents a more hopeful perspective: "When women succeed in maintaining themselves against the animus, instead of allowing themselves to be devoured by it, then it ceases to be only a danger and becomes a creative power."[77] This more hopeful perspective is as encouraging for men in the grip of the anima as it is for women struggling with the animus. The realization and integration of at least some aspects of the anima and the animus can provide both men and women with greater creative capacity and can enable them to realize more of their full potential as human beings. For the anima and the animus, besides constituting a biologically and psychologically necessary bridge to the opposite sex, also may serve, in an individual's later stages of development, as a bridge to the collective unconscious.

Jung's theory of the archetypes of the collective unconscious has its roots in Jung's own experience of the "strange mythology of the psyche." His own dreams and fantasies as well as those of his analysands supplied him with a fund of vividly dramatic psychic images, whose more general and collective significance only became clear to him when he compared the strange mythology of the psyche with the stories and symbols of world mythology. Our next step, then, will be to examine several major sets of archetypal images that have come to constitute the basic categories of the Jungian analysis of myth.

NOTES

1. Jung, *Memories, Dreams, Reflections*, ed. Aniela Jaffé (New York: Vintage Books, 1963), p. 300.

2. *Sacred Narrative: Readings in the Theory of Myth*, ed. Alan Dundes (Berkeley: University of California Press, 1984), p. 245, in his introduction to Jung's essay "The Psychology of the Child Archetype."

3. Ginette Paris, *Pagan Meditations: The Worlds of Aphrodite, Artemis, and Hestia*, trans. Gwendolyn Moore (Dallas: Spring, 1986), p. 184.

4. Jung, letter in English dated February 9, 1960; in *Letters*, II, p. 541.

5. Thus Jung discouraged the use of drugs such as LSD as a means of access to the collective unconscious: "there is no point in wishing to *know* more of the collective unconscious than one gets through dreams and intuition. The more you know of it, the greater and heavier becomes your moral burden, because the unconscious contents transform themselves into your individual tasks and duties as soon as they begin to become conscious. Do you want to increase loneliness and misunderstanding? Do you want to find more and more complications and increasing responsibilities? You get enough of it." (Letter in English dated April 10, 1954; in *Letters*, II, p. 172).

6. Jung, letter dated May 30, 1960; in *Letters*, II, p. 560.

7. Jung, "On the Psychology of the Unconscious, " in *Two Essays on Analytical Psychology*, p. 95.

8. Sam Keen, *Faces of the Enemy: Reflections of the Hostile Imagination* (San Francisco: Harper, 1984).

9. Jung, interview with M.I. Rix Weaver, in *C.G. Jung, Emma Jung and Toni Wolff: A Collection of Remembrances*, ed. Ferne Jensen (San Francisco: Analytical Psychology Club of San Francisco, 1982), p. 92.

10. Jung, letter in English dated March 15, 1954; in *Letters*, II, pp. 160–1.

11. Jung, letter in English dated March 25, 1960; in *Letters*, II, p. 545.

12. Ibid.

13. Jung, *Dream Analysis: Notes of the Seminar Given in 1928–1930*, ed. William McGuire (Princeton, N.J.: Princeton University Press, 1984), p. 76.

14. Jung, as recorded by Suzanne Percheron, in *C.G. Jung, Emma Jung and Toni Wolff*, p. 58.

15. Ibid., pp. 89–90.

16. See Aldo Carotenuto, *A Secret Symmetry: Sabina Spielrein between Jung and Freud*, trans. A. Pomerans, J. Shepley and K. Winston

(New York: Pantheon Books, 1982), with commentary by Bruno Bettelheim. The book is based on correspondence discovered only in 1977. See also Gerhard Wehr, *Jung: a Biography*, trans. David Weeks (Boston and London: Shambhala Publications, 1987), pp. 140–4.

17. Jung, letter dated November 9, 1955; in *Letters*, II, p. 277.

18. See also John A. Sanford's discussion of this tale in his *The Strange Trial of Mr. Hyde: A New Look at Human Evil* (San Francisco: Harper & Row, 1987), as well as in his earlier *Evil: The Shadow Side of Reality* (New York: Crossroad Publishing, 1981).

19. Mrs. Robert Louis Stevenson's "prefatory note" to *The Strange Case of Dr. Jekyll and Mr. Hyde*, in *The Works of Robert Louis Stevenson* (New York: Scribner, 1922), pp. 338–41.

20. Ibid., p. 341.

21. *The Robert Louis Stevenson Treasury*, ed. Alanna Knight (London: Shepheard-Walwyn, 1985), pp. 48–51.

22. Robert Louis Stevenson, *The Strange Case of Dr. Jekyll and Mr. Hyde* (New York: Airmont, 1964), pp. 62–3 ("The Incident at the Window").

23. Ibid., p. 18 ("Story of the Door").

24. Ibid., p. 113 ("Jekyll's Full Statement").

25. Jung, *Psychology and Religion, West and East*, 2nd ed., trans. R.F.C. Hull (Princeton, N.J.: Princeton University Press, 1969), p. 134.

26. Jung, preface (trans. R.F.C. Hull) to Erich Neumann, *Depth Psychology and a New Ethic*, trans. Eugene Rolfe (New York: Harper and Row, 1973), p. 16.

27. Ibid., p. 12.

28. Ibid., p. 40.

29. Ibid., pp. 110–1.

30. Ibid., p. 113.

31. Anthony Storr, *Jung* (London: Fontana/Collins, 1973), p. 23.

32. Jung, *Memories, Dreams, Reflections*, p. 179.

33. Ibid., p. 180.

34. Ibid., p. 181.

35. Ibid., p. 180.

36. Stevenson, *Dr. Jekyll and Mr. Hyde*, p. 13 ("Story of the Door").

37. Ibid., pp. 27–9 ("Search for Mr. Hyde").

38. Ibid., p. 45 ("The Carew Murder Case").

39. Jung mentions Stevenson's famous tale only twice in his works, and then only casually. Perhaps the moral allegory put him off.

40. Jung, *Memories, Dreams, Reflections*, p. 181.

41. Jung, "On the Psychology of the Unconscious" (1916, but revised later, mainly in the 1926 and 1943 editions), in *Two Essays on Analytical Psychology*, pp. 74–5.

42. The association of the savage with "murderous energy" is clear enough in Jung's account of the dream. The dwarf's skin suggests that of an Egyptian mummy; Egypt could have been associated in Jung's mind with the land of ancient wisdom. Hence the possible association of the dwarf with "shadow wisdom."

43. Again, a purely hypothetical interpretation of a dream. Only Jung's personal associations—which he does not produce—could provide the necessary key. But when Jung mentions in the essay "On the Psychology of the Unconscious" "how much antagonism and even hatred lay in what, until now, had passed for love," and the "apostasies of every description" that accompany the "transition from morning to afternoon" in human life (p. 115), it is hard not to think of Freud, of Jung's recent apostasy and of the shadow energy and insight that fueled it.

44. For a rich, if disorganized, presentation see Jung, "Anima and Animus," in *Two Essays on Analytical Psychology*, pp. 188–211.

45. Jung, letter in English dated November 12, 1957; in *Letters*, II, p. 402.

46. Jung, *Memories, Dreams, Reflections*, p. 181.

47. Ibid., p. 185.

48. Jung would later recommend such conversations with the anima as an actual therapeutic technique: see his *Two Essays on Analytical Psychology*, pp. 200–4.

49. Ibid., p. 186.

50. Jung, letter in English dated November 12, 1957; in *Letters*, II, p. 402.

51. Jung, "Approaching the Unconscious," in Jung et al., *Man and His Symbols*, p. 17.

52. Jung, *Two Essays on Analytical Psychology*.

53. M. Esther Harding, *The I and the Not I: A Study in the Development of Consciousness* (Princeton, N.J.: Princeton University Press, 1965), p. 112. See the chapter "Anima and Animus."

54. Bennet, *Meetings with Jung*, p. 108.

55. Virginia Woolf, "Men and Women" [1920], in her *Books and Portraits*, ed. Mary Lyon (London: Triad Grafton, 1979), p. 42.

56. For a recent example of such fascination with a fictional character who has attained quasi-mythical status, see Mario Vargas Llosa, *The Perpetual Orgy: Flaubert and Madame Bovary*, trans. Helen Lane (New York: Farrar/Straus/Giroux, 1986).

57. This observation was the starting point of Alain de Lattre's study *La Bêtise d'Emma Bovary* (Paris: Corti, 1980).

58. Jung, *Memories, Dreams, Reflections*, pp. 171–2.

59. Bennet, p. 75.

60. Jung, *Memories, Dreams, Reflections*, p. 8.

61. Jung, letter in English dated January 30, 1948; in *Letters*, I, p. 493.

62. Jung, *Two Essays on Analytical Psychology*, p. 208.

63. Ibid.

64. Jung, *Nietzsche's Zarathustra*, I, pp. 220–1.

65. See Marie-Louise von Franz, *Problems of the Feminine in Fairy Tales* (New York: Spring Publications, 1976) pp. 43, 69–70, 169.

66. Jung, *Dream Analysis*, p. 97. Von Franz comments on the danger presented by the mother's animus to a son's psychological welfare in her *Puer Aeternus*, 2nd ed. (Santa Monica, CA: Sigo 1981), pp. 127–9.

67. Jung, *Dream Analysis*, p. 97.

68. Von Franz, *The Way of the Dream*, in conversation with Fraser Boa (Toronto: Windrose Films Ltd., 1988), p. 242.

69. Jung, *Dream Analysis*, p. 96.

70. Jung, letter dated January 24, 1959; in *Letters*, II, p. 478.

71. Emma Jung, *Animus and Anima*, trans. Cary F. Baynes and Hildegard Nagel (Zurich: Spring Publications, 1972), pp. 23–4.

72. Jung, *Aion*, p. 22.

73. Harding, p. 112.

74. Emily Brontë, *Wuthering Heights* (Oxford: Oxford University Press, 1981), p. 82 (vol. I, chapter 9).

75. Ibid., p. 160 (vol. II, chapter 1).

76. Emma Jung, pp. 41–2.

77. Ibid., p. 42.

CHAPTER THREE

The Strange Mythology of the Psyche: The Hero, Wise Old Man, Great Mother, Divine Child, and Self

As we have seen, Jungians often find in the archetypal imagery of dreams and fantasies direct analogies to the figures of mythology. Let us return to Jung's dream of the murder of Siegfried (December 18, 1913). It was discussed earlier in terms of the shadow represented by the brown-skinned savage, but it also illustrates another major figure of the strange mythology of the psyche, the *hero*:

> I was with an unknown, brown-skinned man, a savage, in a lonely, rocky mountain landscape. It was before dawn; the eastern sky was already bright, and the stars fading. Then I heard Siegfried's horn sounding over the mountains and I knew that we had to kill him. We were armed with rifles and lay in wait for him on a narrow path over the rocks. Then Siegfried appeared high up on the crest of the mountain, in the first ray of the rising sun. On a chariot made of bones of the dead he drove at a furious speed down the precipitous slope. When he turned a corner, we shot at him, and he plunged down, struck dead.[1]

Jung interpreted his dream as having a collective as well as a personal meaning:

> When I awoke from the dream, I turned it over in my mind, but was unable to understand it. I tried therefore to fall asleep again, but a voice within me said, "You *must* understand the dream, and must do so at once!" The inner urgency mounted until the terrible moment came when

the voice said, "If you do not understand the dream, you must shoot yourself!" In the drawer of my night table lay a loaded revolver, and I became frightened. Then I began pondering once again, and suddenly the meaning of the dream dawned on me. "Why, that is the problem that is being played out in the world." Siegfried, I thought, represents what the Germans want to achieve, heroically to impose their will, have their own way. "Where there is a will there is a way." I had wanted to do the same. But now that was no longer possible. The dream showed that the attitude embodied by Siegfried, the hero, no longer suited me. Therefore it had to be killed.[2]

In August 1956 Jung mentioned to E.A. Bennet some details which differ slightly from the account he gives of the dream in his autobiography. The hero Siegfried is now described not as driving a chariot but as wearing something like skis made out of the bones of the dead, with which he glides down over the rocks.[3] In addition, he appears in full *shining armor*, just as the sun is rising. Furthermore, Jung and the primitive figure of the shadow are armed for hunting chamois. But, as in the account in the autobiography, Jung initially feels great remorse and guilt over the murder of Siegfried and rushes from the scene of the crime. The falling rain may destroy all traces of the murder, but it cannot wash away his feelings of guilt.

Jung's Siegfried dream provides its own critical psychological perspective on the hero myth. The following discussion of its mythological motifs will enable us to place in theoretical perspective the various *contexts* in which the strange mythology of the psyche must be located, in this and in all other cases when a full Jungian analysis of a myth is undertaken.

The *historical context* of the myth of the death of the hero in the dream must be examined first. Just as a myth is expressed in particular ways in a particular culture at a particular moment in its history, so the myth in a dream is dreamt by a particular dreamer at a particular moment in his or her personal history. In addition to personal contents, however, an archetypal dream may establish some connection with the historical situation of the dreamer's community. Jung likes to cite the example of "big" dreams which, in his travels in East Africa, he discovered were traditionally considered to be the kinds of dreams that needed to be shared with others rather than kept to oneself since they had a more general significance for the community as a whole and did not just deal with personal problems. Jung's own "big" dream occurred in December 1913 at a crisis point both in his personal history (the break with Freud, and Jung's "midlife crisis") and in Western history (the tense period just before the outbreak of World War I in August 1914). Jung's interpretation takes both personal and collective elements into account.

Jung's interpretation of his own dream also specifies the *cultural context*. He accounts for the presence of a Germanic hero myth in his dream by alluding to his own close involvement with German culture. As a German-speaking Swiss from the border city of Basel—a traditional crossroads of German, Swiss and French cultural influences—Jung was close enough to Germany to feel threatened, culturally speaking, by German atavistic dreams of bloodlust and conquest.

In addition, although the Wagnerian dimension of the myth of Siegfried goes unmentioned in Jung's autobiography, it is important to attach Jung's Siegfried dream to the possibility at least of a Wagnerian subtext. Wagner's operas had become extremely popular in the early years of the twentieth century, and the myth of Siegfried would have been familiar to most cultivated people of the time through the version presented in the four operas of *The Ring of the Nibelung*, which Jung had already written about in *Symbols of Transformation* (1912). Especially relevant to the interpretation of Jung's dream is the scene in *The Twilight of the Gods*, the fourth and last opera of the series, in which the murder of Siegfried is initially planned to appear as the result of a hunting accident. Furthermore, the emotional impact of Hagen's murder of Siegfried in this opera could not be more shocking, and this sense of revulsion generated by the scene in the opera corresponds to some degree to the emotions generated in Jung by the dream.

For the dream also provides an *emotional context*: the complex welter of Jung's reactions to having participated in the murder of Siegfried. Guilt plagues his mind, and he is "filled with disgust and remorse for having destroyed something so great and beautiful."[4] While mythology constitutes the textbook of the archetypes for Jungian theory, myths and mythologems in

dreams present themselves not in the emotionally neutral format
of a textbook but rather in terms of the individual dreamer's
specific emotional reactions. Thus it is important to clarify the
specific *feeling tone* that reveals the personal position of the
dreamer in relation to the dream. In this case, rather than
jubilation or simply sadness, Jung felt remorse, disgust, and guilt
at the murder of Siegfried.

The *specific imagery* of the dream provides the *thematic
context*. The myth of Siegfried is associated with the image of the
rising sun. In the account of the dream in Jung's autobiography,
he appears "high up on the crest of the mountain, in the first ray
of the rising sun." Bennet's version adds that he is wearing
"shining armour," which reinforces his association with the sun.
This image puts Siegfried into the thematic category of a *solar
hero*, a role that he had played to some degree in Wagner's
conception of him.[5] In a significant fantasy of Jung's several days
earlier (December 12, 1913), the floating corpse of the blond-
haired youth is also associated with a "red, newborn sun, rising
out of the depths of the water."[6] But in the December 18 dream
and the December 12 fantasy the *narrative context* is different. The
fantasy, according to Jung, unveils a symbolic "drama of death
and renewal," with death being symbolized by the dead youth
and the subsequent renewal by the sun. In the dream, however,
the hero Siegfried is linked more directly with the rising sun and
then is killed. There is no expectation of renewal or resurrection,
and, given Jung's intense feeling of guilt, the feeling tone of the
dream is much less hopeful. The dream's narrative context is
thus one of a murder, not of death and resurrection.

Another possibly revelatory detail is that in Bennet's
account Jung and the savage are armed with rifles to hunt
chamois, but it is the hero Siegfried whom they wind up hunting
instead. In other words, Jung and his savage shadow shoot
Siegfried down like an animal. In addition, Siegfried has only his
shield and spear to defend him, while Jung and his shadow have
rifles that give them an unfair advantage. The remorseful *feeling
tone* of the dream, and the suicidal depression that Jung felt
afterwards, can be thus accounted for by the *narrative context*.
The "awful crime" of killing Siegfried appears horrendous partly

because of the unfairness of the fight and partly because of the implicit comparison with the slaughter of a beast.

The context provided by *personal associations*, even in a "big" dream carrying the weight of archetypal collective meaning, is still important for its interpretation. Unfortunately, Jung gives us little to go on. With typical European reserve, he is generally reluctant to reveal much about his private life and personal relations, and even his autobiography, *Memories, Dreams, Reflections*, tells little about his many rich relationships with people.

Still, some speculation on the significance of the name Siegfried seems justified. One possible association for Jung could have been with "*Sig*-mund" Freud, the heroic pioneer of psychoanalysis and certainly the greatest hero of Jung's professional youth. The root Sieg/Sig means "victory"; both Siegfried and Sigmund are *heroic* Germanic names. Jung and Freud had broken off relations by December 1913. Jung had resigned his position as editor of the *Jahrbüch der Psychoanalyse* a few weeks before, in a short and bitter note to Freud dated October 27, which was to be their last communication of a personal nature. Thus it is possible to see in the dream of the murder of the hero Siegfried a reflection of Jung's feelings of guilt and remorse at breaking off relations with the hero of psychoanalysis, who formerly had been such a source of support and inspiration.

But it is equally possible to interpret Siegfried as Jung in his role as Freud's spiritual son, especially since in *The Ring of the Nibelung* Siegfried's father is named Siegmund, Freud's first name in an alternative spelling. It is curious that Freud's first name was not given to him by his parents but rather was the one that Freud gave himself. As a young man Sigismund Freud had been so enthused by the first Viennese performance (1877) of *The Valkyrie* that he changed his name from Sigismund to Sigmund in honor of the hero who dies tragically in this second opera of Wagner's *Ring Cycle*.[7] If Freud is the father Si[e]gmund, then Jung is logically his son Siegfried in the dream. In fact, Jung's biographer Gerhard Wehr claims that Jung's mainly Jewish colleagues in the Psychoanalytic Association called *him* the "blond Siegfried,"[8] and one may speculate that they did so with this Wagnerian father-son association in mind.

It might therefore make even more sense to accept Jung's interpretation of Siegfried as symbolizing not Freud so much as Freud's heroic "son"—his own ambitious and energetic youthful self, the heroic attitude that no longer suited him. To this interpretation could be added, however, the connection between Siegfried and the role of Gentile hero of the predominantly Jewish psychoanalytical movement that Jung played up to the time of his break with Freud. Jung's dream, when interpreted from this perspective, expresses his anguish over abandoning or "killing" that youthful heroic role by bringing his association with—and dependency on—Freud to an end and thereby stepping forward into a lonely independence and an uncertain future.

It is not, however, necessary to discard one interpretation in favor of the other. Dreams, like myths, are *polysemous*: they can harbor a number of meanings and are susceptible to a number of interpretations. Siegfried may symbolize Freud *and* Jung *and* German militarism *and* the heroic attitudes of youth. Furthermore, a remembered dream may contain hesitations and ambiguities as to exact content and detail. Here the two accounts—Jung's in his autobiography, and the version taken down by E.A. Bennet—are sometimes in conflict. As in variants of a myth, a dream's narrative may be remembered in two or more different ways. Siegfried on skis and Siegfried driving a chariot are somewhat different figures. The version in the autobiography is possibly the result of a later mental adjusting of the original dream to the thematic context of heroism since a chariot is a more mythologically heroic means of locomotion than a pair of skis. In both cases, however, the *bones of the dead* are the construction material. These bones might symbolize the murderous aggressiveness of a heroism that seeks only destruction (German militarism) as well as the "dead" quality of attitudes that no longer suited Jung's future growth (Freud's doctrinaire attitudes as well as Jung's own role as the young hero of the Freudian movement).

Finally, there is the *ethical context*. A myth-laden "big" dream not only presents mythic images to be enjoyed aesthetically or interpreted intellectually but also asks the dreamer to deal ethically with the new contents put forward by the unconscious in the form of an archetypal dream. In the case of Jung's dream of killing the hero Siegfried, this ethical dimension was extremely compelling:

> When I awoke from the dream, I turned it over in my mind, but was unable to understand it. I tried therefore to fall asleep again, but a voice within me said, "You *must* understand the dream, and must do so at once!" The inner urgency mounted until the terrible moment came when the voice said, "If you do not understand the dream, you must shoot yourself!" In the drawer of my night table lay a loaded revolver, and I became frightened.[9]

The ethical burden of dealing with the dream was placed on Jung's shoulders in no uncertain terms!

In summary, the heroic myth of Siegfried as presented in Jung's dream must be interpreted in terms of the *historical context* (personal as well as collective), the *cultural context*, the *emotional context* and its *feeling tone*, the *thematic context* and its *specific imagery*, the *narrative context, personal associations,* and the *ethical context.* No doubt there are personal aspects to be analyzed in a myth of the psyche that would usually not be present or knowable in the case of general mythology. Nevertheless, dream myths of the psyche and cultural myths share common features, and in Jungian theory they are thought to derive from a common mythmaking level of the mind. Therefore the study of mythology has much to gain from Jungian perspectives.

One example will serve to illustrate the meticulous concern for detail and context with which Jung analyzes dreams. In the October 30, 1929 session of his seminar on dream analysis, Jung comments on the figure of Christ represented as a hero with a sword in an old German poem as well as in a dream of one of his analysands. The basic Jungian procedure of explicating dreams via the analogies presented with mythology ("amplification") is clearly illustrated, but so is the careful attention to context. Jung notes the particular *historical context* of the dream image, which is, he said, "peculiarly applicable to our Christian nations, just emerging from the Great War."[10] He considers the *cultural context* to be German, though not exclusively so. For the Prince of Peace to be represented as a warrior is a manifestation of "the German warlike quality, the primitive berserker rage that is in Western man in general."[11]

Jung takes a dim view of the hero myth behind Western imperialist power drives, not only because he is Swiss (Switzerland, unlike practically every other Western European nation, had never laid claim to a colonial empire) but also because, having travelled extensively in the non-Western world, he knows how Westerners were viewed by the non-Western peoples they oppressed. His assessment of the myth of Christ the Warrior thus establishes an *ethical context*:

> As soon as I was outside our white civilization, I saw what Europeans are like. We look awful. The Chinese call us devils and it is true, thin cruel lips, and our wrinkles are uncanny. . . . As you approach the coast of Europe from the great flats of Africa, and see the snow-capped mountains, the little bays, etc., you know that this is where the pirates live. . . .[12]

Jung's critical perspective on Western culture is shared to some degree by his analysand, a Swiss businessman who had lived in Africa and whose dream had presented him with a vision of a sheet iron statue of Christ armed with a long sword inside an African hut.[13]

Since we are dealing with only one of the many mythological motifs in the dream, we will not go into the *narrative context*, although Jung establishes it meticulously. It is, for example, of great significance for his interpretation of the dream that the African hut has by the end of the dream become a kind of mosque. The *emotional context* involves the dreamer's emotional reactions both inside the dream and in a waking state, where the dream becomes an object of psychological reflection. Jung considers it important that the Swiss businessman "was born among the Moslems," has lived in Africa, has absorbed non-Western attitudes toward European civilization, and shares "the fear and also the [feeling of] inferiority of the half-primitive man, that peculiar spot which people have who are born in the colonies." The *feeling tone* consists of a "feeling of resentment" that derives from the analysand's standpoint outside of European culture. Given his sympathy for African Moslem culture, Christ's sword is something the dreamer cannot use as his own. In other words, the *ethical context* does not allow him to participate wholeheartedly in the hero myth of the Christian West.[14] As regards the *thematic context* and its *specific imagery*, Jung interprets Christ's sword as also symbolizing the cross and surmises that the dreamer's rejection of the image of the warrior Christ stems from the fact that "the Christian religion is no longer alive to him," whereas "Islam is living in the native side of him."[15] The *personal associations* with Islam and with Africa derive, as we have seen, from the analysand's earlier personal experiences with the Moslem world.

Hero myths frequently involve the killing of a monster. In his Tavistock Lectures given in English in London in 1935, Jung comments on this particular motif in connection with a patient's "big" dream, which ends in the following way:

> In the background there appears a monstrously big crab-lizard. It moves first to the left and then to the right so that I find myself standing in the angle between them as if in an open pair of scissors. Then I have a little rod or a wand in my hand, and I lightly touch the monster's head with the rod and kill it. Then for a long time I stand there contemplating that monster.[16]

Jung thinks that the crab—unlike earlier images in the dream, whose meaning would have to be determined by purely personal association—is an archetypal image. Consequently, it is important for him as an analyst to provide the patient with a mythological context for this part of the dream. Jung interprets the crab-lizard as a variant of the dragon motif: the monster slain by the hero. The dream shows the patient indulging in a hero fantasy, in which, by inflation, he identifies himself with the hero myth.

An apt literary parallel comes to mind: James Thurber's *The Secret Life of Walter Mitty*, in which a henpecked husband imagines heroic roles for himself in his daydreams by way of compensation. Like Thurber's Walter Mitty, however, the dreamer is not really up to such heroic deeds, and the wand he uses instead of a sword to kill the monster is a sign of the fanciful magical means he stupidly imagines will dispose of it. The dreamer is a self-made man who has risen to the directorship of a prestigious public school and who, at age forty, wishes to continue his uninterrupted climb to success by obtaining a chair at the University of Leipzig. His dream, as Jung interprets it, was a warning from the unconscious that such heroic ambitions are unwarranted and unrealistic. But the patient rejects Jung's interpretation, goes to Leipzig, and within three months has lost his position. "He ran up against the fatal danger of that crab-lizard," Jung tells his London audience, "and would not understand the warning."[17] In other words, he did not take the ethical burden of understanding a "big" dream seriously enough.

The Wise Old Man

Jung writes in *Memories, Dreams, Reflections* that

> All my works, all my creative activity, has come from those initial fantasies and dreams which began in 1912, almost fifty years ago. Everything that I accomplished in later life was already contained in them, although at first only in the form of emotions and images.[18]

One of these archetypal images was to be called the Wise Old Man.

In the *katabasis* (descent to the underworld) fantasy already discussed in connection with Salome as a personification of Jung's anima, the figure who accompanied her was the Old Testament prophet Elijah. Jung rejects any personalistic interpretation of the figure: "Naturally I tried to find a plausible explanation for the appearance of Biblical figures in my fantasy by reminding myself that my father had been a clergyman. But that really explained nothing at all. For what did the old man signify?"[19] Since Jung's map of the human psyche is based primarily on his experiences of his own psyche, it is not surprising that he considers the anima as "always associated with the source of wisdom and enlightenment, whose symbol is the Old Wise Man." To come out from under the influence of the anima enabled Jung, and presumably would enable anyone else, to gain access to the wisdom of the Wise Old Man.

There is, however, the possibility of some patriarchal slighting of the feminine involved in defining the male principle as the sole repository of wisdom. Jung tends, especially in his earlier years, to type the ultimate source of wisdom as masculine. For example, in one of his many ambiguously worded judgments about Indian spirituality, he declares that the anima is only "in appearance" the source of wisdom and that "Indian thought (as represented in modern times by Ramakrishna and others) is based on a mentality still contained in the Mother, because the general mood of India is matriarchal."[20] In his later years, however, Jung himself paid homage to the female conception of Divine Wisdom (Sophia), especially in his *Answer to Job*. It is not surprising that later Jungians have paid more attention to representations of the Wise Old Woman as a corrective to Jung's earlier patriarchal disregard of female wisdom.

In giving to the Wise Old Man a unique status as wisdom figure, the younger Jung is probably a victim as much of his family situation as of the patriarchal attitudes of his time. It is surprising, however, that Jung alludes to his own father, Paul Achilles Jung, in connection with the figure of Elijah since the autobiography makes clear how little of the wise mentor figure Jung found in his biological father. Jung's father was a clergyman who could not face up to the consequences of his own loss of faith and who took refuge in conventional theological thinking as a bulwark against his own unbelief. To his son, the father's preaching always sounded "stale and hollow, like a tale told by someone who knows it only by hearsay and cannot quite believe it himself." Later discussions with his father when he was eighteen always "came to an unsatisfactory end: "'Oh nonsense,' he was in the habit of saying, 'you always want to think. One ought not to think, but believe.' I would think, 'No, one must experience and know. . . .'"[21]

Thus, when Jung in his late thirties lets himself descend into the world of the actual experience of the archetypes, it is not the all-too-human Paul Achilles Jung but rather another more exalted archetypal figure who is to become his "spiritual father." This figure, who developed out of the Elijah figure, Jung names "Philemon." He seemed, wrote Jung, "quite real, as if he were a

living personality," and Jung converses with him, "walking up
and down the garden with him," in a way that suggests that,
long after his father's death in January 1898, when C.G. Jung was
twenty-two, and shortly after the painful break with his all-too-
human mentor Freud, Jung had finally found "what the Indians
call a guru."[22]

Years later Jung would explain to his friend, the English
priest Father Victor White, the meaning of a recent dream in
which "a most venerable looking, very old man with white locks
and a long flowing white beard" offers to share a bed with him:[23]

> While I stood before the bed of the Old Man, I thought and
> felt: *Indignus sum Domine* [I am unworthy, Lord]. I know
> Him very well: He was my "guru" more than 30 years
> ago, a real ghostly guru—but that is a long and—I am
> afraid—exceedingly strange story.[24]

In his biography Jung explains that in Hindu religious culture it
is assumed that, while most students have a living human being
as a teacher, a few have "ghostly gurus," that is, they have "a
spirit for teacher." Since this appeared to be his own case with
Philemon, Jung was to find this bit of Hindu lore "both
illuminating and reassuring."[25]

In part, the archetype of the Wise Old Man as represented
by Philemon played a *compensatory* role in Jung's life. His
clergyman father was disappointing as a spiritual guide in his
childhood and adolescence and died before Jung might have
established a more solid rapport with him. By way of
compensation, a dream in Jung's old age represented his actual
father in the guise of the Wise Old Man, who was about to
introduce him into the "supreme presence."[26] A connection
between personal father image and archetypal Wise Old Man
was thus made at least once in Jung's life. There was enough
respect for his father's wisdom for Jung's unconscious to project
the figure of the Wise Old Man onto him in a dream.

As is the case with all other archetypes, the experience of
the Wise Old Man can lead to a state of psychic *inflation*: an
unwarranted and usually unconscious identification with a
mythic representation of the archetype. Jung discusses the
phenomenon of inflation in great detail throughout his
presentation of Friedrich Nietzsche's poetic and philosophical

masterwork *Also sprach Zarathustra* (*Thus Spake Zarathustra*) in a seminar given in English lasting from May 1934 to February 1939. Jung saw in Nietzsche a tragic case of inflation with the Wise Old Man, whom Nietzsche called Zarathustra, the name of an ancient Iranian sage. Unfortunately, Nietzsche fell victim to his own visionary capacities. Jung argued that

> If you have some vision or premonition, you are tempted to assume that you are perhaps the wise old man yourself, and then one calls it an inflation. Nietzsche himself was in the condition for an inevitable inflation. That explains his almost pathological megalomania, which was criticized during his lifetime, that megalomaniac manner of speech was a considerable obstacle in his way; people thought he made tremendous assumptions. It was simply an inevitable inflation through the coming up of that figure [the Wise Old Man] and his identification with it. [27]

The sense of being all wise and all knowing is quite a temptation for a self-confident and even cocky intellectual such as Nietzsche. There is, as Jung wrote, "a very great majesty in inflation, something marvelous."[28] The problem is that it is a potentially dangerous state of mind, in which one rapidly loses touch with one's common humanity. Jung's fascination with Nietzsche involved a blend of feelings of admiration and affection as well as of exasperation. Nietzsche had been a brilliant and highly original professor at the University of Basel, where Jung was later to study, and in Jung's youth the intellectual circles of Basel were still reeling from the impact Nietzsche had made. In addition, Jung felt a particular affinity with one whose works were of such value for modern psychology; Freud also wrote of Nietzsche that his "guesses and intuitions often agree in the most astonishing way with the laborious findings of psychoanalysis."[29]

Thus the "Nietzsche case" was of more than purely academic interest to Jung. He clearly considered him to be a problematic figure for him personally, a brilliant but unbalanced precursor. The advice he would have given Nietzsche (who died insane in August 1900, when Jung had just finished his studies in Basel) is clearly patterned after his own experiences with Philemon, who is Jung's equivalent of Zarathustra. While Jung carried on imaginary conversations with Philemon and loved and revered him as an archetypal teacher of wisdom, he was careful to relate to him with humility as a *figure separate from himself*, whereas Nietzsche *identified* himself with Zarathustra. Thus Jung was to say later that

> if Nietzsche were a contemporary of mine and asked my ideas about it, I would say: "Be your humble self, say you know nothing, you have no ideas, and if you feel there is somebody who wants to talk, give him a chance, clear out of your brain and leave it a while to the old man. Then make notes of it, take it down and see what he says. Then you can make up your mind whether your ideas fit in with it or not. But don't identify with it."[30]

This process of disidentification, which some Jungians call *deflation*, leads to the end of inflation and opens the way to the *integration* of archetypal contents. The active effect of a myth on the mind is thus both desirable and dangerous—dangerous because of the inflated state of mind it can induce, desirable because it is difficult to integrate an archetype without some initial inflation with it.

The Great Mother

Jung writes much about the influence of the mother on the psychological life of her children and is especially sensitive to the dangers of maternal love. He is eloquent in describing the necessity of the victorious combat of the hero with the dragon, who represents the negative aspect of the mother which must be overcome if the son is to establish a broader base of consciousness and come into his own as a man.

This, of course, is primarily a myth of *male* heroism. A woman might feel that it does not fit her psychological needs for growth and individuation at all. Kim Chernin, commenting on the Jungian male heroic paradigm in her book *Reinventing Eve*, finds that Jung is "describing the transformation of a mind far different" from her own. As a mature woman, she no longer identifies herself with "the heroic goddess slayer transforming himself on his road of trials." She exclaims with some indignation: "Why on earth is he killing her [the mother]? If I had the chance to get close to her . . . I'd throw myself into her arms."[31]

Since the mother's effect on the child's life contains both loving and frightening dimensions, the struggle to free oneself from both dimensions, from the positive as well as the negative mother complex, is the mark of the hero, especially of the male hero, whose myth consequently often contains the motif of the dual mother.[32] In Jung's own life it took conscious resistance to the power of his mother's "natural mind," as we have seen, for Jung to carry on with his word association experiments. In a sense, this strange altercation may have expressed one aspect of Jung's own heroic fight with the dragon in the form of his mother.

But we are concerned less with the mother complex of personal psychology than with the mythology associated with the Mother as archetypal figure. And as regards this subject, outside of *Symbols of Transformation* and one short essay on the subject ("Psychological Aspects of the Mother Archetype"),[33] Jung has fairly little to say. It was really left to his disciples, especially Erich Neumann (*The Great Mother*) and M. Esther Harding (*Women's Mysteries, Ancient and Modern*), to attempt a description of the complete spectrum of images and myths associated with the Great Mother/Earth Mother archetype.

This neglect of an important archetype likely stems from the fact that Jung, as a male, had less direct access to feminine psychology, for which the Great Mother/Earth Mother plays a role equivalent to that of the Wise Old Man for males. Jung observed that "the figure of the old wise man is much rarer in a woman and not so typical, because wisdom in her case is usually connected with the archetypal earth mother."[34] In male psychology—in the psychology of men like Jung, we might add, since the statement may not apply equally well to all men—Jung found the earth mother archetype to be "a sort of pale archetype . . . that does not function as it functions in a woman."[35] In Wagner's *Ring Cycle* the god Wotan may have gone to the Earth Mother Erda to learn wisdom, but Jung's path led him to listen to the Wise Old Man Philemon.

Jung's own religious background, like Freud's, was biblical and patriarchal. His anguished struggle in his old age with the problem of the Old Testament Father God in *Answer to Job* testifies to his deep religious involvement with a patriarchal conception of divinity. Like Freud, he also had tremendous respect for modern science. But in the last essay he wrote for publication he states that science has impoverished, mythologically speaking, the once numinous image we now call, not "Mother" but "matter":

> Today . . . we talk of "matter." We describe its physical properties. We conduct laboratory experiments to demonstrate some of its aspects. But the word "matter" remains a dry, inhuman, and purely intellectual concept, without any psychic significance for us. How different was the former image of matter—the Great Mother—that could encompass and express the profound emotional meaning of Mother Earth.[36]

In the second half of his career Jung came to a more balanced position and gave female as well as male archetypal energies their due.

The last thirty years or so of Jung's life were increasingly dedicated to the symbolic interpretation of alchemy and resulted in the publication of *Psychology and Alchemy* in 1944 and of the two volumes of *Mysterium Coniunctionis* in 1955 and 1956. Under the initial inspiration of the Sinologist Richard Wilhelm's translation of the Chinese alchemical treatise *The Secret of the Golden Flower*, on which Jung wrote a commentary first published in 1931, Jung began collecting European alchemical texts and gradually succeeded in cracking the code of their symbols. Alchemy turned out to coincide "in a most curious way" with analytical psychology: "I had stumbled," he wrote, "upon the historical counterpart of my psychology of the unconscious."[37]

Central to Jung's deciphering of the terminology of alchemy was the myth of the *hieros gamos*, the sacred marriage of Sky Father and Earth Mother, of (in alchemical terms) Sol and Luna (Sun and Moon), of Rex and Regina (King and Queen). In the terminology of analytical psychology, the archetypal male and female principles must eventually be brought together and joined. As Jung was already saying in a June 1935 session of his Zarathustra seminar, in which he used the by-now familiar vocabulary of Chinese alchemy, "there are surely two things in the world, the Yang and the Yin, the man and the woman, and if woman is disregarded, it is a mistake."[38] For the alchemists, the production of gold required the union of substances such as iron and copper, which were symbolized in the mythological terminology of alchemy by the god Mars and the goddess Venus; their fusion, their chemical marriage, "was at the same time a love-affair."[39] Thus the feminine principle was given new value for Jung through its role in the central alchemical procedure and the myth of the sacred wedding, or *hieros gamos*.

For Jung, the son of a Protestant clergyman, Protestantism, in breaking with the Catholic devotional tradition centered on the Virgin Mary, has ceased to acknowledge the female component of divinity: "the disappearance of the feminine element, namely the cult of the Mother of God, in Protestantism was all that was needed for the spirituality of the dogmatic image to detach itself from the earthly man and gradually sink into the unconscious."[40] But Protestantism was unable to repress the mother cult completely, and for Jung the attention devoted to the archetypal feminine in alchemy constituted a cultural return of the repressed female principle represented earlier by the Virgin Mary:

> When such great and significant images fall into oblivion they do not disappear from the human sphere, nor do they lose their psychic power. Anyone . . . who was familiar with the mysticism of alchemy remained in contact with the living dogma, even if he was a Protestant. This is probably why alchemy reached its heyday at the end of the sixteenth and in the seventeenth century: for the Protestant it was the only way of still being Catholic.[41]

For the erstwhile Protestant Jung, whose sympathy with the rites and symbols of the Catholic Church grew ever greater over his lifetime, the study of alchemy may have served a similarly compensatory function.

Yet the culminating visions of Jung's life, which occurred as he recovered from a heart attack in 1944 and which he was later to call "the most tremendous things I have ever experienced,"[42] drew their mythological motifs not from the Protestantism of his youth or from the Catholic tradition to which he felt himself increasingly sympathetic but from three non-Christian traditions: Greek, Hindu and Jewish. As described in the "Visions" chapter of his autobiography, the first vision took place a thousand miles above the earth in something that resembled the kind of Hindu rock temple Jung had seen on the coast of the Bay of Bengal. The vision was of a rite of spiritual initiation presided over by "a black Hindu" who "sat silently in lotus posture upon a stone bench." "He wore a white gown," wrote Jung, "and I knew that he expected me."[43] The motifs of the next vision were drawn from classical Greek mythology and medieval Judaism, and represented a *hieros gamos*—the mystic marriage of the Kabbala and the divine intercourse of Zeus and Hera described by Homer in the *Iliad*. [44]

The two visions are clearly complementary. The first, during which Jung felt that "the whole phantasmagoria of earthly existence . . . fell away or was stripped"[45] from him, with the figure of the dark Hindu yogi playing the role of initiator, seems related to motifs associated with the Wise Old Man, embodiment of male *logos*, whose wisdom of renunciation is presented in a Hindu context. The second, with its mystic marriage, is a lesson in the power of female *eros*, of integration rather than renunciation. This wisdom is associated with an epiphany of the Great Mother in the form of the nurse who was attending Jung in the hospital. Yet the symbol is less the nurse herself and more the figure she changed into during his delirium. Jung describes her as "an old Jewish woman, much older than she [the nurse] actually was . . . preparing ritual kosher dishes for me."[46]

Near the end of his life Jung was full of praise for the Papal Bull of Pius XII, *Munificentissimus Deus*, which validated what had been a long-standing belief on the part of many devout Catholic worshippers of the Virgin. The promulgation of the dogma of the Assumption of the Blessed Virgin Mary affirmed that the Virgin Mary had ascended bodily into heaven and, as the Bride of Christ, had joined her Son in the heavenly bridal chamber; this signified that, as Divine Wisdom or Sophia, she was united with the godhead. For Jung, who interpreted the

Catholic dogma symbolically as sacred myth, this meant that the Roman Catholic Church had taken a step toward recognizing a fourth component of the Trinity, a *female* component. By contrast, Protestantism was left "with the odium of being nothing but a man's religion, which allows no metaphysical representation of woman."[47] Furthermore, the Catholic Trinity now had moved in the direction of becoming a *quaternity* (for Jung a symbol of wholeness), having added to itself a fourth figure suggestive of the Great Mother as Divine Wisdom: the Virgin Mary as Sophia.

Jung's extraordinary enthusiasm for this new doctrinal position within the Catholic Church—"the most important religious event since the Reformation,"[48] as he called it—was no doubt linked to his theory that "a myth is dead if it no longer lives and grows."[49] The papal bull of Pius XII had contributed to the growth of the myth of the Virgin Mary, which, at least for Jung, had taken over aspects of the myth of the Great Goddess's union with her Divine Child.

The myth of the Sacred Marriage had particular resonance for Jung in his later years, especially after the impact on him of the visions of 1944. In his hospital room he had been possessed by this myth and found afterwards some echo of his private visionary experience in the religious life of Roman Catholicism, the "maternal character"[50] of which grew more and more congenial to him as he became older.

The Divine Child: *Puer Aeternus*

In *Answer to Job* Jung writes that "The dogmatization of the *Assumptio Mariae* points to the *hieros gamos* . . . , and this in turn implies . . . the future birth of the divine child."[51] Jung himself felt an inner affinity with the divine child, or *puer aeternus*, archetype. At his home in Bollingen, at the end of the path near the boat house, he had carved a small shrine to Attis, the classical representation of the *puer aeternus*. According to E.A. Bennet, Jung "spoke of the story of Attis as one of the most beautiful in antiquity."[52] He responded with great warmth of feeling to the "bewitching beauty" of a photograph someone had given him of a Greek sculptured head, which he identified with Attis, the son and lover of the goddess Kybele. He admired "the erotic element, the feminine sweetness of the face":

> He has, like his *analoga*, viz. Adonis, Tammuz, and the Germanic Baldur, all the grace and charm of either sex. [The head] expresses in a perfect way the feeling an Asiatic Greek would experience in worshipping Attis or one of his equivalents, one of the *pueri aeterni*, being the joy of men and women and dying early with the flowers of spring.[53]

Jung kept this photograph framed on his desk.

Jung spoke at length of the archetype of the *puer aeternus* in the Dream Analysis seminar of 1928–30. He saw it represented in such images as Meister Eckhart's vision of a beautiful naked boy; the dying gods of the ancient Near East; the popular figure of the child or adolescent Eros/Cupid of Greco-Roman and Renaissance iconography; the brownies and pixies of European folklore; and even the Christ Child, the endearing *bambino* of so much Italian church art. In *Essays on a Science of Mythology: the Myth of the Divine Child and the Mysteries of Eleusis*, a 1941 book of essays co-authored with the Hungarian classicist Carl Kerényi, Jung provided an extensive psychological commentary on mythological representations of the *puer aeternus*.

The *puer aeternus*, says Jung elsewhere, "is simply the personification of the infantile side of our character, repressed because it is infantile."[54] But Jung also stresses the positive dimensions of the figure and thereby offers a radical revaluation of the infantile dimension of adult psychic life, which Freudian psychology dismisses as a purely regressive phenomenon. For Jung, what is "infantile, childish, too youthful in ourselves" is also what carries the promise of future development: "the Puer Aeternus means really your most devoted attempt to get at your own truth, your most devoted enterprise in the creation of your future; your greatest moral effort."[55]

No doubt Jung was also aware of the dangers of the archetype of the puer, which, like any other archetype, has a negative as well as positive pole. In a session of the Zarathustra seminar of June 1935 Jung said that the psychological dimension of the problem of Nazi Germany could be envisaged in mythological terms as the result of the activation of the *puer aeternus* by itself—without the salutory wisdom of the Wise Old Man. Without this wisdom German psychology was the collective equivalent of a young boy's psychology, heavily dependent on authority.[56] But it was really left to Jung's disciple Marie-Louise von Franz[57] to anatomize the dangerous flight from reality and responsibility represented by the cult of eternal youthfulness in modern culture.

Flying through the air, untouched by the trammels of earth, the *puer aeternus* may experience, as in the myth of Icarus, a fall that is all the more painful for being totally unexpected. The opening scenes of Salman Rushdie's recent novel *The Satanic Verses* (1988) provide a present-day example of the puer perplex. Two puer protagonists pushing forty are catapulted from their dreams of innocence and happiness by the explosion of a bomb in the airliner in which they have been flying. Their fall through the clouds and their miraculous landing unscathed on a beach mark the end of their youthful innocence and the beginning of their engagement with some of the unsolved business of their actually quite complicated lives and situations.

As for the novelist himself, still as of 1994 under a sentence of death decreed by the grim old man of the Iranian revolution, the Ayatollah Khomeini, Salman Rushdie may be viewed—with the greatest sympathy—as having experienced a puer tragedy of mythological proportions. He incurred the murderous wrath of a *senex* ("old man") figure in the form of Khomeini—the *senex* as archetypal Mean Old Man and the *puer aeternus* constituting polar opposites of youth and age. From great expectations of uncomplicated literary success he was thrown into the horrors of constant threats of death. For Rushdie, a most talented and innovative proponent of magical realism, the "Rushdie affair" must seem at times to be a magical realist mythological drama come to life.

The Self

In his autobiography Jung writes that "a characteristic of childhood is that, thanks to its naivete and unconsciousness, it sketches a more complete picture of the self, of the whole man in

his pure individuality, than adulthood."[58] Thus the archetype of
the divine child may be seen as leading the way to the archetype
of the Self, "the whole man, whose symbols are the divine child
and its synonyms."[59] For Freud, the ego is the center of the
individual's sense of self. For Jung, the foundation for the
conscious experience of individual existence lies in the
unconscious archetype of the Self. The Self operates as the
unconscious inner core of an individual's being, as the ultimate
principle of harmony and unity. Perhaps inspired by the Hindu
term "Atman" (literally "Self" in Sanskrit), which designates the
transpersonal oneness of identity for all beings in the nondualist
metaphysics of Vedanta, Jung calls this new center the *Self*,
although for him it is a psychological rather than a metaphysical
concept.

The archetype of the Self can express itself through a
number of archetypal images, and Jung did not limit the
archetype of the Self to representations of the "divine child and
its synonyms." Once again, the dreams and fantasies of the
period of World War I were crucial for the development of his
concept of an archetype. In 1918–19 Jung took to drawing small
circular drawings which he called "mandalas," using the
traditional Sanskrit iconographical term. In a mandala the
implied center of the circle or diagram symbolizes the
unconscious core dimension of individuality. Jung came to be
more and more impressed with the significance of his drawings
as representations of what he called "the wholeness of the
personality."[60]

Jung's ideas and images of the Self correspond to some
degree with those concerning the ultimate source of self-
consciousness in Eastern mystical thought. Jung was therefore
especially heartened when in the late 1920s the German
Sinologist Richard Wilhelm presented him with the translation
he had made of the Chinese Taoist alchemical treatise *The Secret
of the Golden Flower* and urged him to write a psychological
commentary on it. Jung did so and concluded that the text
"confirmed [his] ideas about the mandala and the
circumambulation of the center." In fact, so important was this
confirmation of his personal inner life through the establishment
of an affinity with an external cultural form that Jung called it

"the first event that broke through my isolation."[61] To find in Chinese Taoism this external parallel for some of his own ideas and experiences of the symbology of the Self was a great relief. The universal dimension of the archetype became even clearer when he was able to connect it with the symbolism of the Atman of the Hindus, the Buddha of the Buddhists, and Tifereth in the Jewish Kabbala as well as with the Christ figure in Christianity.[62]

Throughout his life Jung was determined not to become a slavish disciple of Eastern wisdom. In his address "In Memory of Richard Wilhelm" (1930) Jung expatiated on the dangers of imitating the East blindly, and he excoriated Western attempts to expropriate its psychological treasures:

> What it has taken China thousands of years to build cannot be grasped by theft. We must instead earn it in order to possess it. What the East has to give us should be merely help in a work which we still have to do ourselves. Of what use to us are the wisdom of the Upanishads or the insight of Chinese yoga, if we desert the foundations of our own culture as though they were errors outlived and, like homeless pirates, settle with thievish intent on foreign shores?[63]

Initially somewhat sceptical concerning its value to the West, Jung devoted an immense amount of time and energy in the 1930s to understanding Eastern mysticism. His journey to India in 1938 resulted in invaluable impressions of a rich Asian culture which until recent times had developed largely in isolation from Western cultural traditions. Eventually he became less apprehensive of what he had initially decided was the unassimilable nature of the Eastern "Wisdom of the Self." By the 1940s he was more open to Eastern ways of thinking. He could now write that "the wisdom and mysticism of the East have . . . very much to say to us" and that "the philosophy of the East, although so vastly different from ours, could be an inestimable treasure for us too." He still added, however, that "in order to possess it, we must first earn it."[64]

When it came to his study of the archetype of the Self, it is clear that Jung felt that he had his own thinking to do. Thus when he comments on mandala symbolism in his late essay "A Study in the Process of Individuation" (1955), rather than drawing his examples from the "treasure" of Eastern symbolism and mythology, he focuses attention on the paintings made many years before by an educated American woman who in the late 1920s had come to him for help. Jung had diagnosed her problem as one of *individuation*—of her coming into her own as a unique individual through a "transformation process that loosens the attachment to the unconscious."[65] At first she had tried to paint human figures, but this did little to free her from the grip of the unconscious. Then she felt drawn to the mandala image of the sphere, much as Jung himself had been ten years before. The symbol of the sphere helped her as an individual to become whole—to integrate the archetype of the Self which had already been constellated in her.

The integration of the Self is no easy task. In fact, it can be quite daunting. The constellation of the archetype of the Self, Jung writes, "hits consciousness unexpectedly, like lightning, and occasionally with devastating consequences. It thrusts the ego aside and makes room for a supraordinate factor, the totality of a person, which consists of conscious and unconscious and consequently extends far beyond the ego."[66] Yet coming to terms with the Self is an essential psychological task for some individuals. Whether they fulfill this task or not has great importance for the rest of humanity, since what is done even by a few individuals makes an impression on the collective mentality and paves the way for others.

Indeed, the process of individuation is for Jung the key to world peace. It is his conviction that "the masses are not changed unless the individual changes."[67] The successful freeing of the individual psyche from fatal compulsions, the loosening of its attachment to the unconscious, is the necessary first step toward world peace. If this process of individuation does not occur in the lives of a significant number of persons, the rest of humanity, tyrannized by the disharmony created in the psyche by the absence of the Self as a harmonizing archetypal force, will have no option but to replicate its inner drama of tyranny and oppression on the world theater of politics. In the nuclear age this replication could result in a tragic mythological drama of world destruction—a drama we could ill afford to witness, since we would also be its victims.

In *The Undiscovered Self*, a book written when he was eighty, Jung reveals the cure that he felt would go far in healing the tragic split between self and world, and between consciousness and unconsciousness. He calls for a religious attitude toward life and defines religion as "the careful observation and taking account of certain invisible and uncontrollable factors."[68] This religious attitude would allow human beings to become aware of something beyond the external world and its political conflicts—the Self as an inner harmonizing principle—that would enable them to keep their balance and move toward wholeness. In so doing they would affect in a subtle way the world they live in and be able to act as bringers of peace in a world on the edge of nuclear war. Thus for Jung the wholeness symbolized by the living archetypal images of the Self, and the detachment from unconscious compulsions and projections created by the process of individuation, represent a challenge to which individuals must respond for their own good as well as for the good of humanity.

NOTES

1. Jung, *Memories, Dreams, Reflections*, p. 180.
2. Ibid., p. 180.
3. Bennet, *Meetings with Jung*, p. 61.
4. Jung, *Memories, Dreams, Reflections*, p. 180.
5. See Jean-Jacques Nattiez, *Wagner Androgyne*, trans. Stewart Spencer (Princeton, N.J.: Princeton University Press, 1993), p. 31.
6. Ibid., p. 179.
7. Nattiez, p. 362.
8. Wehr, *Jung*, p. 145.
9. Jung, *Memories, Dreams, Reflections*, p. 180.
10. Jung, *Dream Analysis*, p. 337.
11. Ibid.

12. Ibid.

13. Ibid., p. 317.

14. Ibid., p. 338.

15. Ibid., p. 339.

16. Jung, *Analytical Psychology: Its Theory and Practice* (New York: Pantheon Books, 1968), p. 96.

17. Ibid., p. 105.

18. Jung, *Memories, Dreams, Reflections,* p. 192.

19. Ibid., pp. 181–2.

20. Jung, letter in English dated April 21, 1948; in *Letters,* I, p. 498. Jung usually uses the English term Old Wise Man; later Jungians have adopted the form Wise Old Man, which I take as standard.

21. Ibid., p. 43.

22. Ibid., p. 183.

23. Jung, letter in English dated December 19, 1947; in *Letters,* I, p. 481.

24. Jung, letter in English dated January 30, 1948; in *Letters,* I, p. 491.

25. Jung, *Memories, Dreams, Reflections,* p. 184.

26. Jung, *Letters,* I, p. 491.

27. Jung, *Nietzsche's Zarathustra,* I, p. 133.

28. Ibid., p. 134.

29. Sigmund Freud, *An Autobiographical Study* (1925), quoted in Anthony Storr, *Freud* (Oxford and New York: Oxford University Press, 1989), p. 122.

30. Jung, *Nietzsche's Zarathustra,* I, p. 135.

31. Kim Chernin, *Reinventing Eve: Modern Woman in Search of Herself* (New York: Harper & Row, 1987), p. 48. The subtitle is a witty allusion to the title of the much reprinted collection of Jung's essays *Modern Man in Search of a Soul* (New York: Harcourt, Brace, 1933).

32. See especially the chapters "The Battle for Deliverance From The Mother" and "The Dual Mother" in Jung, *Symbols of Transformation,* 2nd ed., trans. R.F.C. Hull (Princeton, N.J.: Princeton University Press, 1967), pp. 274–393.

33. In Jung, *Four Archetypes,* pp. 7–44.

34. Jung, *Nietzsche's Zarathustra,* I, p. 523.

35. Ibid., p. 524.

36. Jung, "Approaching the Unconscious," in Jung et al., *Man and His Symbols*, pp. 84–5.

37. Jung, *Memories, Dreams, Reflections*, p. 205.

38. Jung, *Nietzsche's Zarathustra*, I, p. 535.

39. Jung, *Mysterium Coniunctionis*, 2nd ed., trans. R.F.C. Hull (Princeton, N.J.: Princeton University Press, 1970), p. 457.

40. Ibid., p. 361.

41. Ibid., pp. 362–3.

42. Jung, *Memories, Dreams, Reflections*, p. 295.

43. Ibid., p. 290.

44. Ibid., p. 294.

45. Ibid., pp. 290–1.

46. Ibid., p. 294.

47. Jung, *Answer to Job*, 2nd ed., trans. R.F.C. Hall (Princeton, N.J.: Princeton University Press, 1973), p. 103.

48. Ibid., p. 102.

49. Jung, *Memories, Dreams, Reflections*, p. 332.

50. Jung, *Answer to Job*, p. 104.

51. Ibid., p. 105.

52. Bennet, p. 107.

53. Jung, letter in English dated April 22, 1955; in *Letters*, II, p. 244.

54. Jung, *Dream Analysis*, p. 175.

55. Ibid., p. 279.

56. Jung, *Nietzsche's Zarathustra*, I, pp. 533–5.

57. See von Franz, *Puer Aeternus*.

58. Jung, *Memories, Dreams, Reflections*, p. 244.

59. Jung, *Answer to Job*, p. 106.

60. Jung, *Memories, Dreams, Reflections*, p. 196.

61. Ibid., p. 197.

62. See Jung, *Flying Saucers*, trans. R.F.C. Hull (New York: Harcourt Brace, 1959), p. 104.

63. Jung, commentary to *The Secret of the Golden Flower*, trans. Richard Wilhelm (New York: Harcourt Brace Jovanovich, 1962), p. 144.

64. Jung, *Psychology and the East*, trans. R.F.C. Hull (Princeton, N.J.: Princeton University Press, 1978), pp. 184–5. The allusion is to Goethe's

Faust, *Part I*, 682–3: "Whatever you have inherited from your fathers—
you must earn it in order to possess it."

    65. Jung, *Mandala Symbolism*, trans. R.F.C. Hull (Princeton, N.J.:
Princeton University Press, 1972), p. 9.

    66. Ibid., p. 20.

    67   Ibid., p. 65.

    68. Jung, *The Undiscovered Self*, p. 15.

CHAPTER FOUR

The Jungian Analysis of Myth

At a meeting of the Basel Psychology Club in 1958 someone asked Jung whether a myth could be equated with a collective dream. He answered as follows:

> Strictly speaking, a myth is a historical document. It is told, it is recorded, but it is not in itself a dream. It is the product of an unconscious process in a particular social group, at a particular time, at a particular place. This unconscious process can naturally be equated with a dream. Hence anyone who "mythologizes," that is, tells myths, is speaking out of this dream, and what is then retold or actually recorded is the myth. But you cannot, strictly speaking, properly take the myth as a unique historical event like a dream, an individual dream which has its place in a time sequence; you can do that only *grosso modo*. You can say that at a particular place, at a particular time, a particular social group was caught up in such a process. . . .[1]

Until this point in the book what has been emphasized is the *intrapsychic* dimension of the Jungian approach to mythology, concerned as it is with "the strange myths of the psyche," the mythology associated with the inner archetypal images found in dreams and fantasies. When Jung and his followers scrutinize the mythologies created by various cultures past and present, they discover analogies with the mythology of the psyche. The presence of these correspondences between an individual's dream and fantasy motifs and the motifs of world mythology constitutes the basis for a specifically *Jungian* analysis of myth. For Jung and the Jungians, the outer world of social myths and rituals and the inner world of the strange mythology of the psyche are connected. Public and intrapsychic worlds meet at the point where the human imagination creates myths and symbols that correspond both to social needs for harmony and to individual needs for growth and individuation.

Jung viewed the discovery of these correspondences as a tremendous breakthrough in the elaboration of the fundamental procedures of analytical psychology. He would frequently cite the example of a schizophrenic patient of his whose fantasy of the sun possessing an erect penis "that was where the wind came from" was eventually found to correspond with the solar tube which was the origin of wind in Greco-Roman Mithraic mythology.[2] This discovery, and others like it, were at the origin of Jung's theory that the intrapsychic world and the world of mythology share common motifs because they derive from the same source: the world of the archetypes of the collective unconscious.

As a medical student at the University of Basel, Jung wrote a thesis on the strange case of his cousin Helene ("Helly") Preiswerk, who was a medium. In her spiritualist seances the young girl was alleged to speak with the voices of the departed. Jung explained these voices as spontaneous dramatic improvisations expressing unconscious components of her personality—dramatized representations of what he would have later called her *shadow*. The attention he paid to the voices of "Fräulein S.W.," as he dubbed his cousin in his thesis *On the Psychology and Pathology of So-Called Occult Phenomena*, revealed to him that spiritualist occultism and scientific psychology were not worlds apart and that the psychological interpretation of occult phenomena could shed light on hitherto ignored or misunderstood aspects of the human psyche. Unlike Freud, who feared what he called "the black flood of occultism," Jung was drawn to the study of the human psyche in all of its dimensions, even when it contained much that seemed frighteningly bizarre.

Already in his early years at Burghölzli, the prestigious psychiatric clinic of the University of Zurich, Jung had paid careful attention to the apparently meaningless ramblings of his patients, listening closely and discovering gradually that in their chaotic and sometimes amusing babble lay meaningful narratives and mythological motifs. For example, a young catatonic woman under his care imagined that she was living on the moon among people threatened by a terrible vampire from which she intended to free them. This hero fantasy with which she identified herself was, on the one hand, an insane delusion, a case of possession by a myth and its archetypal contents—an extreme state of inflation. But on the other hand, Jung concluded, the myth allowed her to feel exalted and special and so to escape from her humiliating memories of childhood incest and abuse. Somewhat paradoxically, the hero fantasy she was able to articulate was the door to her eventual cure. Seeing this archetypal fantasy as functioning as a potentially salutary personal myth enabled Jung to enter into her mythological world and ultimately to lead her out of her insanely inflated state. In time, he was able to tell her that she could no longer live on the moon but must return to earth. Her telling of her private myth, and Jung's listening to it seriously, had a cathartic effect, and subsequently she was able to lead a normal life.[3]

In the course of his clinical activity, Jung found that his patients' major problem was being gripped by something of which they were wholly unaware:

> When we are unconscious of a thing which is constellated, we are identified with it, and it moves us or activates us as if we were marionettes. We can only escape that effect by making it conscious and objectifying it, putting it outside of ourselves, taking it out of the unconscious.[4]

Becoming aware of the nature of what was constellated in the unconscious proved to be a vital first step in freeing persons from its harmful influence.

The Jungian technique of paying special attention to the correspondences of patients' fantasies and dreams with myths is designed to help bring about a raising of the level of an individual's consciousness through a process that Jung calls *amplification*. This process of objectifying and externalizing unconscious contents as mythic fantasies enables patients to get a grip on what grips them.

Mythic dreams and fantasies are thus sources of energy and adaptation for individuals struggling for greater awareness. A myth may enter an individual's life spontaneously at some moment of crisis and enable him or her to make decisions and take action. An especially vivid example of this may be found in a text published too late for Jung to have known about it, an autobiographical memoir by Dr. Rudolf Pekar. Pekar had been posted as a German military physician during World War II to the concentration camp at Ebensee, Austria. Early in 1945, as the Allied forces drew closer and were expected to liberate the camp in short order, his superior officers had devised a diabolical scheme to lure the camp's prisoners into an underground shelter under the pretext of protecting them from bombing attacks but actually in order to blow them up before they could be liberated. Pekar knew that any sign of resistance to this massacre meant instant execution. Thus he faced an agonizing dilemma: should he attempt to save the lives of others by risking his own, or, by remaining silent and doing nothing, should he save his own life but betray his deepest beliefs in human solidarity?

Pekar's account of his moral crisis includes the following revelation of the power of mythic fantasy in the individual's struggle for awareness:

> I remembered that on the edge of the road stood a tall fir tree. According to a belief handed down by the folk tradition, trees can give people strength. With arms stretched out wide I embraced its trunk and leaned my head on its bark. Then I spoke to the tree: "give me some of your earthly and cosmic strength, so that I may find a way to remain a man of faith who believes in something."[5]

He then came to the decision to go ahead with a plan to stop the massacre, a decision which eventually helped save the lives of hundreds of prisoners.

The fantasy that enabled Pekar to decide to do this heroic act was related to the folk myth that "trees give people strength," which occurred to him spontaneously at his moment of deepest agony. Although any further attempt to interpret Pekar's mythic fantasy can only be tentative, it is worth noting that Jung once interpreted the tree as a symbol of "spirituality" or "transcendental experience."[6] Since Jung often emphasizes that the collective unconscious usually becomes conscious only in moments of crisis, it seems clear that it was Pekar's state of spiritual crisis (he wished desperately to remain a "man of faith") that drew forth from the collective unconscious a spiritual symbol that strengthened his resolve to act in accordance with his faith.

For Jung, a myth can come alive only when reclaimed and vivified by the human psyche. A myth originates or takes on new life and meaning when an individual mind attempts, sometimes desperately, to respond adequately to pressures from the world and from the collective unconscious. The subjective factor is consequently far more important for Jungian theory than for other theories of myth.

The subjective factor is important in two different ways. First of all, a myth must have a numinous and emotional impact on the individual's psyche in order to be experienced and understood as a genuine myth: the individual is *moved* by the myth. Second, even in the course of analyzing a myth as the object of a purely academic investigation along Jungian lines, the researcher must respond emotionally to the myth. Emotional response is part and parcel of the process of interpretation. This almost scandalous emphasis by Jung on the subjective factor has probably done much to perplex and discourage readers and researchers from fields dominated by the ideal of objectivity. Nevertheless, a Jungian analysis of mythology must constantly refer back to the individual psyche, or cease to be Jungian.

Much of what has been too loosely called "archetypal criticism,"[7] including the notable work of synthesis of Joseph Campbell,[8] lacks this characteristic Jungian emphasis on the individual psyche, on the scandalous subjective factor. For the Cambridge school of archetypal theorists (Jane Harrison, Francis Cornford, Gilbert Murray, and A.B. Cook) and such later archetypal literary critics as Northrop Frye, Jung may be said to have been "a common resource" but "not really a source."[9] As for Joseph Campbell, Robert Segal considers his brand of psychology to be non-Jungian and attributes this to the fact that Campbell gave little importance to the individual's conscious ego, which for Jung was of the greatest importance as the mediator between the world and the unconscious.[10]

The Role of Myth in Culture:
Myth as Compensation

Given the strong emphasis on the individual psyche, it might seem difficult to imagine how Jungian theory could deal with mythology as a cultural and collective phenomenon. Still, if myths can play such an energizing and even a galvanizing role in an individual's psychological life, it would seem likely that mythology might play an analogous role in the cultural life of a collectivity. Yet Jung was ordinarily far from sanguine about the effects of group mentality and tended to see all aspects of collective life as regressive in their effects on the individual's psychology.

In spite of these misgivings, Jung did feel that rituals, and by extension the myths which they enacted, had the potential to raise the level of an individual's level of consciousness and energy by encouraging and enabling the assimilation by the individual of constellated unconscious contents needed for the growth and development of the culture:

> The inevitable psychological regression within the group is partially counteracted by ritual . . . [which] prevents the crowd from relapsing into unconscious instinctuality. By engaging the individual's interest and attention, the ritual makes it possible for him to have a comparatively individual experience even within the group and to remain more or less conscious.[11]

But does the individual—as opposed to the culture—really benefit from such collective experiences? Jung's grave suspicions regarding the dangers of mass psychology and the lowering of consciousness (*abaissement du niveau mental*) in groups made it difficult for him to say much in the way of unqualified praise for ritual and collective experiences of the numinous in terms of their value for the individual.

As Jung grew older, his position shifted somewhat. The value for the individual of collective religious practices, with their emphasis on shared mythology and ritual, grew more and more evident to him, in spite of his bias in favor of individual experience. The mythology and ritual of the Catholic Mass in particular drew his sympathetic attention and concern.[12] As we have seen, so did the newly promulgated doctrine of the Assumption of the Virgin Mary, with its myth of the *hieros gamos*.

However much it is mediated by individual consciousness, mythology does have a valuable *social* function for Jungian theory: that of *compensation*. Just as dreams and fantasies, by bringing in material that needs to be assimilated for the sake of greater psychological equilibrium, may be said to constitute an attempt on the part of the unconscious to compensate for imbalanced aspects of the individual conscious mind, so myths may be conceived of as compensating for a culture's dangerously one-sided attitudes. This particular function of cultural *compensation* is clearly demonstrated in Jung's discussion of the modern myth of Flying Saucers.

In 1951 Jung wrote to an American colleague about some recent purported sightings of "flying saucers" (unidentified flying objects, or "UFOs") as they had been reported in the news media:

> I'm puzzled to death about these phenomena, because I haven't been able yet to make out with sufficient certainty whether the whole thing is a rumour with concomitant singular and mass hallucination, or a downright fact. Either case would be highly interesting.[13]

Seven years later he published *Flying Saucers: A Modern Myth of Things Seen in the Skies*.

Jung considered UFOs to be the product of *projection*, which occurs when a constellated content of the unconscious is seen as an external happening. Projection happens all the time; our perception of the external world is constantly colored by our intrapsychic world. But the archetypal projection that produces myths is on a different scale of magnitude. As in the case of UFOs, the projection is not only individual but collective. In the letter just quoted, Jung sees the possibility of "mass hallucination." But there is more than hallucination at work. To explain UFO's from the standpoint of Jungian theory is also to endow them, as projections resulting from a disturbance in the collective unconscious, with the potential for generating collective meaning.

As regards the cause of this disturbance, Jung felt that the Cold War tensions of the 1950s were the conscious political symptoms of humanity's unconscious psychological compensatory need for wholeness when faced with the Cold War's frightening spectacle of a world divided into two hostile parts— two nuclear superpowers prepared to annihilate each other with a push of the button. As a fairly conservative-minded Swiss with little sympathy for the Soviet Union and its policies, Jung suggested that "the basis for this kind of rumour is an emotional tension having its cause in a situation of collective distress or danger, or in a vital psychic need. This condition undoubtedly exists today, insofar as the whole world is suffering under the strain of Russian policies and their still unpredictable consequences."[14] However one might in retrospect apportion political responsibility for Cold War tensions (the West certainly had its share), one may still accept Jung's thesis that this "vital, psychic need" for psychological wholeness could express itself in compensatory visions of symbols of wholeness such as the round "saucers."

Flying saucers, for Jung, are the modern counterpart of the traditional symbol of wholeness, the *mandala*, which he had studied at length in two essays published in 1950, the first (based on a lecture given in 1933) entitled "A Study in the Process of Individuation" and the second called "Concerning Mandala Symbolism."[15] Visual designs organized around a center (the Sanskrit word *mandala* originally meant "circle"), mandalas have been used for centuries in many religious practices as a means of centering and calming the mind. Flying saucers are distinctly modern because of their technological prowess; they are considered by many to be the spaceships of extraterrestrial beings whose technology surpasses that of humanity. Jung remarks with a bit of sarcasm that "anything that looks technological goes down without difficulty with modern man" and that the archetypal image of the UFO seems all the more real, since it avoids the "odiousness of mythological personification."[16]

But what is so "odious" about "mythological personification" for modern man? In Jungian theory an archetypal image is the product of the interaction of a constellated archetype—here, the archetype of wholeness, or the Self—with the consciousness of a particular age and culture. Our own age no longer believes in personifications of psychic forces in the form of gods or spirits of other kinds. For that reason, when the UFO as a modern projected image of wholeness is visualized in terms of the modern mythological imagery of contemporary science fiction, it can easily become part of a modern mythic narrative. The modern mind will reject a traditional myth dealing with the descent to earth of celestial divinities, but it will accept a myth of close encounters with extraterrestrials endowed with superior wisdom and technology. Furthermore, since UFO buffs frequently believe that these extraterrestrials have come to Earth not with hostile intent but rather with messages of hope for the survival of the human race, Jung seems justified in seeing in the UFO myth a modern restatement of the old myth of *epiphany*, in which gods or angels would visit the earth with promises of "peace on earth, good will to men."

The element of *compensation* in this myth is clear. In the nuclear age that had just opened, humanity, divided into hostile halves, had for the first time in history the capacity to destroy itself completely. The terror of such a self-inflicted fate was one that humanity had never faced before, since the worldwide nature of the ideological confrontation and the scale of the forces of destruction were without precedent. In a world threatened by a nuclear holocaust, any message of hope would be welcome. The appeal of a modern epiphany myth such as that of the flying saucers would originate in this desperate need for reassurance in the face of an imminent apocalypse.

Still, the depth of response evoked by the UFO as *symbol* has far outweighed the impressions left by the naive content of the extraterrestrials' "messages." Thus it was the *myth*, and not the *message*, that played a compensatory role during the first shockwaves of the nuclear age. In particular, the sheer force of the image of the UFO as represented in supposedly unretouched photographs published in the world press gave great public notoriety to the "sightings." Jung felt that, for those who were acquainted with the history of symbols of totality, the UFOs could easily be conceived as "gods." He called them "impressive manifestations of totality" and saw in their "simple, round form" an archetypal image of the Self. In a world torn apart by psychological and political tensions, the archetype of the Self "plays the chief role in uniting apparently irreconcilable opposites and is therefore best suited to compensate the split-mindedness of our age.[17]

Jung also studied UFOs that appeared in the dreams of his analysands and indeed wrote one correspondent about a UFO dream of his own. The UFO turned out to be the circular lens of a kind of slide projector (magic lantern) which projected Jung himself as an image, just as a slide projector projects images on a screen.[18] The obvious interpretation, consonant with the emphasis that Jung gave to the process of individuation in his therapeutic practice, was that the timeless archetypal Self—the lens—was the true creator of the little concrete historic entity known as C.G. Jung. We can see that the UFO as an image representing the religious instinct for wholeness was operative in Jung's psyche as well, and this certainly explains some of the intense interest he devoted to the study of the UFO phenomenon.

Jung paid some reluctant attention—but not enough attention, from a Freudian perspective, at least—to the fact that some UFOs appear cylindrical or cigar-shaped. These shapes easily suggest a phallic dimension. Jung did admit that there was something to be said for a sexual interpretation of the symbology associated with the UFOs: "However unsatisfactory a sexual interpretation may be in this case, the contribution it makes should not be overlooked and must be given due consideration [since] a very powerful instinct like sexuality has its share in the structure of the phenomenon."[19] Still, Jung's reluctance to continue interpreting along these lines is disappointing. It must be said to his credit that he at least discerned in the compensatory myth of flying saucers a "close association between the sexual instinct and the striving for wholeness."[20] Unfortunately, he did not elaborate on these remarks.

Jung's first presentation of the theory of the compensatory function of myth in culture is to be found in a 1922 essay entitled "On the Relation of Analytical Psychology to Poetry." Writing of the social significance of art, he concludes:

> [Art] is constantly at work educating the spirit of the age, conjuring up forms in which the age is most lacking. The

unsatisfied yearning of the artist reaches back to the primordial image in the unconscious which is best fitted to compensate the inadequacy and one-sidedness of the present.[21]

In a subsequent essay on "Psychology and Literature" (1930, revised 1950), Jung applies his theory of compensation to the myth that perhaps more than any other had influenced his life and thought: the myth of Faust, above all as represented in Goethe's famous poetic drama. In Goethe's *Faust* Jung locates the compensatory function in the symbol of the Eternal Feminine, "the highest manifestation of the anima," which provides a "compensation [for] Faust's inhumanity."[22]

Jung takes a similar tack in his 1932 essay on Joyce's *Ulysses*. He interprets the novel's apparent "lack of feeling" as compensation for the "false feeling" and "hideous sentimentality" of the period during and following World War I. If he is not always enthusiastic about *Ulysses* as a literary work—he misses its comic dimension completely—he does appreciate the way its compensatory dimensions constituted an implicit protest against the "lamentable role of popular sentiment in wartime" and the "sentimentality hoax of gigantic proportions" that left a generation of young men dead in the trenches or maimed for life.[23]

Although Jung does not apply his theory of compensation consistently and at length to any one myth until his essay "Flying Saucers," the theory sheds light on certain aspects, especially political, of the study of mythology. It provides a psychological and critical perspective on propagandistic imagery and myths—on the *misuse* of archetypal representations to inflame mass hatred and parochial enthusiasms. At the same time it opens the way to a sympathetic analysis of culture in which new attitudes are seen finding their way into the cultural mainstream through an appeal to countercultural symbols and mythic narratives. In both cases, however, it is important to remember that, no matter how numinous or psychologically compelling a myth may be, one must adopt an ethical attitude toward it. A myth can be turned to good or bad uses, depending on how it is handled.

Myth and Inflation

In a short poem entitled "Sils Maria" (after the name of the Swiss village in the Engadine where he spent several summers beginning in 1881) Friedrich Nietzsche evokes the memory of a crucial visionary event in his psychological life—the epiphany of the ancient Persian sage Zarathustra (Zoroaster):

> Da, plötzlich, Freundin! wurde eins zu zwei—
> —Und Zarathustra ging an mir vorbei . . .
> (There all at once, my friend, one became two,
> When Zarathustra crossed my path . . .)

Zarathustra became for Nietzsche a compelling image of the Wise Old Man, and he would make him into the mouthpiece for his philosophy of the Superman in *Thus Spake Zarathustra*. According to Jung, Nietzsche's Zarathustra served as a mythic double—mythic in the sense that, although Nietzsche's presentation of the figure owed fairly little to the teachings of the historic Zoroaster, the founder of Zoroastrianism, the figure embodied for him the numinous qualities of the archetypal prophet and sage. Nietzsche was henceforward prone to identify the essence of his role as a philosopher with the figure of Zarathustra. In other words, Nietzsche became *possessed* by the archetype of the Wise Old Man.

As noted, Jung's term for this process of identification with a mythic double or archetypal image is *inflation*. Inflation results in a bloated ego—a "swelled head," as the popular expression puts it—and can lead to tragedy, if the ego, rather than recognizing the nature of the archetypal content as distinguished from itself, remains identified with it. In the case of Nietzsche, to whose rhapsodic philosophical work *Also Sprach Zarathustra* (*Thus Spake Zarathustra*) Jung dedicated an English-language seminar held in Zurich over a five-year period (1934–1939), Jung concluded that the German philospher failed to distinguish himself sufficiently from the archetype of the Wise Old Man manifested in the guise of the ancient sage Zarathustra.

It is true that for Jung the *integration* of an archetype usually requires some degree of *identification* with it first. But, having identified oneself with it at first, one must go on to *disidentify* with it. The resulting state of *deflation* allows for the integration of some of the archetypal contents—the depth of vision of the sage, for instance. But for this to happen, the ego must remain aware of its own all-too-human limitations and must stay humble in relation to the potentially overwhelming numinosity of the archetypal content. Only in this way can true sanity be maintained.

In other words, the ego should neither blithely ignore the archetypal content nor identify with it rashly. Once an archetype has been constellated, it is as dangerous to attempt to repress it completely as it is to identify with it totally. In *The Bacchae* of Euripides King Pentheus is unwilling to accept the divinity of Dionysos and as a consequence is destroyed by the power he refuses to acknowledge. At the opposite extreme, Pentheus' mother, Agave, identifies herself totally with Dionysos. While thus possessed by the god and in a state of divinely induced inflation and frenzy, she unknowingly kills her son. In this tragedy of under- and over-identification, only the two old men, Cadmus and Teiresias, are able to integrate something of the Dionysian frenzy—if only by doing a little dance in honor of the god! Their wisdom is the modest wisdom of the middle path: to identify with it—since some degree of inflation is inevitable, once an archetype has been constellated—but also to preserve a humble sense of one's common humanity in the process.

Jung notes that therapists are particularly prone to inflation with the Wise Old Man, partly because their patients often expect them to be wise in a superhuman way and so project such images onto them. If therapists succumb to the suggestive power of such projections, says Jung, "they are poisoned, and as a rule they become sensitive and susceptible, difficult to deal with."[24]

But things may turn out well if the therapist's uninflated sense of ordinariness and humility can be regained. In the process, it is true, the salutary, if often embarrassing, effects of deflation may assume comic dimensions, as the following anecdote by an American Jungian therapist illustrates rather nicely:

> On a hot summer day a number of years ago, I wore white clothes to my office. A patient told me I looked like a guru and in fact had long felt that I actually was a master. While

I made an obligatory comment about it only being a projection, in fact I was secretly pleased and became identified with the image of the master. I pontificated quite proudly about many subjects related to the nature of existence, not only till the end of that session but for two sessions afterwards. I finally disidentified with the priestly archetype when I went to lunch and took a bite out of my hamburger and ketchup squirted on my white shirt. This experience brought me back to my more mundane state with a sense of my only too human ridiculousness.[25]

As we have seen, Jung was fascinated with Nietzsche's problem of over-identification and inflation partly because he himself had gone through a similar process of finding a spiritual guide in a mythic figure—for him, not Zarathustra but Philemon. But through painting and through imaginary conversations with Philemon Jung came to realize the crucial and sanity-saving distinction between himself and the image of the mythic sage. As a result of this disidentification, he was able to realize that "it was he who spoke, not I."[26]

Myth and Politics

For Jung, the Nazi period in Germany was a psychological as well as a political catastrophe for European civilization. For over a decade a state of inflation had overtaken an entire nation, and human evil had assumed mythical dimensions. A culture famous for its poets and thinkers became possessed by the demon of destruction.

In 1936 Jung dedicated a major essay, "Wotan," to the subject of the Germanic "god of storm and frenzy, the unleasher of passions and the lust of battle, . . . the superlative magician and artist in illusion."[27] Jung saw Nazism as the manifestation of the power of this mythical figure operating behind the scenes during the tremendous political and social upheavals in Germany in the 1930s. Years before, Jung had read Bruno Goetz's 1919 novel *Reich ohne Raum* (*The Kingdom without Space*), which he regarded as a prophetic book. Its vision of Wotan's return seemed to Jung to be "a forecast of the German weather."[28] Just before writing his own essay, he had been reading Martin Ninck's scholarly monograph *Wodan und german-ischer Schicksalsglaube* ("Wotan and the Germanic Belief in Fate"), which impressed him as a "really magnificent portrait" of the god. Finally, in 1945, in "After the Catastrophe," Jung returned to the topic of National Socialism, after the full horrors of Nazi rule had been brought to light. These essays are the key texts for the study of the Jungian analysis of political events.

What Jung's analysis of the Wotan myth elucidates is the all-too-unconscious nature of the forces that move human history. From a Jungian perspective, the history of consciousness and culture is more often than not the history of better-late-than-never conscious adaptations to changes in the collective unconscious. These conscious adaptations are essential, Jung explained in a letter written shortly before his death, for "when an archetype is unconsciously constellated and not consciously understood, one is *possessed by it* and forced to its fatal goal."[29] While he is vague regarding the conditions that constellated the Wotan archetype—he rarely gives economic and social considerations much account—the following extract from a letter written in his old age might be said to represent Jung's definitive formulation of the interaction between the collective unconscious and human history:

> Our consciousness only imagines that it has lost its gods; in reality they are still there and it only needs a certain general condition in order to bring them back in full force. This condition is a situation in which a new orientation and adaptation are needed. If this question is not clearly understood and no proper answer given, the archetype which expresses this situation steps in and brings back the reaction which has always characterized such times, in this case Wotan.

Jung concludes with more than a little fatalism that man is "a being operated and manoeuvered by archetypal forces." He is "not the master in his own house and . . . he should carefully study the other side of his psychic world which seems to be the true ruler of his fate."[30]

In retrospect, it is surprising and somewhat alarming to realize that Jung himself was somewhat caught up by enthusiasm for the power of the Wotan archetype in his 1936 essay, which ends lyrically by quoting some verses from the Norse *Poetic Edda*. More importantly, he seems to absolve the Germans of responsibility for their actions when he states that "it has always been terrible to fall into the hands of a living god. . . . We who stand outside judge the Germans far too much as if they were responsible agents, but perhaps it would be nearer the truth to regard them also as victims."[31] As a Swiss onlooker, living in a country whose political instincts were far healthier, Jung perhaps believed that Germany's inflated state of mind would eventually pass without creating too much misery for the rest of the world.

Jung's particular theory of German culture and its disastrous degeneration under Nazism needs to be examined critically. By the early 1920s, with the horrors of World War I in perspective, Jung had already formulated a theory concerning the "mutilation" of the Germanic soul that a violent imposition of Christianity on the Germanic tribes had produced: "a wholly incongruous Christianity, born of monotheism on a much higher level," had been grafted onto the primitive Germanic religion, a "state of polydemonism with polytheistic buds." The natural development of Germanic culture from barbarism to civilization was interrupted by this imposition of the higher culture of Mediterranean Christianity, with the result that a veneer of civilization concealed a fair amount of uncivilized attitudes—a problem that was to continue to plague Germanic culture down through the centuries. In modern times, wrote Jung as a German-speaking Swiss sharing somewhat in this dilemma, "there is a whole lot of primitivity in us to be made good."[32] Jung believed that further progress toward civilization would involve going back to those neglected primitive roots and "giving the suppressed primitive man in ourselves a chance to develop."[33]

But in Jungian theory the need to come to terms consciously with a constellated archetype is a cultural task for individuals, not for undifferentiated groups. Jung's psychological individualism was allied with a profound distrust of groups and of group mentalities: "all human control comes to an end when the individual is caught in a mass movement," wrote Jung already in his 1936 essay. Later, after World War II, the

Holocaust, and the onset of the nuclear age had shaken his faith in humanity's capacity for good, Jung was even more cautious about political ideologies and collective action. In *The Undiscovered Self* (1957) he urges a raising of the consciousness of individuals as the sole means of averting worldwide nuclear disaster. Why, then, did he suggest earlier, in the case of the trials and travails of Germanic arrested cultural development, that a collective political response to a psychological disturbance could take the place of psychological integration on the level of the individual psyche?

It may be that in the 1930s Jung, like so many others, had not made up his mind as to the value of ideological mass movements based on psychic possession by unconscious myths. Writing in 1939 to his Jewish colleague and former student Erich Neumann, who had had a dream which featured a motif of the Wotan myth, Jung noted that the figure of Wotan had been appearing in the dreams of his German and German-Jewish clients alike. Jung seemed undecided as to the ultimate value of this archetypal presence. On the one hand he referred to the "Teutonic regression in Germany," with the word "regression" bearing a clearly negative connotation; but on the other hand he also saw Wotan as symbolizing "a spiritual movement affecting the whole civilized world (Wotan as wind-god = pneuma [spirit])."[34] In short, it is not clear whether Jung viewed Wotan as a force for good or for evil.

Jung also seemed undecided as to whether Wotan was the manifestation of an archetype specific to a particular race (since in the 1936 essay he makes reference to a racial unconscious, a concept he later abandoned) or a particular culture's image of a universal archetype of the spirit. The infuriating confusion between *archetype* and *archetypal image* leads to a needless confusion between Wotan as an allegedly Germanic archetype, "a living and unfathomable tribal god," and Wotan as a universal archetypal image of the spirit represented in terms of a particular cultural myth. In the latter case, Wotan, though the creation of the mythic imagination of the pagan Germanic tribes, would have had his ultimate roots in the universal archetype of the spirit, represented elsewhere and at other times in other different ways—for example, by Dionysos in ancient Greek religion and by "the wind that bloweth where it listest" in the Bible.

In the 1930s Jung clearly hoped that, since the myth of Wotan contained positive as well as negative elements, the positive elements would prevail. His 1936 essay stresses the dual nature of the deity: Wotan as storm god on the one hand but as god of intuitive wisdom on the other. This ambivalent appraisal went hand in hand with a dangerously ambivalent attitude toward National Socialism. Jung, like many apolitical or politically naive people of his day, had some expectations that National Socialism might turn out to be a peculiar but relatively harmless phase of German history. Subsequent events no doubt proved him totally wrong, but it is also true that he could not benefit from hindsight and judge Nazism in 1936 from the perspectives of 1945. In 1936 Jung thought that "the unfathomable depths of Wotan's character explain more of National Socialism than all three reasonable factors [economic, political, and psychological factors] together." From the standpoint of this political analysis of myth it was still possible to hope that the "ecstatic and mantic qualities" of Wotan would come to the fore, overshadowing the destructive elements of the storm god, and that "National Socialism would not be the last word."

But Jung's analysis of the myth of Wotan as the myth of Nazism proved to be limited in its psychological as well as political insights. It was to become clear to him only later that Wotan was not, as he had thought in 1936, "the truest expression and unsurpassed personification of a fundamental quality that is particularly characteristic of the Germans"[35] but rather an unusually virulent mythic manifestation of a constellated universal archetype of the spirit. In the German cultural context of the 1930s Wotan's positive wisdom-bearing dimension could not be integrated because of the low level of psychological, political, and spiritual culture existing in Germany at that time. Rather, what the myth of Wotan symbolized had to be feared and dealt with in terms of its unassimilated dimension as a demonic embodiment of evil. That it was not so dealt with was to prove to be the "spiritual catastrophe" that Jung foresaw for Germany.

After the war Jung no longer held to his analysis of the Wotan myth as a bipolar phenomenon. In the 1945 essay "After the Catastrophe" he barely mentions Wotan, and when he does, it is not as the dual-natured god of storm *and* intuitive wisdom but as the storm god only. Instead of explaining Nazism as the political manifestation of a collective psychological possession by Wotan, with his bipolar archetypal potential for good as well as for evil, Jung characterizes the relationship the Germans had unconsciously established with Wotan during the Nazi period as a Faustian *pact with the devil.*

Whether from political naivete or lack of foresight, Jung "slipped up," as he himself admits, in his early assessment of Nazism. But with the theoretical thrust of his analysis—that Nazi Germany was *in the grip of a myth*—Jung opened up a field of research that needs to be developed much further: the psychological analysis of political movements and of their latent mythologies.

Neumann and Myths of the Great Mother

Jung was fortunate in having a number of pioneering students who, after absorbing the lessons of the master, went on to push back the frontiers of Jungian psychology. Some have done this by extending the range of material covered; others by rethinking and reorienting certain theoretical positions; some have done both. To this last group Erich Neumann belongs. Within the limitations of a short introductory study devoted to Jung and the Jungians as theoreticians of myth, it is possible only to highlight some aspects of the rich and original thinking of this highly gifted Jungian.

Neumann was born in Berlin in 1905, studied with Jung between 1934 and 1936, and spent most of his career in Israel, where he died prematurely in 1960. His book *The Great Mother* (1955) was dedicated "to C.G. Jung, friend and master, in his eightieth year." It constitutes a major reorientation in the field of the Jungian study of myth, highly original in its theoretical assumptions and daring in the range of its material. In spite of his openness to the feminine side and to the problems of the anima, Jung himself had relatively little to say about the Great Mother archetype. He was much more concerned with archetypal images of the Wise Old Man and, in his later years, with the Old Testament myth of the father god Yahweh, with which he wrestled in his controversial 1952 book *Answer to Job*. Jung—and Jungian psychology during his lifetime—always remained somewhat patriarchal in orientation. (There is a striking photograph of Jung at age eighty-five surrounded by a small crowd consisting of his children, grandchildren, and great-grandchildren, in which he seems the very image of the archetypally prolific patriarch.)[36]

Neumann's particular originality as a Jungian lay in his countering of latently patriarchal attitudes with a new emphasis on the power of the Feminine. As a German Jew who lived and wrote in Israel, the traditional land of the Old Testament father god, Erich Neumann was drawn, perhaps by way of compensation, to the force of ancient associations of Near Eastern lands with the cult of the Magna Mater that early Judaism, Christianity, and Islam had suppressed. He made it his creative task at the end of his life to study the many representations of the neglected archetype of the Great Mother.

As in his earlier magnum opus, *The Origins and History of Consciousness* (1949), Neumann was initially concerned with the *development over time* of the mythology associated with the Great Mother: from the Uroboros, the circular snake biting its own tail, which symbolizes the united primordial parents; to the archetypal feminine and then to the Great Mother, whose emergence signifies separation from the Great Father; to the further distinctions of Good Mother and Terrible Mother. Such speculations made a name for Neumann since they gave the Jungian study of myth a plausible scenario for the prehistoric development of mythology as well as an easily visualizable schema for the understanding of how one set of mythological images could have emerged from another. That schema was not a rigidly chronological evolution, however, but rather a process in which history and psychology merged to produce "psychohistory."

But what made Neumann's later book, *The Great Mother*, even more epoch-making than *The Origins and History of Con-*

sciousness was the radical nature of his critique of patriarchal consciousness: "the peril of present-day mankind springs in large part from the one-sidedly patriarchal development of the male intellectual consciousness, which is no longer kept in balance by the matriarchal world of the psyche."[37] At a time when Jung was looking to the modern myth of flying saucers in order to address the problem of a split world in search of wholeness, Neumann turned to the neglected storehouse of compensatory myths about the Great Mother, convinced that only a new consciousness which acknowledged feminine as well as masculine values would allow for the development of psychic wholeness. This *reorientation* of Jungian thought toward seemingly archaic matriarchal modes of thought and the myths that expressed them was an original step. Neumann's work has done much to encourage Jungians to value the feminine not merely as a necessary unconscious compensation for masculine consciousness—the function of the *anima*—but also in and of itself. The *anima* functions in males at least partially as an individual male's female subpersonality; a male may correctly refer to her as "*my* anima." By contrast, the Great Mother dwells in the unsounded depths of the collective unconscious, belonging to no gender in particular, mother of all.

Neumann was adamant in maintaining that his research, for all its complex presentation of primeval images and myths, was never antiquarian in purpose. Although he was directly inspired by J.J. Bachofen's classic study of the primitive matriarchy *Das Mutterrecht* (*Mother Right*), Neumann viewed the importance of his own work differently. Bachofen, for all the attention he gave to matriarchy, viewed matriarchal "lunar" consciousness as not only *prior* to but also *inferior* to the later, patriarchal, "solar" spirit. For Bachofen, matriarchy is a stage of the development of culture. For Neumann, it is also a permanent aspect of the psyche:

> "early mankind" and "matriarchal stage" are no archaeological or historical entities, but psychological realities whose fateful power is still alive in the psychic depths of present-day man. The health and creativity of every man depend very largely on whether his

consciousness can live at peace with this stratum of the
unconscious or consumes itself in strife with it.[38]

In statements like these one realizes the full originality of
Neumann's position. He sees "matriarchal consciousness," for all
its primitive roots, as something desperately needed as an
antidote to the hypertrophy of a one-sidedly patriarchal modern
consciousness, which denies the unconscious and emphasizes
abstract conceptuality and "pure spirit." The lunar spirit of
matriarchy, as opposed to the solar spirit of patriarchy, accepts
the twilight world of consciousness resting on and permeated by
the world of the unconscious. It does not set up matter and spirit
as irreconcilable principles. By encouraging spontaneity and
receptivity, it fosters human creativity and wholeness.

But Neumann's originality was not absolute. In one sense
one can see him in the 1950s as carrying on independently from
his teacher Jung some of the same kind of psychological research
that motivated Jung's alchemical studies culminating in
Mysterium Coniunctionis (1955–7), in which Jung discussed such
topics as the marriage of Sol and Luna, the re-valuation of
Materia, and the joining together of consciousness and the
unconscious. Just as Jung was enthralled, as we have seen, by the
newly promulgated Roman Catholic doctrine of the Assumption
of the Virgin Mary and its myth of the *hieros gamos*, so Neumann
was taken up with his studies of the mythology of the feminine
in the Great Mother section of *The Origins and History of Consciousness* (1949), *Amor and Psyche* (1952), his essay on Leonardo
da Vinci and the Mother archetype, *The Great Mother*, and his late
work on the maternal archetype and the sculpture of Henry
Moore. Both Jung and Neumann were shocked by the
psychological and social cataclysm of World War II into the
realization that masculine technocratic heroic solar consciousness had produced not just a modern scientific civilization but
also the possibility of its total annihilation. Both Jung and
Neumann reacted to this dangerously unbalanced situation by
seeking compensatory mythologies as a means of stimulating the
culture into making conscious adaptations in the established
modes of thought. Jung found such compensatory myths
primarily in the neglected texts of alchemy, from the early
medieval period through the eighteenth century; Neumann, in

the ancient Mediterranean and Near Eastern mythological realm of the Magna Mater.

Still, it seems fair to say that Neumann went much further than Jung in stressing the *maternal* dimension of the needed change in psychological orientation. It is in order to stimulate a vivid and salutary sense of the archetypal power of the maternal archetype that *The Great Mother* takes the reader on a guided tour of the various manifestations of the Mother, from the most primitive (The Great Round) to the most highly evolved, as in the figures of Divine Wisdom and Sophia. Of Sophia, Neumann writes: "This feminine-maternal wisdom is no abstract, disinterested knowledge, but a wisdom of loving participation . . . the spiritual power of Sophia is living and saving; her overflowing heart is wisdom and food at once."[39] The full impact of this reorientation of Jungian theory in the direction of a "wisdom of loving participation" has yet to be measured, although its importance is already firmly established.

"The Purest Expression": Von Franz on Fairy Tales

"Fairy tales are the purest and simplest expression of collective and unconscious psychic processes," writes Marie-Louise von Franz in *An Introduction to the Psychology of Fairy Tales*. "Therefore their value for the scientific investigation of the unconscious exceeds that of all other material."[40] This bold assertion underlines the originality of her contribution: the displacement onto fairy tales of the attention once given to myths.

Since fairy tales "represent the archetypes in their simplest, barest and most concise forms,"[41] free from the overlay of cultural material that myths carry with them, von Franz thinks that they constitute a mirror of the psyche of unparalleled clarity. Furthermore, since each fairy tale taken individually contains one essential meaning in symbolic form, the analysis of fairy tales becomes a key element in the training of Jungian analysts.

Nevertheless, there is a disturbing element of reductionism in von Franz's claim for the value of the study of fairy tales. "After working many years in this field," she writes, "I have come to the conclusion that all fairy tales endeavor to describe one and the same psychic fact."[42] For her, this fact is the archetype of the *Self*. Thus all fairy tales, according to von Franz, deal with the process of *individuation*. If so, this particular symbolic focus would seem to distinguish fairy tales radically from the multireferential world of mythology.

Just as one notes in the work of Joseph Campbell a pronounced tendency to reduce all myths to symbolic statements of a single universal religious outlook or monomyth,[43] so one frequently finds von Franz reducing the vast and variegated world corpus of fairy tales to allegories of Jungian individuation. Like Campbell, von Franz favors a synthetic approach to the study of fairy tales; like Campbell, she can be criticized for imposing a single pattern on a vast amount of disparate material. As she herself admits, the danger with too theoretical an approach to an archetype is that "everything becomes everything." Yet in actual practice, von Franz's various studies of fairy tales do not seem to be as relentlessly centered on a single theme as her theoretical statements might lead us to expect. Although she does have the tendency to put things in categories and then to put everything in one ultimate category ("fairy tales as descriptions of the Self"), in fact she remains quite aware of the limitations of a rigidly monolithic approach.

The charm and the psychological acuity that characterize her writings have made "Marie-Louise" for many readers the archetypal Jungian Wise Old Woman. Her mind and feelings seem well integrated, and her wisdom is that of the heart. She held various notable seminars in the 1950s and 60s, transcriptions of which were revised later for publication, including *An Introduction to the Psychology of Fairy Tales* (1970), *Puer Aeternus* (1970—a study of Saint-Exupéry's modern fairy tale *The Little Prince*), *Problems of the Feminine in Fairy Tales* (1972), *Shadow and Evil in Fairy Tales* (1974), and *Individuation in Fairy Tales* (1976). In these works von Franz allies a vision of a systematic approach to the Self through such standard Jungian mythic categories as shadow, anima/animus, and the archetypal quest for the treasure with a highly developed presentation of the intricacies of the human psyche, of its labyrinthine complexities and its emotional richness.

It is perhaps quite apt that, as a woman, von Franz should have picked as the focus for her research the study of fairy tales, whose original storytellers were frequently women. In particular, the Grimm fairy tales, to which she often refers, are mainly known through versions told by women ("in general women were the best informants,"[44] writes a biographer of the Grimm brothers); and "Old Marie" Mueller, a pious widow in her sixties and housekeeper for the family of one of the neighbors of the Grimms in Kassel, was the source for about one quarter of the fairy tales in the first volume (1812).

It is also rather surprising that von Franz says nothing about all this! For just as Neumann wound up stressing the relationship between modern psychological awareness and archaic matriarchal consciousness, so von Franz might be said to have brought the integrative wisdom of humble wise old women of the German past into the forefront of modern psychological research—without really acknowledging what she was doing. With von Franz, as also with Neumann, one has the impression that each is a bit overly fascinated with the perspectives of the opposite sex. For instance, her classic study *Puer Aeternus* has nothing to say about the phenomenon of the female *puella*!

In any case, the originality of both Neumann and von Franz in the area of the Jungian analysis of myth is based to a great extent on the daring nature of the theoretical positions they took up in relation both to Jungian psychology and to the need to continue the work of the Master without living under his shadow. Neumann, the German Jew from Berlin and later the Tel Aviv Israeli, and von Franz, the strong-minded Austrian Catholic from Vienna, were uniquely qualified by both individual temperament and culture to push back the frontiers of the depth psychology of C.G. Jung, the Swiss Protestant patriarch from Basel. It is a sign of Jung's own broadmindedness and capacity as a teacher that both were able to develop in their own original ways.

Alchemy and Psychology

The particular archetypal image that Jung struggled to come to terms with in his alchemical studies was the *coniunctio*, or the joining of opposites. The myth that expresses this archetypal image is the *hieros gamos*, the sacred marriage of male and female principles. In his eightieth year he brought to a close the research that he had undertaken from 1941 to 1954. The results were published as *Mysterium Coniunctionis: An Inquiry into the Separation and Synthesis of Psychic Opposites in Alchemy* (1955). Here he notes, in the midst of a painstaking and elaborate explication of the psychological import of alchemical texts dating mainly from the late Middle Ages to the seventeenth century, that the particular myth of the *hieros gamos* is still alive in the modern psyche, as witnessed by the case of the newly promulgated Roman Catholic dogma of the Assumption of the Virgin Mary, who enters the heavenly bridal chamber and is symbolically united with Christ the Son.

For Jung, such symbols as the *coniunctio* "are tendencies which pursue a definite but not yet recognizable goal and consequently can express themselves only in analogies."[45] In contrast to Freud, Jung takes symbolically rather than literally the incestuous nature of the mother/son or sister/brother sexual union in myths representing the *coniunctio*. Moreover, whereas for Freud the problem of incestuous desire centered on the Oedipus myth constitutes a psychological malady to be overcome, for Jung the constellation of "the archetype of incest" (the first archetype to be discovered, and discovered by Freud, as he liked to say) accompanies the onset of the individuation process. Coming to consciousness in the form of various numinous symbols of incestuous union, the *coniunctio* as the archetypal image of incest serves a symbolic representation of that process of reconciliation of opposites and of psychic union.

For Jung, the alchemist's work (*opus*) was of the nature of a psychological and, indeed, religious quest. It was a series of rituals performed secretly, not publicly, and performed by an individual, not a congregation. It was undertaken by individuals who "staked [their] whole soul for the transcendental purpose of producing a *unity*. It was a work of reconciliation between apparently incompatible opposites."[46] But what the alchemists sought largely unconsciously, analytical psychology, taking up "the trail that had been lost by the alchemists,"[47] could pursue with a far more conscious sense of the inner psychological dimension of the work.

Both alchemy and analytical psychology seek to produce a unity out of opposites. For the alchemists, this unity was symbolized by the production of "gold" (*philosophical gold*, not the "vulgar gold" of the miser's delight). For Jung, it is the completion of the individuation process:

> We can see today that the entire alchemical procedure for uniting the opposites . . . could just as well represent the individuation process of a single individual, though with the not unimportant difference that no single individual ever attains to the richness and scope of the alchemical symbolism.[48]

But were the alchemists at all aware of the psychological import of their experiments? Recent scholarship seems to support Jung's psychological reinterpretation of the alchemists' passionate quest to the extent that it may be said to illuminate the inner dimensions of the *opus*. At least for such alchemists of the late Renaissance and seventeenth century as John Dee and Gerhard Dorn, according to one recent authority, the ultimate goal of the *opus* was the transformation of the alchemist himself into a "living philosophical stone." Alchemy, as a "philosophy of transformations," used "chemical terms" hermetically in order to "expound a spiritual system."[49]

The possibility of a psychological and spiritual interpretation of alchemical texts with their rich symbolism enabled Jung to anchor his own theory of the individuation process, not in Oriental conceptions of the Self such as the *atman* of Hindu religious philosophy and the *tao* of the Chinese alchemical text *The Secret of the Golden Flower* but in Western texts that constituted for Jung a "local" tradition.[50] These key alchemical texts were published in collections in Jung's own city of Basel (*Ars Chemica* [1566]); in Strasbourg (the last three volumes of *Theatrum Chemicum* [1613, 1622, 1661]), just down the Rhine from Basel; in nearby Geneva (*Bibliotheca Chemica Curiosa* [1702]); and in Frankfurt (*Musaeum Hermeticum* [1678]). Jung considered

Goethe's *Faust*, one of his favorite books from his early years onwards, the culmination of this alchemical tradition, its "highest poetic expression."[51] (There was even a family myth that Jung's paternal grandfather—after whom he was named— was Goethe's illegitimate son.) Through Goethe's *Faust*, especially the second part, alchemy became for Jung the ancestor of his own depth psychology.

One might categorize Jung's later works, including his work on alchemical and Gnostic texts, as religious thought with a *psychological*, not a *metaphysical*, foundation. Jung's autobiography, *Memories, Dreams, Reflections* goes into great detail concerning the dreams, visions and fantasies that constituted his *psychological* experience of the divine. The key word for Jung in matters of religion was *experience*, not faith: "the arch sin of faith, it seemed to me, was that it forestalled experience."[52] He wrote these words thinking of the loss of faith that plagued his father, a Lutheran minister who in the face of scientific materialism had found no religious experience with which to confirm his faith and who died without resolving this soul-wrenching problem. In an interview given the year (1959) before his death for the BBC television program "Face to Face," an interview that probably brought Jung to the attention of more people than anything before or since, there is a riveting moment when Jung replies to the question, "Do you now believe in God?":

> Now? [Pause.] Difficult to answer. I *know*. I don't need to believe. I know.[53]

Such a statement may strike the reader as pretentious, to say the least. But what in someone else's case might seem the height of presumption may be taken in Jung's case as a candid revelation. The "Visions" chapter of his autobiography gives an extraordinary account of the dreams and visionary experience that Jung had in the first months of 1944, during his stay in a hospital after a heart attack. At the end of his life he wrote that "they were the most tremendous things I have ever experienced."[54] Most of them concerned mythic representations of the *hieros gamos*, whether in the form of the marriage of Tifereth and Malchuth (the male and female principles of the Godhead in Jewish Kabalistic doctrine), the Marriage of the

Lamb, or the divine marriage of Zeus and Hera as described in the *Iliad*. Such accounts leave little doubt that Jung must be considered a genuine visionary and that his involvement with myths of the *hieros gamos* in alchemy was partially motivated by the *visionary experience* of such myths during the early years of the research which led to *Mysterium Coniunctionis*. As Jung was to say in the last pages of his autobiography, the "dividing walls" that separated his conscious ego from the world of the unconscious were "transparent." This transparency enabled him to "perceive the processes going on in the background," an experience that gave him a kind of "inner certainty."[55] These words may be said to constitute a paradigmatic description of the visionary mode.

The Holy Grail

In *Memories, Dreams, Reflections* Jung notes his fascination with the Grail legend. He retrospectively identifies his youthful self with the hero Parsifal, forced to witness in silence the painful existence and unhealed wounds of Amfortas, the "fisher king." In the case of his own Lutheran clergyman father Achilles, Jung considered these sufferings to be an unconscious living out of the sufferings of the Christian in general, without his father ever "becoming aware that this was a consequence of the *imitatio Christi*."[56]

Jung himself wrote little on the Grail, but his wife, Emma, made it her life's task as a scholar. Jung later admitted that "had it not been for my unwillingness to intrude upon my wife's field, I would unquestionably have had to include the Grail legend in my studies of alchemy."[57] Emma Jung died in 1955, before completing her magnum opus; it was Marie-Louise von Franz who brought it to completion and saw it published in 1958. *The Grail Legend* thus has a dual authorship. Since it is impossible to disentangle the contributions of Emma Jung from those of von Franz, I will attribute quotations and ideas simply to "the authors."

For the authors, the myth of the quest of the Holy Grail played a *compensatory* role for medieval Christianity. Christian dogma based on the teachings of Jesus and of the Fathers of the Church was balanced by images and rituals that *compensated* for its one-sided attitudes. Thus early on in the history of Christianity the figure of the historical Jesus came to be associated with an increasing number of archetypal images and symbols, to the point where the Christ image worshiped by Christians became a richly symbolic image of the Self. This traditional process of *amplification* of the Christ image through the accretion of such numinous symbols of the Self as the Cross, the Lamb, and the Fish was continued by the medieval Grail legend. The authors account for the growth of the myth in the following manner:

> fantasies, feelings and emotions rising up from the unconscious, as well as audacious new thought contents, had a better chance of finding expression . . . so that it could in fact be said that the living essence of Christ, his blood, lived on especially intensively in such interpretations, and that in transforming itself it also developed further.[58]

But the spiritual teachings of Christianity and the warrior ethic of medieval knighthood were potentially at odds, and this latent conflict threatened the integrity of the medieval Christian world vision. The need to bring Christianity into harmony with feudal thought and experience was answered by the creation of new myths concerning the knightly quest—a quest not for love, fame, and fortune but for the mysterious Grail.

What exactly was this Grail? According to the authors, in the various versions of the myth the true nature of the Grail was deliberately kept a mystery, "an archetypal image of polyvalent meaning."[59] In that way it could continue to entrance and fascinate the medieval mind and draw to itself not only Christian but also pre-Christian contents. As a ritual object suggesting the *chalice* (ciborium), the Grail reawakened the awe that medieval Christians wished to feel concerning the central mystery of the Mass. It symbolized the vessel containing the transubstantiated wine of the Mass, the veritable blood of Christ. In this sense, the Grail was a transparently Christian allegory, representing in terms of a knightly quest one of the sacred objects of the Mass.

But the Grail's meaning was not exhausted by the chalice of the Mass, for its symbolism resonated far beyond the range of orthodox medieval theology. As archetypal *vessel*, the Grail evoked a primal image of the Great Mother; as *stone*, it represented "an inner readiness for relating to the archetype of the Self."[60] With its central images of vessel and stone, together with other elements (the Lance, the Sword, the initiatic ordeal, the Fisher King), the Grail legend predates Christianity and sinks its roots in a Celtic and Germanic pagan past. By awakening such primal images, the Grail Legend helped graft Mediterranean Christianity onto the half-pagan mind of Northwestern Europe, only recently Christianized. It allowed for a deeper spiritual appropriation of the new faith through emotional conviction and not merely through dogmatic assent; it engaged the heart as well as the mind.

The authors analyze the various symbols of the Grail Legend at great length, giving numerous parallels from the storehouse of Celtic and Germanic mythology—at times one even wishes for less! Still, the central issue of the Grail legend as a compensatory myth is usually kept in view. Like alchemy, the Grail legend dealt with the problems of the assimilation of what medieval Christianity tended to reject: matter and evil. Matter was dealt with by the evocation of material images of the Self, the Grail being represented as sacred material object or stone, as opposed to the spiritualized Christ image. Evil was given a necessary compensatory role in the myth by the episode of the mysterious wounding of the Grail King by an enemy.

What is essential for the authors in the Grail legend is "the form in which the essential psychic life of the figure of Christ continues to exist and what it means."[61] Insofar as the Grail legend continues to fascinate contemporary minds, one may be allowed to speculate that the myth still has some role to play in contemporary religious consciousness.

NOTES

1. Jung, *C.G. Jung Speaking*, p. 371.

2. See Jung, *Symbols of Transformation*, p. 101.

3. See Jung, *Memories, Dreams, Reflections*, pp. 128–30.

4. Jung, *Dream Analysis*, p. 217.

5. Dr. Rudolf Pekar, "Ein Arzt Erinnert Sich" ["A Doctor Remembers"], in Edeltraud Kendler, *Nie Wieder! Das Konzentrazionslager Ebensee* [*Never Again! The Ebensee Concentration Camp*] (Bad Ischl, Austria: Blick Verlag, 1988), p. 99 [my translation].

6. Jung, *Nietzsche's Zarathustra*, II, pp. 1433–4.

7. See Richard F. Hardin, "Archetypal Criticism," in *Contemporary Literary Theory*, ed. G. Douglas Atkins and Laura Morrow (Amherst: University of Massachusetts Press, 1989), pp. 42–59.

8. See Robert A. Segal, *Joseph Campbell: An Introduction*, rev. ed. (New York: New American Library/Mentor Books, 1990 [1987]).

9. Hardin, p. 47. On the influence of Jungian psychology on the Cambridge ritualists, see Robert Ackerman, *The Myth and Ritual School: J.G. Frazer and the Cambridge Ritualists*, Theorists of Myth Series, vol. 2 (New York: Garland, 1991), pp. 65, 149, 152, 167, 189, 197.

10. See Segal, ch. 12 ("Campbell as a Jungian").

11. Jung, *The Archetypes and the Collective Unconscious*, 2nd ed., trans. R.F.C. Hull (Princeton, N.J.: Princeton University Press, 1968), p. 61.

12. See Jung, "Transformation Symbolism in the Mass," in *Psyche and Symbol*, ed. Violet S. de Laszlo (Garden City, N.Y.: Doubleday, 1958), pp. 148–224.

13. Jung, letter in English dated February 6, 1951; in *Letters*, II, p. 3.

14. Jung, *Flying Saucers*, p. 13.

15. Jung, *Mandala Symbolism*, pp. 6–70 and 71–100.

16. Jung, *Flying Saucers*, p. 22.

17. Ibid., p. 21.

18. Jung, letter dated January 16, 1989; in *Letters*, II, p. 477. See also Jung, *Memories, Dreams, Reflections*, p. 323.

19. Jung, *Flying Saucers*, p. 44.

20. Ibid., p. 38.

21. Jung, *The Spirit in Man, Art, and Literature*, pp. 82–3.

22. Ibid., p. 99.

23. Ibid., p. 122.

24. Jung, *Nietzsche's Zarathustra*, I, p. 154.

25. Warren Steinberg, "The Therapeutic Utilization of Countertransference," *Quadrant*, 22 (1989), 25.

26. Jung, *Memories, Dreams, Reflections*, p. 183.

27. Jung, *Essays on Contemporary Events*, p. 13.

28. Ibid., p. 15.

29. Jung, letter in English dated September 14, 1960; in *Letters*, II, p. 594.

30. Ibid., pp. 594–5.

31. Jung, *Essays on Contemporary Events*, pp. 23–4.

32. Jung, letter dated May 26, 1923; in *Letters*, I, pp. 39–40.

33. Ibid., p. 40.

34. Jung, letter dated December 16, 1939; in *Letters*, I, p. 280.

35. Jung, *Essays on Contemporary Events*, p. 17.

36. In *C.G. Jung: Word and Image*, ed. Aniela Jaffé (Princeton, N.J.: Princeton University Press, 1979), p. 145.

37. Erich Neumann, *The Great Mother: An Analysis of the Archetype*, 2nd ed., trans. Ralph Manheim (Princeton, N.J.: Princeton University Press, 1963 [1955]), p. xlii.

38. Ibid., pp. 43–4.

39. Ibid., pp. 330–1.

40. Marie-Louise von Franz, *An Introduction to the Psychology of Fairy Tales* (Dallas: Spring, 1970), p. 1.

41. Ibid.

42. Ibid.

43. In Campbell's case, probably a reflection of his interest in the "harmony of religions" taught by Ramakrishna, which stressed the basic unity of all religions—the paradigm of "one truth expressed various ways." Campbell was a friend and associate of Swami Nikhilananda of the New York Ramakrishna-Vivekananda Center.

44. Murray B. Peppard, *Paths Through the Forest: A Biography of the Brothers Grimm* (New York: Holt, Rinehart and Winston, 1971), p. 51.

45. Jung, *Mysterium Coniunctionis*, p. 468.

46. Ibid., p. 554.

47. Ibid.

48. Ibid., p. 555.

49. Charles Nicholl, *The Chemical Theatre* (London: Routledge & Kegan Paul, 1980), p. 54.

50. Jung likewise interpreted ancient Gnostic texts as symbolic expressions of the individuation process and valued them for anchoring his theory in the Western tradition. See Robert A. Segal, ed., *The Gnostic Jung* (Princeton, N.J.: Princeton University Press, 1992), esp. pp. 19–48.

51. Jung, *Mysterium Coniunctionis*, p. 554.

52. Jung, *Memories, Dreams, Reflections*, p. 94.

53. Jung, *C.G. Jung Speaking*, p. 428.

54. Jung, *Memories, Dreams, Reflections*, p. 295.

55. Ibid., p. 355.

56. Ibid., p. 215.

57. Ibid.

58. Emma Jung and Marie-Louise von Franz, *The Grail Legend*, trans. Andrea Dykes (London: Hodder and Stoughton, 1971), p. 111.

59. Ibid., p. 121.

60. Ibid., p. 144.

61. Ibid., p. 109.

CHAPTER FIVE

New Orientations and Developments

Like other vital and developing fields, analytical psychology has produced its fair share of creative extensions, controversial popularizations, and changes of orientation. This chapter will examine some of the ones most germane to the study of mythology. It will also provide a theoretical framework for the different kinds of Jungian symbolic interpretations likely to be encountered in the course of researching a particular myth.

Sometimes one of the ideas spun off by Jung with astonishing profusion only later inspired, or at least confirmed, a Jungian procedure that otherwise might appear to be without precedent or authority. In such a case I have presented Jung's own particular contribution to later "Jungianism" without apology for the seeming anachronism.

Archetypal Dimensions of Daily Life

Jungian theory views myth as ultimately based on the extraordinary experience of archetypal numinosity in dreams, fantasies, and visionary states of consciousness. But what of daily life? Does the dull, daily grind have an archetypal dimension? Does ordinary experience harbor a "mythic" potential?

In *Jung and the Post-Jungians* (1985) Andrew Samuels argues for the presence of archetypal experience in ordinary perceptions:

> There is a general move in analytical psychology away from single, big, decorous, numinous expectations of archetypal imagery. The archetypal may be said to be

found in the eye of the beholder and not in that which he
beholds. . . . The archetypal is a *perspective* defined in terms
of its impact, depth, consequence and grip. The archetypal
is in the emotional experience of perception and not in a
pre-existing list of symbols.[1]

Samuels' "expansionist" theory of archetypes allows archetypal
experience to be described and accounted for on the basis of
ordinary perception. The experience of the archetypal is no
longer restricted to dreams, visions, or synchronistic phenomena; rather, daily life can provide its own opportunities for
sensing the archetypal in the midst of otherwise ordinary
experiences. This experience of the archetypal does not require
correlation with a standard list of "Jungian archetypes." The
particular theoretical interest of such an approach is that it
eliminates the need to pigeonhole the *particular archetype* that has
been constellated in a given situation and allows us to "ask
ourselves with regard to any phenomenon: what is the part
played by *the archetypal*?"[2]

    Samuels gives an example of such an experience. A
Jungian group was discussing the psychological traumas
resulting from the experience of bombing raids in Lebanon.
What turned out to be archetypal for the participants was not the
actual topic discussed but rather the "wordy" dimension of the
discussion. "*Wordy*," comments Samuels, "was, just then, an
archetypal image." Following Samuels' lead, one might easily
conclude that when one speaks of "the power of language," or
when one notes in mythology the motif of the magical effect of
words or the motif of speaking too little or too much, the
ultimate reference would be to something of the sort Samuels
experienced: the numinous effect of words.

    According to this theory, daily life—and not just dreams,
visions, and extraordinary states of mind—provides numerous
occasions for the intrusion of the archetypal into ordinary
perception. We know that falling in love, for instance, is clearly
an archetypal experience, since in that extraordinary state of
mind even a person of limited insight into the unconscious
experiences for a while the numinous fascination of the anima or
animus. But there exists a much greater range of tamer
experiences not easily catalogable that may provide numinous

experiences: a sudden silence in nature, a nagging feeling of dread, or an unexplained sense of happiness. Everything, in other words, that we might label "poetic" or "emotional" has the potential for being interpreted as an archetypal experience.

The mythological patterns manifested in our daily lives are the subject of a popular book by Carol Pearson, *The Hero Within: Six Archetypes We Live By* (1989). Pearson uses the hero archetype as a container for a spirally oriented map of the heroic quest. Her mythological terminology replaces what she calls "limiting stereotypes" with "empowering archetypes" that are "active in our *conscious* lives." Since Pearson focuses her attention on ordinary conscious experience rather than on the unconscious, she believes that "the myths that govern our lives" require "ordinary, well-known words to describe them rather than the exotic names of ancient gods and goddesses or psychological terms such as anima and animus, which may seem intimidating to some." Having eliminated traditional Jungian terminology at one stroke, and having replaced it with six archetypes with unintimidating names (the Innocent, the Orphan, the Martyr, the Warrior, the Wanderer, and the Magician), Pearson leads the reader into a novel perspective on mythology, according to which "the archetypes are fundamentally friendly," since "in honoring them we grow."[3]

It remains to be seen, however, whether Pearson's use of the term "archetype" constitutes anything more than a friendly nod in the direction of Jungian psychology. Unlike Robert Moore, whose recent book *King, Warrior, Magician, Lover* (1990) is closely linked with the theoretical foundations of Jungian psychology, Pearson seems determined to replace the emphasis in depth psychology on the collective unconscious with a psychology of archetypes of *conscious* life. Whether successful in this attempt or not, her work exemplifies a recent trend to move archetypal psychology into the arena of the practical psychology of everyday life.

Gods and Goddesses in Everyone

The mythology associated with the names of ancient gods and goddesses is not, however, too "exotic" for all Americans, many of whom seem quite capable of taking an interest in the significant archetypal patterns and meaningful imagery that traditional myths reveal when interpreted psychologically and symbolically. In fact, a number of popular books published in recent years have encouraged readers to identify themselves, their problems, and their potentials with the myths of ancient deities. The basis for the popularity of these books might be accounted for somewhat cynically by the pleasant fantasy of deification: whereas once one was branded a neurotic, now one is hailed as a god. But there is no doubt that these books have struck a chord in the hearts of a large number of readers.

Nowhere has the incitement to archetypal inflation been greater than in those books touched by currents of modern feminism and the New Age mystique of a return of a religion of the Goddess. In this category we might place such books as Ginette Paris' *Pagan Meditations: Aphrodite, Hestia, Artemis* (1986) Sylvia Brinton Perera's *Descent to the Goddess: A Way of Initiation for Women* (1981), Christine Downing's *The Goddess: Mythological Images of the Feminine* (1984), Jean Shinoda Bolen's *Goddesses in Everywoman: A New Psychology of Women* (1984), Nancy Qualls-Corbett's *The Sacred Prostitute: Eternal Aspect of the Feminine* (1988), and Jennifer Barker Woolger and Roger J. Woolger's *The Goddess Within: A Guide to the Eternal Myths That Shape Women's Lives* (1989). The same mythological amplification of everyday problems and concerns characterizes the basic procedure of other studies oriented around the psychology of men. One finds the same concern with "empowering archetypes" that was noted in the case of Carol Pearson's *The Hero Within*, minus the fear that ancient myths might prove in any way "intimidating." Such studies as Eugene Monick's *Phallos: Sacred Image of the Masculine* (1987), Sherry L. Salman's "The Horned God: Masculine Dynamics of Power and Soul" (1986), Irene Gad's "Hephaestus: Model of New-Age Masculinity" (1986), and Jean Shinoda Bolen's *Gods in Everyman: A New Psychology of Men's Lives and Loves* (1989) show the same relationship to the growing men's movement as the earlier titles do to the more firmly established feminism of the last several decades. Both sets of works testify to the coming of age of a new sense of the archetypal in daily life.

Lest the reader conclude prematurely that these studies represent nothing more than a breezily optimistic, overly casual, and typically American approach to mysteries of the psyche, it is only fair to add that this popularizing trend has caught on in German-speaking lands as well, including Jung's own Switzerland. There we find adultery, for instance, anatomized in terms of a psychological interpretation of the myth of Zeus and Semele (Hans Jellouschek, *Semele, Zeus und Hera: Die Rolle der Geliebten in der Dreiecksbeziehung* [1987]), androgyny discussed in terms of the myth of the Sphinx (Helmut Remmler, *Das Geheimnis der Sphinx: Archetyp für Mann und Frau* [1988]), and other problematic aspects of love examined in terms of the myths of such divine couples as Shiva and Shakti, and Ishtar and Tammuz in Verena Kast's *Paare* (1984), recently translated into English as *The Nature of Loving: Patterns of Human Relationship* (1986). Given the earlier extensive published research of Marie-Louise von Franz on fairy tales, and given of course the enduring fascination of such stories in the cultural homeland of the brothers Grimm, it is not surprising that psychological interpretations of fairy tales (e.g. Lutz Müller, *Das tapfere Schneiderlein: List als Lebenskunst* ["The Brave Little Tailor: Cunning as an Art of Living"] [1985]) have also proved popular. Continuing this trend in the Far East, the Japanese Jungian Hayao Kawai has analyzed some of the psychological dimensions of his own culture in *The Japanese Psyche: Major Motifs in the Fairy Tales of Japan* (1988).

These psychologizing meditations on myths do not really constitute a radical departure from the spirit of Jung's own occasional therapeutic advice. Consider the following advice that Jung gave a young Greek girl who had written him about a dream she had had of "two feminine figures in their long Grecian robes, one of whom was the goddess Demeter." Jung felt that the dream was trying to draw her attention to what he called a "great mythologem so important for a woman's psych-ology." His advice to her was "to follow the suggestion of the dream and to meditate on all the aspects of the myth of Demeter and Persephone"[4] in order to find out out what Demeter had to convey to her. This psychological meditation on myth can be taken as a model for what some later Jungian writers have urged on their readers.

The use of mythological figures as aids to psychological development and self-knowledge is based on what some consider a fringe, but others a major, development in Jungian psychology. David Miller has dubbed it "the new polytheism." In Miller's opinion, Jewish and Christian myths have so permeated our cultural consciousness from childhood onwards that they are less useful in pointing out undiscovered or neglected aspects of the Western psyche. Such myths suffer from overfamiliarity as well as from overabsorption by the culture. By contrast, the myths associated with the Greek gods and goddesses, precisely because "they are not a part of our remembered history," can help us toward an expanded consciousness and a "remythologization of life."[5] Their very lack of familiarity, at least to present-day Americans, makes them more effective in pointing out unfamiliar areas of the psyche and in stimulating psychological insight and growth.

The leading figure of this myth-oriented Jungianism is James Hillman, whose original and complex theory deserves a lengthy study in its own right. Hillman believes that myths generate "healing fictions." By this term he means that the mythical stories we tell ourselves about our lives can bring order to chaos and hope to despair. In order to regenerate our capacity for "story-awareness," something that so many of us lose after childhood, a re-mythologization of consciousness is needed. And for this Hillman believes that both classical and biblical myths can come to our aid. Myths can "direct fantasy into organized, deeply life-giving psychological patterns."[6]

For this reason Hillman has reoriented his "archetypal psychology" in the direction of polytheistic imagination, as opposed to the obsessive circling around "self and monotheism" that he sees as the latent weakness of Jung's own theoretical orientation.[7] For Hillman, the problem lies not so much with Jungian theory itself as with the co-option of the Jungian individuation process by Western monotheistic culture, especially by the Protestant culture from which Jung came. For

Hillman, the result of this co-option is that Jungian theory has been given an inappropriately religious slant that is foreign to its originally nonmetaphysical, even anti-metaphysical, orientation: "When our model of individuation is governed by monotheistic psychology in its Protestant direction, every fantasy becomes a prisoner for Christ."[8]

And yet the "New Polytheism" itself may in fact be seen as subtly religious in orientation, especially when Hillman makes such statements as "depth psychology believes in myth, practices myth, teaches myth" in the context of affirming that "psychoanalysts are the myth-preservers in our culture." The line between the analytical and the priestly vocations may seem dangerously thin when too much hostility to monotheistic Protestantism seems to manifest the antagonism of one religious position toward another rather than a recognizably analytical concern with the symbolic interpretation of myths and religious iconography for the light they shed on the nature of the psyche. Hillman's taking up of arms in order to defend classical forms of pagan religious sensibility is something that has not been seen since the artistic neo-paganism of the Renaissance—a time of great cultural ferment when the greatest French poet of the period, Pierre de Ronsard, could be accused of sacrificing a goat to the Greek god Dionysos!

More than any other Jungian analyst, Hillman has a refined and educated literary perspective which makes him especially vulnerable to the charge of estheticism.[9] Nevertheless, it is fair to say that mythological consciousness, however much it may have been lost in our culture at large, was always preserved by the poets, and Hillman in that sense deserves to be called, as Ronsard was earlier, the "prince of poets," at least among Jungians. His writings should be of increasing interest to literary critics and to classicists since they develop the theory that the ancient gods and goddesses and the mythologies associated with them are not dead but continue to live on as images of the living processes of the psyche. A purely historical and antiquarian approach to mythology needs to be vivified by a feeling for the texture of living myths and for the perennial significance they contain.

Symbolic Interpretation and the
Remythologization of Religion

Even to the casual reader, the religious orientation of so many aspects of Jung's later thought is inescapable. Was Jung himself a mystic? Certainly the dreams and visions of 1944 as recounted in *Memories, Dreams, Reflections*, permeated as they are with the imagery of the Book of Revelation and the Jewish Kabala, suggest this possibility. Aniela Jaffé, his secretary and close associate in his old age, has written recently that "Jung was a highly gifted dreamer" and that "what distinguished [him] from the mystics in the usual sense of the word was that he acknowledged the epistemological limitation."[10] That is, Jung claimed to have experienced *psychological image* and not *metaphysical fact*.

However one resolves the issue, it seems clear that Jung allied a naturally religious temperament with a strong visionary capacity. At the same time he found it impossible to live within the confines of the Christian faith of his childhood—or of any other traditional religious or mythological framework, for that matter. As an empiricist, he was extremely distrustful of the formulations of theologians, who, in his opinion, argued over metaphysical ideas when they should have been seeking to understand religious experience. Writing late in his life to an Italian correspondent, he maintained that "we need religion, which means a careful consideration of what happens . . . and less sophistry, i.e., overvaluation of the rational intellect."[11] This hostility to the *furor theologicus* ran deep with Jung, and theologians tended to repay him in kind. Nothing distressed him so much in later years as his inability to gain understanding from the religious intellectual community, which, he felt, ought to have been the first to hail his great expectations of the future role of religion in the life of modern humanity. Even his extensive correspondence with Father Victor White, in which many major differences were openly debated—not least the bombshell effect which Jung's *Answer to Job* had had on religiously minded readers—finally ended in silence and White's withdrawal from communication.

What exactly were Jung's ideas about religion? How have they been received in the period after his death? First of all, Jung, as noted, valued *experience* over *belief.* Writing to an American correspondent, he claimed that religion "is not at all a matter of intellectual conviction or philosophy or even belief, but rather a matter of inner experience," although, as he notes wryly, "this is a conception which seems to be completely ignored by the theologians in spite of the fact that they talk a lot about it."[12] Religious experience was something he conceptualized as the numinous experience of the archetypes of the collective unconscious.

Jung did not, however, promote the casual or premature search after such experience. As he wrote to Father White concerning Aldous Huxley's enthusiasm for mescalin-induced visions, "there is no point in wishing to *know* [= experience] more of the collective unconscious than one gets in dreams and intuition." The reason for this, he wrote, is that "the more you know of it, the greater and heavier becomes your burden, because the unconscious contents transform themselves into your individual tasks and duties as soon as they begin to become conscious."[13] Other than in "dreams and intuition," the direct experience of the collective unconscious was more than something Jung could recommend as a goal for those motivated primarily by mere curiosity. Rather, since it laid such a heavy burden of responsibility on those who had such experience given to them by fate (as Jung seemed to have considered was his own case), it was something less to be sought after than to be endured if it could not be avoided.

Second, Jung was quite aware of the fact that "inner experience" is ultimately uncommunicable except in terms of *myth.* "Myth," he wrote, "gives the ultimately unimaginable religious experience an image, a form in which to express itself."[14] Myths are descriptions of psychic processes "told by the many and heard by the many"; myth, since it is a primal form of human communication, "makes community life possible."[15] Thus for several reasons Jung was not in favor of what seemed to be a progressive and enlightened trend in theology at the time: Rudolf Bultmann's attempt to distance religion from its mythological components by translating them into existentialist terms. Nor could Jung sanction the attempt to produce through *demythologization* what Dietrich Bonhoeffer had called a "faith without religion." Such a demythologization, felt Jung, would privilege belief over experience and would eliminate the one means—myth—by which experience could be communicated.

Given what he considered to be the desperate spiritual needs of the nuclear age, Jung favored a rehabilitation of religious myths, but not in terms of outdated *concretistic* (literal) or historic interpretations that are unacceptable to the scientific empiricist. Rather, Jung favored a psychological rather than metaphysical and a *symbolic* rather than literal interpretation of religious myths and symbols. Such interpretation is always tentative, since it relies heavily on the changing subjective responses of the interpreter, not on some fixed system of belief or on some traditional symbolic code. When Maud Oakes sent him her interpretation of the symbols and inscriptions that Jung himself had carved on a stone monument outside his house at Bollingen,[16] he discouraged her from seeing in them "metaphysical assertions" or "a sort of confession or a belief." "I have no religious or other convictions about my symbols," he wrote. "They are mere allusions, they hint at something, they stammer and often they lose their way." Stressing the "tentativeness" of all such attempts to interpret images, myths and texts symbolically, Jung added that even his own symbolic products were "nothing but humble attempts to formulate, to define, to shape the inexpressible."[17] Thus Jungian psychological symbolic interpretation makes no claims to metaphysical truth.

This *tentative* symbolic mode of interpretation is what Jung struggled to illustrate in such late essays as "Transformation Symbolism in the Mass" (1954) and *Answer to Job* (1952). But it may take a while for Jung's psychological point of view to make much headway against the metaphysical bias of orthodox theologies.

By now Jung's call for symbolic remythologization from a psychological perspective has been heeded by at least a few religious thinkers, and it seems likely that interest from that quarter will continue to grow. John Sanford, an Episcopal priest who received a letter from Jung just before his death praising an essay he had written on the importance of dreams (see Sanford's book *Dreams: God's Forgotten Language* [1968]), has continued to interpret religion and religious myths from a Jungian standpoint in such books as *The Kingdom Within: A Study of the Inner Meaning of Jesus' Sayings* (1970), *The Man Who Wrestled With God: Light from the Old Testament on the Psychology of Individuation* (1974), and *King Saul the Tragic Hero: A Study in Individuation* (1985). A Carmelite priest, John Welch, published a study of the inner journey entitled *Spiritual Pilgrims: Carl Jung and Teresa of Avila* (1982), which won the National Catholic Book Award for the Best Adult Book of that year. Apparently without offending too many theologians, Welch was able to support Jung's position that, as a "symbol of the Self," as "a symbolic representation," "the figure of Christ points not only to the historical Jesus and the resurrected God-man but also to the inner life and goals of all men and women."[18] Ann and Barry Ulanov's *Religion and the Unconscious* (1975) also reaffirms the value of Jungian symbolic interpretation: "Meditating over the symbols of the human unconscious opens one to meditations connecting one to the divine and ultimately to the world of sacrament."[19] The Jungian analyst Edward Edinger has published both *The Bible and Psyche: Individuation Symbolism in the Old Testament* (1986) and *The Christian Archetype: A Jungian Commentary on the Life of Christ* (1987). That Jung's procedures are at last on the way to becoming respectable among Christian theologians and religious scholars seems supported by the assertion, in Wayne G. Rollins' book *Jung and the Bible* (1983), that "Jung had a biblical understanding of the world . . . and . . . a sense of God—the numinous, the holy, at the center of things."[20]

Jung's longstanding interest in Eastern religious traditions such as Hinduism, Yoga and Chinese Taoism has been well documented in the text as well as the annotated bibliography of Harold Coward's *Jung and Eastern Thought* (1985). Some East-West perspectives on Buddhism as well as a Jungian commentary on the famous Zen Oxherding Pictures may be found in *Buddhism and Jungian Psychology* (1985) by J. Marvin Spiegelman and Mokusen Miyuki. Here, too, in the area of flourishing non-Western faiths, one can reasonably expect a further rapprochement between Jungian and traditional religious positions.

Jungian Primitivism

The term "primitivism" is typically used in two distinct but related senses. First of all, it designates a *sentimental* approach to archaic and pre-industrial cultures. However, this seemingly sympathetic perspective in fact contains not only a veiled contempt for the simple-minded "primitive" but also a demeaning colonialist or neo-colonialist program of subjugation and exploitation: the primitive is a child who requires parental (i.e., colonialist) supervision. Seen from this perspective, the primitive can only be an anachronism, who embodies what "advanced" Western civilization has left behind. As Marx said of the Homeric epics, primitive cultures represent "the childhood of humanity." However appealing they may seem, they exist at a "lower" stage of development and represent a species of barbarism that the civilizing mission of the West has a duty to raise to a "higher" plane. Thus Jung, employing the condescending colonialist vocabulary of his age, described primitive cultures as "descending to a . . . lower cultural level," while actually valuing them rather highly.[21]

But if the primitive frequently represents the secretly despised Other for the modern Westerner, there is a second version of primitivism which sees that Other *as* Us, or rather, *in* Us. In this *idealizing* version of primitivism the primitive is seen as holding the key to the modern Westerner's deepest sense of identity: the primitive becomes a symbol of the unconscious psychic core, the primordial self covered over by layers of civilization. The primitive *in us* is more authentic, more in contact with the wellsprings of life—in Jungian terms, more in contact with the archetypes of the collective unconscious.

The modern primitivist fantasy of identification with the primitive runs deep in the modern psyche, where it plays a *compensatory* role of major proportions. It compensates for the stresses of the industrial and corporate workplace, for the destruction of the natural world, for the loss of small-scale community life, and for the loss of leisure and the spirit of playfulness. Whether embodied in the Native American warrior, the Stone Age cave dweller, or the African witch doctor, the consoling fantasy of the primitive plays counterpoint to the problems of modern civilization. This idealizing version of primitivism might appear to be some new version of pastoral— with the modern Westerner happily playing at primitive, just as Marie Antoinette once played at shepherdess. But one should be careful not to dismiss it out of hand as pure fantasy, as "myth, not reality," for fantasies and myths contain significant compensatory images that can enlighten and enrich cultural consciousness.

These two versions of primitivism—the sentimental and the idealizing—may coexist in the Western mind without arousing any sense of their contradictoriness. One finds both of them in Jung's writings. A genuine psychological appreciation of the value of primitive cultures is rarely dissociated in Jung's own work from the colonialist view of them as "lower" and less culturally evolved than modern cultures. Still, Jung's chief claim to originality lies in his clear sense of the link between modern and primitive psychological life—a link forged through myth above all.

Jung noted two excellent reasons for studying the mythology of primitive cultures. First, the study of primitive cultures provides an outside standpoint from which to judge modern Western culture and its idiosyncrasies. It enables us to glimpse our own cultural shadow, to which we are so often blind. Second, primitive myths are alive in our psyches. The voice of the unconscious may speak to modern human beings through very unmodern myths!

Jung's earliest opportunity to see Western civilization as others see it came in 1924–25 during a trip to the American Southwest. There he was able for the first time to speak at length (and in English, without an interpreter) with an outstanding representative of a primitive culture, a chief of the Taos Pueblo Indians, Ochwiay Biano (Mountain Lake). In the course of getting to know him and his culture, Jung came to realize how white men looked from the standpoint of the Indian: as men with cruel faces and maniacal stares, whom the Indians could only consider to be insane. This glimpse of the Western cultural shadow prompted Jung to redefine the history of Western civilization's imperial progress from Roman times onwards as a history of rapine and brutality and to see the other face of

Western civilization as "the face of a bird of prey seeking with cruel intentness for distant quarry—a face worthy of a race of pirates and highwaymen." He added that "all the eagles and other predatory creatures that adorn our coats of arms [an American thinks immediately of our national bird the Bald Eagle] seem to me apt psychological representatives of our true nature."[22]

Jung also felt deeply the sense of dignity that an archaic culture rooted in its own mythological vision could give its members. At the same time he gained a valuable critical perspective on the contrasting rootlessness of modern Western culture, psychologically impoverished since the Renaissance by its break with the mythic world and suffering from a dangerous split between the conscious world of modern rationalism and the shadow world of the unconscious.

The other great benefit of studying primitive cultures lay for Jung in the paradoxical discovery that primitive myths could speak to him on a most intimate, personal level. A trip to Africa the next year brought him into contact with the Elgonyi, a Masai tribe living on the slopes of Mt. Elgon in British Kenya. Here, too, he was able to converse at length (albeit with a translator) with representatives of a primitive culture that had not yet totally succumbed to Western cultural imperialism. As in the American Southwest, one of the things that impressed him most was the solar mysticism that pervaded the culture. The people of the Taos Pueblo, as Jung had discovered after his talks with Ochwiay Biano, considered themselves to be children of the Sun. They believed that the sun's daily course across the sky—and, by extension, the continued existence of life on earth—was made possible by their rituals and religious devotion. Jung found a similar sense of connection via myth and ritual with the sun as the principle of light with the Elgonyi. They lived according to what Jung dubbed "the Horus principle," the mystery of the newly risen divine light, as exemplified by the god Horus in ancient Egypt. Jung discovered something more: that the mystery of the birth of light, of the birth of consciousness, was a mythological drama "intimately connected with me [and] with my psychology."[23] Jung's expedition to Africa had thus turned into "not so much an objective scientific project as an intensely personal one."[24]

The year before, Jung had envied the spiritual self-confidence, in spite of years of Anglo cultural and social oppression, of the beleaguered people of the Taos Pueblo—a self-confidence based on their conviction that their rituals and religious devotion were essential to the course of the sun across the sky and to the maintenance of the universe. Now in Africa Jung intuited for the first time what became for him the meaning of human consciousness: that it was consciousness which endowed the world with objective reality. This meaning for Jung was contained within a myth of participation in the creation of the world: "Man is indispensable for the completion of creation . . . in fact, he himself is the second creator of the world, who alone has given to the world its objective existence."[25] Man is thus the Second Creator; Man is co-partner with God.

In this myth Jung was to find great personal significance and satisfaction, especially in his later years. Human consciousness allows the creator god "to become conscious of His creation, and man conscious of himself. This was, wrote Jung, "the explanatory myth which [had] slowly taken shape within me in the course of the decades."[26] This myth, which Jung spelled out above all in *Answer to Job*, satisfied his need to see meaning in the existence of human consciousness as part of the cosmos. It was in many ways his personal myth. It was for him a compensatory myth that dominated his thought in his old age. It developed at a time when the Cold War and the nuclear threat had all but extinguished his hopes for the future of humanity. But its origin, as we have seen, stems from his earlier contact with primitive cultures of Africa and of the American Southwest.

With the model of Jung's psychologically oriented primitivism behind them, it is not surprising that later Jungians have devoted attention to primitive cultures and mythologies. Joseph Campbell, although not strictly speaking a Jungian,[27] has probably done the most to popularize and illustrate the thesis that the mythologies of primitive peoples—for Campbell, the myths of the American Indians above all—have much to teach the modern psyche. Campbell's syncretic account of world mythology has received posthumous expression in his *Historical*

Atlas of World Mythology, a beautifully illustrated and clearly written multivolume compendium, which, along with the 1988 filmed series of interviews with Bill Moyers, *Joseph Campbell and the Power of Myth*, has probably brought his primitivistic vision to its high point of popularity and influence.[28]

But Campbell is not the only one to have followed the lead of Jung and to have explored the far reaches of the primitive psyche in search of buried treasure for the myth-starved modern world. The Jungian analyst Joseph L. Henderson read a paper on the Hopi snake dance for the Analytical Psychology Club in London in 1932, several years after Jung had made his momentous journey to the American Southwest. Henderson's lifelong fascination with primitive cultures and especially with their rites of initiation may be best represented in his essay "Ancient Myths and Modern Man" in *Man and His Symbols* (1964) and in his book *Thresholds of Initiation* (1967). *Betwixt and Between: Patterns of Masculine and Feminine Initiation* (1987), a volume of essays edited by Louise Carus Mahdi, Steven Foster, and Meredith Little, illustrates the continuing wealth of reflection that Jungian primitivism is capable of inspiring; it opens with a notable statement by the eminent anthropologist Victor Turner.

In a set of interviews with Jean-Marc Pottiez published under the provocative title of *A Walk With a White Bushman* (1986) Sir Laurens van der Post, a friend of Jung's old age, looked back on his own rich experience of a primitive culture, beginning with his infancy in South Africa. The first human face van der Post remembers is that of a Bushman nurse, Klara, "a Stone Age person," as he puts it at the opening of the first interview. His fascination with Bushman culture has resulted in several books, most recently *Testament to the Bushmen* (1984), which he co-authored with Jane Taylor. While much of what he has written about the Bushmen has value as a vivid description of a primitive culture from the standpoint of an intelligent and sympathetic observer who has deep respect for their culture, van der Post's particularly Jungian emphasis on the inner link between the primitive and the modern psyche is found in such a provocative statement as "the greatest damage we are doing to the Bushmen is to the Bushmen inside ourselves. Because what you do to another human being you do to yourself."[29] The primitive side of the modern psyche that van der Post calls "the Bushman inside ourselves" corresponds to what Jung had earlier called "the million year old man" or (with an even less credible sense of chronology) "the 2,000,000-Year-Old-Man."[30]

For van der Post, the mythology of the Bushmen proved inspiring because he saw in it "the deep inner meanings the psychologists talk about," and the Bushmen themselves represented "something which we now find only in our dreams." His assertion that "it is by making what is first and oldest new and contemporary that we become creative" may be said to constitute an admirably concise manifesto of primitivism, all the more impressive because of the actual experience of a primitive culture that lies behind it. Van der Post's attempt to "translate this Stone Age idiom into a contemporary one" was inspired by his feeling that the "primitive" Bushman was in fact "a walking pilot scheme of how the European man could find his way back to values he had lost and he needed for his renewal."[31] The mythology and the rock art of the Bushmen have the capacity to constellate the "Bushman within ourselves" and to sponsor within the modern Western psyche a new awareness of the unity of life and the sacredness of the natural world.

Other Jungians have continued the project of relating primitive mythological modes of thought to the conceptual system of analytical psychology. For Esther Leonard De Vos, for example, Haitian Voodoo provides a rich field of comparative psychological research. De Vos writes that "it would not be straining credibility to propose that the contents of the collective unconscious are experienced as *loa* by those whose belief system is Voodoo, and as archetypes by those whose belief system is analytical psychology."[32] Janet O. Dallett, in the midst of a personal and professional crisis, found wisdom and inspiration in the mythic consciousness of the Native Americans of the Pacific Northwest.[33] M. Vera Buhrmann, who has studied with the Xhosa healers of South Africa, has discovered that their mythological worldview presents striking affinities with that of analytical psychology.

Behind these and other ongoing Jungian primitivist attempts to bridge the gap between the modern and the primitive psyche stands the earlier research of the British anthropologist and Jungian John Layard. In his 1948 article "The Making of Man in Malekula" Layard describes "the making of woman in man" as the coming to awareness of the anima in a megalithic setting of the New Hebrides; in Malekula "achieving full manhood" involves "ritually experiencing the 'woman within'."[34]

Much still remains to be done in the area of theorizing the primitive Other as modern Self. A "Jungian anthropology" which would link primitive and modern worldviews in terms of shared archetypal patterns needs to be developed. One wonders, for example, how a Jungian approach would interpret the beautiful "spirit-lover"[35] figures of the Baule people of the Ivory Coast. According to one authority, the carvings are intended to assuage "the jealousy of the spirit-lover." To a Jungian, this sounds like an attempt to deal with anima/animus problems through the medium of art. Of one of these intriguing spirit-lover figures, the Baule artist Lela Kouakou has said that it represents a man's spirit wife (*blolo bla*, "bush spouse"). He explains that "some people left a husband or wife behind in the other world when they were born," and the troubles they experience in later life when this spirit spouse gets angry can be dealt with better when such an image is carved.[36] A close parallel with Jungian anima and animus figures could be established from a psycho-anthopological study of such figures.

As the fields of anthropology and analytical psychology continue to share insights, it is likely that more will be done in the way of asserting the basic psychological acuteness of much "primitive" mythological culture. Through a recognition of the inevitability and indeed the desirability of the subjective psychic factor—the scandalous element that Jungians have learned to value so highly—Western researcher and native informant may be seen as linked psychologically and as responding in different ways to the same archetypal world. Seen from this Jungian angle, the modern Westerner is also a "primitive," one possessing a limited field of consciousness floating on the vast ocean of the collective unconscious. Yet the "primitive" is wise in the ways of psychology, capable of establishing a relationship with the archetypal world.

Jungian primitivism at its best thus offers a vision of humanity united not only across geographical space but also across developmental time. It often succeeds in distinguishing itself from both sentimental and idealizing versions of primitivism, in that it defines the primitive not as something childish and outside of us—the sentimental approach—but as something already in us, which is, however, as *problematic* for us as it is for members of primitive cultures.

For the collective unconscious does not cease to be a problem once one leaves the modern West behind. Members of primitive cultures are *not* children. They have the same kinds of problems as Western adults, which they deal with in a number of more or less effective ways. Our sense of the value of surviving primitive and myth-oriented cultures is, therefore, enhanced when we discern in them the presence of *valuable psychological procedures*. And these procedures not only arc valuable for the native informants but also prove instructive for the modern researchers and their modern psyches.

Thus, rather than encouraging the shedding of crocodile tears over the passing of once pristinely primitive ways of life, Jungian primitivism encourages us to learn from myth-oriented cultures and to do what we can to help them survive in a modern context. There is some hope at least for the preservation of primitive cultures when the modern psyche, the psyche of the voting public as well as of the economic managers and the politicians, can find reasons to respect them and to acknowledge their psychological value.

Jungian (Archetypal) Criticism

Outside of the immediate circle of Jungian analysts and analysands, the effect of Jung's thought has been most pervasive in the field of literary criticism. Jung himself took the first step when in *Psychological Types* (1921) he analyzed the work of Carl Spitteler, a Swiss poet who had just won the Nobel Prize for literature. Jung paid special attention to his *Prometheus and Epimetheus*, which he considered as illustrating his own theory of introverted versus extroverted psychological attitudes. But this move into the field of criticism was not an auspicious one. As Jung recounts in *Memories, Dreams, Reflections,* after he had sent Spitteler a copy of *Psychological Types,* the now famous Nobel Laureate did not even favor Jung with a reply but stated in a public lecture shortly thereafter that his *Prometheus and Epimetheus* "meant" nothing and that in terms of meaning he might just as well have sung something as insignificant as "Spring is come, tra-la-la-la-la."[37]

Jung was not a critic, but his later writings, especially the four essays collected in *The Spirit in Man, Art, and Literature,*[38] show him to be a cultivated European at home in the arts, both curious about contemporary developments and bold enough to take controversial positions. No doubt his heart lay with the culture of the German nineteenth century from Goethe's *Faust* to Nietzsche's *Zarathustra,* and he had a peculiar liking for the novel *She* of the once popular Victorian author Rider Haggard. But his personal taste as well as his broad appreciation of literature enlivened his writings, and even his casual conversation was peppered with literary allusions.

In the light of Jung's own strong literary interests, it is not surprising that Jungian criticism, which is often called "archetypal criticism," has come to flourish over the years, from Barbara Hannah's lectures on the Brontës in the early 1930s (*Striving Towards Wholeness,* published only in 1971), to Bettina L. Knapp's recent books,[39] which range widely over the field of both literature and the other arts. The richness of the field is reflected in the many entries discussed in the sophisticated reference work compiled by Jos van Meurs with John Kidd: *Jungian Literary Criticism 1920–1980: An Annotated, Critical Bibliography of Works in English (With a Selection of Titles after 1980).* A good sampling of recent Jungian essays may be found in *Jungian Literary Criticism,* edited by Richard P. Sugg.

Perhaps the greatest contribution that depth psychology has made to literary criticism is to have provided *a language for the symbolic interpretation of intrapsychic images* which can also be used to interpret the images represented in literary texts. Such symbolic images occur spontaneously in dreams and fantasies, appear as components of culturally elaborated myths, and serve as an important source of inspiration for literary representation.

Since both literary criticism and depth psychology deal with the interpretation of symbolic images—in texts and in dreams—there would seem to be an easy bridge from the interpretive strategies of psychoanalysis to those of literary criticism, from the interpretation of dream imagery to the interpretation of literary imagery.

However, the bridge is more like a razor's edge. The significance of intrapsychic symbolic images is, of course, stressed by all schools of depth psychology. But in the wake of Freud and Jacques Lacan many critics are locked into a totally linguistically oriented world view. Language, not image, is the key factor; the word is seen as constitutive of the visual image, not the reverse. And language itself is seen as fundamentally self-referential. Thus the psyche, like the rest of "reality," is regarded as a mere construct of language.

In addition, the psyche was not recognized as a living creative factor in much of earlier, especially Freudian, literary criticism. The literary text was analyzed as a coded personal confession that revealed the author's neuroses and complexes in a way that the critic attempted to decode. Such reductive criticism attempted to explain the text primarily in terms of the author's psychobiography. It failed to value the text as an original contribution to psychology, as psychological research in a literary mode.

Jungian criticism, if anything, has gone to the opposite extreme: the psyche and its imagery often seem to overshadow both the linguistic dimension of the text and the personal psychology of the author. As the Jungian analyst Edward Edinger puts it in his study of Melville's *Moby Dick*: "Rather than being an expression of the author's personal neurosis, a great work of art is a self-revelation of the transpersonal objective psyche."[40] Jungian criticism may deal with literary texts as though they were spontaneous psychic events rather than consciously crafted verbal artifacts.

The preoccupation in Jungian criticism with creative unconscious processes, and the shift in emphasis from verbal sign to psychic image, may be hard to accept completely. In the eyes of its detractors, Jungian criticism may fail to draw a clear enough distinction between intrapsychic imagery and aesthetic imagery. Intrapsychic imagery is a spontaneous product of the unconscious. Aesthetic imagery, for all the analogies it presents to intrapsychic imagery, is a product of literary tradition and conscious literary elaboration. To put the criticism bluntly: a literary text is not an archetypal dream and should not be interpreted as though it were one.

In spite of these difficulties, there are some advantages in considering literature as if it were the creative product of the psyche—as indeed it is, since all human cultural artifacts derive some of their vitality from the relationship they maintain with the psyche. For example, an archetypal critic might consider Dante's Beatrice, a scolding, guilt-inducing figure in the *Purgatorio*, as a complex image of the spiritual anima. This could generate a further recognition of the significance of the peculiar psychological tone of the purgatorial world represented in Dante's symbolic imagination. Purgatory thereby becomes a therapeutic place where criticism and chastisement lead to salvation, not depression. Jungian criticism could reveal the analogies in Dante's medieval theological and mythological world to the world of modern psychotherapy. In such an interpretive framework, which allows the modern reader to read the *Purgatorio* from a psychological perspective, the much delayed and long awaited appearance of Dante's anima figure Beatrice seems psychologically appropriate. A psychological reading of the text does not, however, displace other readings; rather, it enriches the interpretation of the text in unexpected and original ways.

Jungian criticism assumes that psyche is as real as history. Consequently, the world of the psyche is as adequate a reference point for criticism as the world of ideas, class struggle, religion, or literary intertextuality. Admittedly, only those for whom there is already some experience of the reality of the psyche will be likely to find the Jungian approach plausible and interesting. And it goes without saying that some Jungian criticism will prove congenial only to those who already respond with enthusiasm to the overall Jungian concern with the archetypes of the collective unconscious.

Jungian criticism encourages a specific kind of *symbolic reading* of texts. But in spite of this narrow focus a broad spectrum of literary texts may benefit from its perspectives. Not only fairy tales or texts with obvious mythic subtexts such as *Moby Dick* but even such a text as Flaubert's *Madame Bovary*, which on one level of interpretation presents a seemingly realistic anatomy of the adulterous life of an ordinary provincial bourgeois housewife in nineteenth-century France, may benefit from a symbolic reading. In the light of archetypal criticism Emma may be seen as carrying a problematic burden of anima eroticism, always ambiguous and somewhat "off," as Jung would say, because it is tragically unrelated to the demands of practical reality. This anima quality may account for the peculiar fascination Emma Bovary has had on readers, an anima fascination with unconscious impulses and erotic yearnings rejected by a common sense view of the universe. However ironically presented in the text, her quasi-religious enthusiasms and incipient erotic mysticism are given an intensely inward dimension. She may be said to symbolize at times the possibility of a connection of the erotic with the spiritual that the novel ostensibly rejects. Yet the suggestion of this latent theme is subtly unfocused and ambiguous. There is, in other words, a tension between realist description and psychic suggestiveness in *Madame Bovary* that is surely one of its strengths as a complex work of literature.

Many works of literature, of course, have clear mythic subtexts and the interpretation of *mythic patterns* is a correspondingly central feature of Jungian criticism. To take only one illustration, Edward Edinger's discussion of Captain Ahab in Melville's *Moby Dick* as a solar hero is at once bold and nuanced. Such a symbolically rich work clearly calls for myth criticism, from whatever particular perspective.

Generally speaking, however, the field of Jungian or quasi-Jungian myth criticism has suffered from a tendency toward facile reductionism, whether under the inspiration of Erich Neumann's developmental schema in *The Origins and History of Consciousness* or spurred by Joseph Campbell's synthetic vision of the hero's quest in *The Hero with a Thousand Faces*. The temptation to apply Neumann's or Campbell's grid mechanically to a literary text has often proved irresistible. But complex literary texts are not, for the most part, easily reducible to clear mythic patterns. It would have been beneficial if the neglected work of Charles Baudouin, a francophonic Swiss popularizer of Jungian perspectives had been absorbed into the mainstream of Jungian myth criticism. In his remarkable book *The Triumph of the Hero,* [41] the myth of the hero is embedded in epic texts but does not determine their structure since the *literary deviation from mythic pattern* is what differentiates a literary text from a myth in the first place.

Jung's theory of *compensation* has not had the impact on Jungian criticism that it deserves. Despite Jung's discussion in a number of places of the compensatory effects of Goethe's *Faust* and of the Faust myth, his theory has not inspired the kind of detailed cultural studies that one would have expected. The challenge presented by Jung's daring analysis of the compensatory aspects of Joyce's *Ulysses*—its apparent "lack of feeling" compensating for the false sentimentality of the period of World War I, for example—has yet to be taken up in a large-scale analysis. Perhaps the reason is the tendency on the part of Jungian criticism to ignore specific historical and cultural contexts in favor of the relative timelessness of archetypal reality and to privilege the theme of individual development over that of social and cultural evolution.

Like all other criticism, Jungian criticism must meet a criterion of usefulness. It must enrich the understanding of a text and increase the fund of perceptions associated with our reading. Whenever a Jungian grid is mechanically super-imposed on a text, the text is interpreted reductively, as though it had been written especially for a discussion of some aspect or other of Jungian psychology; such criticism results in a relative impoverishment of the text. Reductive interpretation may be useful in discussions of psychological matters, but it does not make for good literary criticism. A literary critic's first duty is to the text.

At its best, Jungian criticism enables us to spot things in the text we might not have seen from any other perspective. For example, in the fifteenth book of Homer's *Odyssey* Telemakhos is about to sail home after a journey in quest of news of his father, Odysseus, who has been missing for twenty years. Although Telemakhos does not know this yet, Odysseus has arrived home before him and is already making plans to slaughter Penelope's suitors and regain his kingdom. For Telemakhos, this plan is going to be fraught with anxiety. The suitors have been like older brothers to him as he was growing up. Nevertheless, these are the men he will be expected to help his father kill.

At this point, while Telemakhos' ability to handle this new role is still uncertain, the stranger Theoklymenos enters his life. Theoklymenos is a man on the run. He badly needs Telemakhos' protection, since he is being hunted down for having killed a kinsman. As a fugitive from justice, Theoklymenos is a puzzling person for Homer to add to the narrative just at the moment when Telemakhos is about to return to his homeland. The appearance of Theoklymenos is usually accounted for by mentioning his prophetic abilities, since at a particularly dramatic moment later on in the narrative he will prophesy the slaughter of the suitors. But is this explanation sufficient?

A Jungian approach may make more complete sense out of this new character's sudden appearance in the narrative. Symbolically, Theoklymenos may be said to supply Telemakhos with some needed shadow energy—in particular, the savage capacity to slaughter kinsmen or quasi-kinsmen like the suitors without pity. Looked at from a Jungian perspective, one of Theoklymenos' functions in the epic narrative appears to be to symbolize intrapsychic shadow content—to put Telemakhos in contact with the cruel shadow energies he will have to draw on in order to help his father regain his kingdom. This symbolic function—Theoklymenos as Telemakhos' shadow side—is something the reader would be unlikely to discover without the aid of Jungian criticism, and thus we may say that in this particular instance Jungian criticism has met the criterion of usefulness.

Jungian art criticism owes something, no doubt, to Jung's short 1932 essay on Picasso as well as to Jung's own talent for visual representation, whether expressed in painting or later in his life in the stone carvings at Bollingen. He had genuine creative talent, although it did not necessarily result in what his troublesome anima would have called "art."

But it was Erich Neumann who really initiated the serious application of Jungian theory to the visual arts. In his essays on

Chagall (in *Creative Man*, 1979) and Leonardo da Vinci (in *Art and the Creative Unconscious*, 1959), and especially in his book *The Archetypal World of Henry Moore* (1959), Neumann applied his own original perspectives, especially regarding the importance of the archetype of the Great Mother, to the field of artistic representation. Finally, the multi-authored volume *Man and His Symbols* (1964) is illustrated throughout with examples of representations of archetypal images drawn from the realm of art, and Aniela Jaffé contributes to it a major essay on "Symbolism in the Visual Arts." Jungian commentary on visual art has continued unabated—without, however, the richness and profusion which have characterized Jungian literary criticism.

Recent Controversies and Debates

Recent developments of a more controversial nature bear witness to the fact that the Jungian study of myth is a field that continues to expand and mature, both consolidating and refining its traditional theoretical positions and setting out in new directions. But what is maturity for some may seem to represent senility and regression to others, and what is expansion for some may signify for others a misuse of the term "Jungian" or even the betrayal of basic principles. Those not professionally involved in the heat of these controversies, however, can still appreciate the results of this fruitful clash of ideas.

As noted in the section on the archetype of the *puer aeternus*, Jung was capable of responding intensely to the "truly bewitching beauty," with "all the grace and charm of either sex," of mythical figures such as Attis and Adonis, "the dying son-gods of the Near East,"[42] and the Germanic Balder—all symbolic representations of the eternally youthful spirit of joy and creativity.

But this archetypal image of the *puer aeternus*, like every other archetypal image, has negative as well as positive dimensions.[43] In recent years a controversy has arisen around the issue of the *puer* and the role this Peter Pan figure may play in modern psyche and society. In twelve lectures given at the C.G. Jung Institute in Zurich during the winter of 1959–60 Marie-

Louise von Franz subjected the figure of the *puer*, as represented mainly by the title figure in Saint-Exupéry's popular tale *The Little Prince*, to what one can only call a scathing analysis. For her, the figure corresponds to "a certain type of young man who has an outstanding mother complex." She goes on to make the provocative assertion that "the man who is identified with the archetype of the *puer aeternus* remains too long in adolescent psychology."[44] Symbolizing the unwillingness to grow up, the *puer* becomes, in von Franz's perspective, the inspiration not for joy and creativity but for all kinds of manifestations of supposed psychological immaturity such as distaste for work, Don Juanism, homosexuality, and the "misunderstood genius" syndrome.

In the wake of von Franz's vigorous critique, the term *puer* (and the corresponding female term *puella*) has even become a term of psychological insult among Jungians, almost as common as the term "neurotic" is among Freudians. In polar opposition to the *senex* or "Old Man," the *puer* for von Franz symbolizes youthful irresponsibility refusing to face up to the demands of adult life. The *puer* perplex is the culprit in the creation of individual pathologies as well as of more general and widespread problems of social adaptation. For von Franz, the *puer aeternus* is mainly a problem, and "not only a personal one, but a problem of our times."[45]

James Hillman sees von Franz's critical anatomy of the *puer* as the result of her overemphasizing the contamination of a praiseworthy archetypal figure by familial, neurotic factors. Hillman sets about to reestablish the balance, and in the process he becomes the champion of the *puer*. In addition, he comes to see the *puer* problem not so much in the *puer* itself as in the opposing figure, the *senex*, which in its negative aspect we might designate as the Mean Old Man.

In an essay published in 1967, the year before the great youth revolts of 1968, Hillman wrote that the negative *senex* "is the senex split from its own puer aspect." The problem of the *puer-senex* polarity (the *puer* and *senex* as the opposite poles of a single archetype) is primarily lodged in the rigid and authoritarian thinking of the paternal *senex*: "without the enthusiasm and eros of the son, authority loses its idealism," and this leads to "tyranny and cynicism."[46] The *puer*, by contrast, is praised by Hillman because "puer impulses" may be conceived as "messages from the spirit or as calls to the spirit"[47]—a spiritual aspect of the archetypal figure ignored by von Franz. Hillman defends the *puer* and *puer* values with great personal intensity, and his own later work may be said to be marked by the signs of the *puer aeternus*—playfulness, elusiveness, irreverence, and originality.

The *puer* controversy continues among Jungians. Jeffrey Satinover has written about the *puer* problem in terms that reinstate von Franz's misgivings, with emphasis on its collective as well as individual dimensions. When, he says, the *puer* functions in the individual as pathology, "the traditional Jungian solution" is a "re-linking . . . to the archetypes in what may be thought of as a more modern, psychologically attuned form of worship." But Satinover distrusts this quasi-religious procedure, finding it of little value for those for whom religion is no option, those for whom "the archetypes cannot be projected onto a transcendental screen," and who consequently must bear the burden of a god who has become a disease.[48] If *puer* worship is an ambiguous solution to the *puer* problem, it is because "the price paid for the religious solution to narcissistic conflict is a degree of irrationality"[49] that may eventually lead to fanaticism, especially if one attempts to justify one's beliefs by appealing to the authority of science and reason. Since the projection of one's *puer* problem onto the mythic screen of a dying and resurrecting god, as in traditional Christianity, is less and less possible for scientifically minded persons, Satinover concludes that the *puer* constitutes a *collective* problem for which no easy solution exists.

The title of a recent workshop given by Satinover offers a glimpse of a political dilemma as seen from the angle of Jungian psychology: "No One at the Helm: the Triumph of the Eternal Adolescent in American Society." His conclusion is that the hidden power of the *puer* archetype "brings with it not only the personal problems that we suffer at the hands of those who have remained children too long, it brings with it as well an outlook, a set of expectations about life, a body of opinion, and an unarticulated philosophy of civics, which is no more mature or functional in the social sphere than it is in the personal."[50] Thus the archetype of the Eternal Adolescent, the archetypal source of creativity and inspiration in its positive aspects, can also be the basis for an alluring *myth of irresponsibility and idleness*. The numinous force of the *puer aeternus* creates problems for modern Peter Pans, who, inflated with a sense of archetypal youthfulness, feel justified in never wanting to grow up. In modern society the same myth works to discourage initiative and to block the empowerment of the oppressed, depriving them of the sense of responsibility for improving their lot. The myth does this, paradoxically and tragically in Satinover's view, by shifting the burden of responsibility onto a mythical *senex* government in whose incompetent hands ultimate power is seen to rest. Thus, as with Hillman, the bipolarity of the archetype is a partial key to the issue. But Satinover concludes that it is the Eternal Adolescent, not the Mean Old Man, who is at fault.

Satinover thus joins hands with von Franz, in opposition to Hillman, in seeing the *puer aeternus* as above all a source of trouble. But this critique has problematic theoretical ramifications. That an archetypal force such as the *puer*, operating in the context of modern political and cultural life, could produce a myth which, far from being a numinous revelation of primordial psychic energies potentially beneficial to society and the individual, could come to constitute a rather shallow mythic rationalization of psychologically and socially regressive tendencies is puzzling. What went wrong? How did a myth become merely obfuscatory rather than creatively compensatory?

A closer look at the the interaction between culture and myth is clearly in order. Recently, Joseph Henderson[51] has proposed a theory of a *cultural unconscious* that may help explain how myths, far from simply giving expression to the archetypal forces of the collective unconscious directly, are in fact often highly transformed by a particular culture. They may even fall back into the shadow side of the culture, to be rediscovered in dreams and fantasies expressing the shadow side of individuals. Henderson cites certain images of China that appeared in the dream of one of his analysands, where these images were linked to associations with wisdom and with the reconciliation of the opposites Yin and Yang—associations that derived from "unconscious cultural conditioning" and from modern Western projections, not from any universal myth of wisdom. Henderson's theory would thus distinguish between myths of the *cultural unconscious*—myths which are tied to their own particular time and culture—and myths of the *collective unconscious*—myths which are less specific and more universal. In his response in the same issue of *Quadrant* to Henderson's paper, Harry Prochaska speaks of "cultural attitudes" that "filter the images welling up from the cultural unconscious and provide the forms for our experience of archetypal images." Henderson's theory of the cultural unconscious, he concludes, "is a major contribution to the structure of Jungian theory" because "his formulation provides that intermediate layer in which the archetypal precipitates into cultural forms"[52]—what another commentator aptly calls "the middle ground of enculturement."[53]

An example will demonstrate the usefulness of this theory. When the archetypal image of the *puer* is filtered through the peculiarly American cultural unconscious of the mid-twentieth century, it results in the ambivalent but extremely compelling *puer* image of "The Teenager"—a cultural image that the rest of the world has acknowledged as typically American, although Satinover is quick to criticize its accuracy. This particular manifestation of the *puer aeternus* is not, however, unprecedented. Ancient Greece, a major source of inspiration for modern American cultural images, had its own youth culture and sponsored a veritable cult of youth under the spell of its own images of the *puer* represented by such figures as the god Hermes and by statues of ideally handsome young athletes. In both ancient Greece and modern America we find a love of sports allied with a youth culture oriented around numinous images of the *puer*.

Given the American infatuation with the Eternal Adolescent, it is perhaps not surprising to observe to what extent the public image of former president George Walker Bush, youthful looking and ready to jog, was compounded of *puer* elements, some of which were no doubt strengthened by their associations with a myth of Texas origins and by his earlier sidekick role in the myth of the Santa Barbara cowboy-president,

Ronald Reagan. Given the much older appearance of his wife Barbara (who laudably did nothing to disguise her age), their public appearances together must have given at least some television viewers the rather startling impression of a Good Old Boy who had married his mother. Jungian viewers would have noted, of course, that the *puer* in myth is often represented as the son-lover of the Great Mother. Bush's cheerful brand of politics could be called either "the politics of *puer* playfulness" or (if one reacts unfavorably to their calculated disregard of traditional liberal concerns with social justice) "the politics of *puer* irresponsibility." Either way, the *puer* in the White House certainly witnessed to the pervasive power of the *puer aeternus* archetype in modern American culture.

Venturing into the realm of political mythology and controversy has become increasingly popular with Jungians. Jung's own somewhat apolitical and Old World preoccupation with the inner realm of psychic imagery perhaps could not be expected to survive untouched in the context of the more extroverted culture of the New World. One political issue in particular has provoked more Jungian interventions than any other: the threat of nuclear war. Jung had already expressed his anxiety concerning the future of mankind in *The Undiscovered Self* and *Answer to Job*. It has taken his followers a while to come to terms with the apocalyptic visions of nuclear destruction that haunt our age.

The Nuclear Age may be said to have opened with a mythological allusion. J. Robert Oppenheimer, the moment following the first flash of the first atomic bomb explosion at Los Alamos, claims to have remembered how Krishna, in the *Bhagavad Gita*, revealed to Arjuna his most fearsome form, saying, "Now I am become Death, the destroyer of worlds." This allusion, as well as the one in the *Gita* to "the light of a thousand suns," links the spectacle of the explosion of the first atom bomb with an ancient Hindu myth of divine epiphany. This "regression" to mythological thinking on the part of a leading scientific mind at the moment when the experiments with atomic power had resulted in the unleashing of a deadly force, whose full effects were as yet unknown but were clearly unprecedented, may be seen in fact as typical of the way the human psyche has spontaneous recourse to myth in conditions of extreme stress.

Oppenheimer's intriguing allusion to a classical Hindu myth to explain the most modern of Western scientific phenomena has itself attained a kind of modern mythic status. It thus could properly serve as the epigraph to a recent collection of Jungian essays entitled *Nuclear Peril and the Psyche*.[54] One contributor analyzes symbolically the problem of "binding" the "expansive, reckless, heroic energy" of the Nuclear Age in terms of the Greek myth of the binding of Prometheus.[55] Another turns our attention to the myth of the scapegoat, reminding us that the nuclear "holocaust" we fear is the projection of our own desires to rid ourselves of our own evil via a scapegoat sacrifice, which in this case would be tantamount to collective suicide.[56] A third analyzes the myth of the apocalyse in terms of our unconscious equation of ourselves with God and points out our need to integrate more loving aspects of the deity into our lives—in particular, the feminine qualities of wisdom, compassion, and respect for life associated with the figures of Sophia and the Shekinah.[57]

Modern American feminism has recently questioned some of the underlying assumptions of Jung's theory of *anima* and *animus*, and since these terms have already proved useful in the Jungian symbolic interpretation of myth and fairytale, this revisioning ought to prove useful, too. Demaris Wehr, for instance, has described the "tragic irony" in the lack of consistency between Jung's description of the *anima*, a most powerful force in male psychology, and his descriptions of women and the feminine in terms of emptiness, passivity, and lack of creativity. The irony appears all the more pronounced when one takes into account the fact that so many of Jung's eminent students were women not the least bit lacking in creative spirit. Wehr may be right when she sees many female Jungians as having "corroborated Jung's devaluation of women because their own internalized oppression [was] reassuringly in tune with his opinions."[58] That Jung's thinking was partially a victim of the casual misogyny of his age and professional circles can hardly be questioned. In the late twentieth century it is all the more necessary to challenge the androcentric assumptions that preside over some of his pronouncements, to the extent that they tend to disempower women even as they exalt the power of the feminine in terms of the *anima*.

In contrast to his nuanced appreciation of the power of the *anima* in men, Jung distrusts the *animus* and usually fails to give emphasis to more positive images of its power in women. For Wehr, his "discussions of the animus-possessed woman are neither neutral nor compassionate."[59] But the issue is a delicate one, for Jung's reverence for the power of the feminine *in the psyche* is just as real as his insensitivity to the relative power-lessness of women *in society*. One might ask: did marrying a wealthy wife blind him to the economic and social oppression of women? Correcting the subtle misogyny and androcentrism of Jungian psychology, Wehr concludes, "will be an essential step toward making Jung's the holistic psychology and spirituality women need it to be."[60]

In Jungian theory *anima* and *animus* are seen as the arche-types presiding over heterosexual love. The question arises, however, as to just what archetype presides over homosexual passion and pairing. Mitchell Walker[61] suggests that there exists an archetype of the *double* that supplies the energy and fascination for a number of psychological relations based on feelings of affinity or identity (the "just like me!" syndrome), including passionate sexual attachment to a person of the same sex. He gives various mythological examples of the figure, from Enkidu in the *Epic of Gilgamesh* to the faithful servant Sam in Tolkien's *The Return of the King*. He specifies that "the double motif may include a tendency to homosexuality, but is not necessarily a homosexual archetype."[62] The figures of Huck and Jim in Mark Twain's masterpiece represent the most famous American instance of this archetypal motif.

As Robert Hopcke has demonstrated recently,[63] Jung's own conventional homophobia did not prevent analytical psychology from being more tolerant of homosexuality than most psychoanalytical theories of the time. And today, now that Jungian theory has begun to respond to the Gay Liberation movement, new symbolic interpretations of myth become possible. For example, Hopcke analyzes the film *The Wizard of Oz*, a cult classic in the San Francisco gay community, as a representation of a myth of the integration of masculine qualities and of the redemption of the feminine. Dorothy's visit to Oz is interpreted as symbolizing the "psychological femininity" foisted on gay men by heterosexual society and then internalized by them. The "redemption of the feminine" analyzed from a feminist perspective by Ann Belford Ulanov[64] as part of a myth of animus integration can thus come to signify for male homosexuals the grand finale of a heroic myth in which the castrating power of the Wicked Witch of the West is overcome and valuable inner masculine qualities, symbolized initially in their unintegrated dimension by the Scarecrow, Tin Woodsman, and Cowardly Lion, can be integrated. For Hopcke, *The Wizard of Oz* contains a myth that illustrates symbolically "the development of a positive, differentiated inner masculinity."[65]

Besides giving careful attention to the homosexual context in which archetypes of the feminine and the masculine may operate, Hopcke also deals with the archetype of the androgyne. But here, as elsewhere, he moves the discussion away from the question of the focus of desire (which may be heterosexual, homosexual or lesbian in various modalities) to a vision of sexual orientation as "a fertile crossroads of various archetypal energies,"[66] as a static condition crying out for an archetypal label. In the wake of Hopcke's book, one now waits for an equally sophisticated and nuanced study of some of the myths associated with lesbian love. As usual, the androcentrism of Jungian psychology seems to have resulted in an etiquette of "gentlemen first." Still, since Jungian feminism has been able to establish a strong foothold already, Jungian lesbian studies are probably just around the corner.

One new area of gender studies that has welcomed Jungian perspectives enthusiastically is the so-called "mythopoetic" wing of the Men's Movement. Much of this Jungian influence has come from Robert Bly, a great admirer of von Franz—or "Marie-Louise," as he likes to call her. Bly has taken her symbolic interpretation of fairy tales several steps forward in his detailed analysis of a Grimms' fairy tale in *Iron John* (1990), a book that has had great popular appeal, and has confirmed Bly's status as one of the major spokesmen of the Men's Movement. In the tale the young prince's initiation is presided over by a Wild

Man mentor figure named Iron John, who represents the archetypal masculine energies the prince needs to integrate. Bly realizes that "the Wild Man's qualities, among them love of spontaneity, association with wilderness, honoring of grief, and respect for riskiness, frightens many people."[67] Nevertheless, he is convinced that the initiated male who integrates these energies properly will be of benefit to society, will avoid sexist attitudes and actions, and will exemplify a post-patriarchal model of positive masculinity.

The Jungian therapist Robert Moore has also established an important Jungian position within the growing Men's Movement. Along with the mythologist Douglas Gillette, he has written *King Warrior Magician Lover: Rediscovering the Archetypes of the Mature Masculine*, a book the authors have dedicated to Bly. Developing Jung's theory of a quadripartite structure of the psyche, Moore and Gillette have set up an original typology of the deep inner structures of masculinity. Like Bly, they are careful to emphasize that patriarchy is based on "boy psychology" and that the mature, initiated masculine self is not to be identified with patriarchal images of manhood that are "abusive of others, and often of self."[68] It is the initiatic process that makes men out of boys through the "accessing" of the mature masculine energies of the psyche. These energies, when accessed and balanced, result in a harmonious development of the mature male personality. Unlike Jung's theory of the anima, their theory does not spell out the role of the relationship with the feminine in masculine psychological development. Moore and Gillette—and Bly, to a lesser extent—are more concerned with the problems of male integrity than with problems of male-female relationships. This slighting of the feminine dimension may constitute a flaw in their otherwise groundbeaking theory of the structure of the male psyche.

The mythopoetic Jungian imagination is now active in the area of modern American feminism, where initial resistance to the Wild Man has perhaps stimulated the birth of the Wild Woman. In fact, no sooner had Robert Bly's *Iron John* disappeared from the New York Times best-seller list than *Women Who Run With the Wolves* took its place, where it stayed for over a year. The author, the Jungian analyst and storyteller Clarissa

Pinkola Estes, has brought together from a number of sources what she calls "myths and stories of the Wild Woman." Her immensely popular book was designed, she writes, to restore "women's flagging vitality" by "psychic-archeological" explorations of "the natural instinctive psyche,"[69] especially as it is personified in the Wild Woman. Her next book will constitute a mythopoetic rehabilitation of the Wise Old Woman, a figure analyzed by Rix Weaver in her book of the same name.

As we have seen throughout this chapter, the Jungian theory of myth can be applied to the social and political concerns of our modern world as well as to the study of traditional mythology. In fact, its strength is that it enables a psychologically oriented mythological awareness to stimulate new thought on a variety of issues. It is impossible to predict what issues it will latch onto next, but a recent collection of essays entitled *A Testament to the Wilderness* suggests that it may make a valuable contribution to the modern ecological move-ment by emphasizing the inner, psychological dimension of the resistances we have to taking proper care of Earth. One contributor to this volume makes the point succinctly when she writes that "only when the creative potential of the inner wilderness is realised will the global wilderness be allowed to flourish and the earth allowed to breathe."[70]

This sense of the relevance of myths for the survival tasks of humanity is perhaps the greatest cultural contribution that Jungian theory can make today. The "strange mythology of the psyche" is a unique record of human evolution over the millennia. At the same time it constitutes a potential blueprint for human adaptation to a modern world from which we often feel psychologically alienated. In other words, humanity can trust its instincts, but it needs to become more conscious of them. This raising of the level of psychic consciousness has an effect on the world just as much as what happens in the world has an effect on the psyche. Nature and psyche are not two separate realms.

NOTES

1. Andrew Samuels, *Jung and the Post-Jungians* (London: Routledge & Kegan Paul, 1985), p. 23.

2. Ibid., p. 52.

3. Carol S. Pearson, *The Hero Within: Six Archetypes We Live By* (San Francisco: Harper & Row, 1989), pp. xx, xxvii–xxviii.

4. Jung, letter in English dated October 14, 1954; in *Letters*, II, p. 188.

5. David L. Miller, *The New Polytheism: Rebirth of the Gods and Goddesses* (Dallas: Spring, 1981), pp. 99–100.

6. James Hillman, *Loose Ends: Primary Papers in Archetypal Psychology* (Dallas: Publications, 1975), p. 3.

7. See Hillman's appendix "Psychology: Monotheistic or Polytheistic" to Miller, *The New Polytheism*, pp. 109–42.

8. Ibid., p. 122.

9. See V. Walter Odajnyk, "The Psychologist as Artist: The Imaginal World of James Hillman," *Quadrant*, 17 (1984), pp. 39–48.

10. Aniela Jaffé, *Was Jung a Mystic? and Other Essays*, trans. Diana Dachler and Fiona Cairns (Einsiedeln, Switzerland: Daimon Verlag, 1989), p. 27.

11. Jung, letter dated September 21, 1955; in *Letters*, II, p. 272.

12. Jung, letter in English dated October 2, 1954; in *Letters*, II, p. 183.

13. Jung, letter in English dated April 10, 1954; in *Letters*, II, p. 172.

14. Jung, letter dated February 12, 1959; in *Letters*, II, p. 486.

15. Ibid.

16. See Jung, *Memories, Dreams, Reflections*, pp. 226–34.

17. Jung, letter in English dated February 11, 1956; in *Letters*, II, p. 290.

18. John Welch, *Spiritual Pilgrims: Carl Jung and Teresa of Avila* (New York: Paulist Press, 1982), p. 191.

19. Ann and Barry Ulanov, *Religion and the Unconscious* (Philadelphia: Westminster, 1975), p. 115.

20. Wayne G. Rollins, *Jung and the Bible* (Atlanta: John Knox, 1983), p. 8.

21. Jung, *Memories, Dreams, Reflections*, p. 246.

22. Ibid., pp. 248–9.

23. Ibid., p. 274.

24. Ibid., p. 273.

25. Ibid., p. 256.

26. Ibid., p. 338.

27. In a late interview Campbell stated: "I'm not a Jungian!" But then he added: "As far as interpreting myths, Jung gives me the best clues I've got." *An Open Life: Joseph Campbell in Conversation With Michael Toms* (Burdett, N.Y.: Larson Publications, 1988), p. 123.

28. See Segal, *Joseph Campbell: An Introduction* for a critical appraisal of Campbell's work.

29. Laurens van der Post in conversation with Jean-Marc Pottiez, *A Walk with a White Bushman* (London: Penguin, 1988), p. 29.

30. Jung, *Dream Seminar*, p. 77. See also ibid., note 6.

31. Van der Post, p. 26.

32. Esther Leonard De Vos, "Voodoo: Our Link with the Occult," in *The Analytical Life: Personal and Professional Aspects of Being a Jungian Analyst*, ed. New England Society of Jungian Analysts (Boston: Sigo, 1988), p. 40.

33. Janet O. Dallett, *When the Spirits Come Back* (Toronto: Inner City Books, 1988).

34. In *Eranos-Jahrbüch*, 16 (1948), p. 283.

35. Werner Gillon, *A Short History of African Art* (New York: Facts on File Publications, 1984), p. 141.

36. Lela Kouakou in conversation, in *Perspectives: Angles on African Art*, ed. Center for African Art (New York: Abrams, 1987), p. 153.

37. Jung, *Memories, Dreams, Reflections*, p. 207.

38. Jung, "On the Relation of Analytical Psychology to Poetry" (1931), "Psychology and Literature" (1950), "'Ulysses': A Monologue" (1934), and "Picasso" (1934), all in *The Spirit in Man, Art, and Literature*.

39. See in particular Bettina L. Knapp, *A Jungian Approach to Literature* (Carbondale: Southern Illinois University Press, 1984), *Music, Archetype, and the Writer: A Jungian View* (University Park: Pennsylvania State University Press, 1988), and *Machine, Metaphor, and the Writer: A Jungian View* (University Park: Pennsylvania State University Press, 1989).

40. Edward F. Edinger, *Melville's Moby Dick: A Jungian Commentary* (New York: New Directions, 1975), p. 3.

41. Charles Baudouin, *Le Triomphe du* Héros (Paris: Plon, 1952).

42. Jung, letter in English dated April 22, 1955; in *Letters*, II, p. 244.

43. See Robert A. Segal, "Adonis: an Ancient Peter Pan," *Psychological Perspectives*, 24 (1991), pp. 124–32.

44. Marie-Louise von Franz, *Puer Aeternus: A Psychological Study of the Adult Struggle with the Paradise of Childhood*, 2nd ed. (Santa Monica: Sigo, 1981 [1970]), p. 1.

45. Ibid., p. 291.

46. James Hillman, "Senex and Puer: An Aspect of the Historical and Psychological Present (1967)," in *Puer Papers*, ed. Hillman (Irving, Tex.: Spring, 1979), pp. 20–1.

47. Ibid., p. 23.

48. Jeffrey Satinover, "Jung's Relation to the Mother," *Quadrant*, 18 (1985), p. 11.

49. Jeffrey Satinover, "Decline of Art in Pursuit of Eternal Adolescence," *Quadrant*, 17 (1984), p. 31.

50. Sheet presented at a workshop given April 16, 1988, at the C.G. Jung Foundation, New York.

51. Joseph L. Henderson, "The Cultural Unconscious, " *Quadrant*, 21 (1988), pp. 7–16.

52. Harry Prochaska, "Response to 'The Cultural Unconscious,'" *Quadrant*, 21 (1988), p. 19.

53. Genevieve Geer, "Through the Prism of America," *Quadrant*, 21 (1988), p. 21.

54. *Nuclear Peril and the Psyche*, ed. Jerome S. Bernstein, special issue of *Quadrant*, 18 (1988).

55. Donald E. Kalsched, "Fire From the Gods: How Will Prometheus Be Bound?," pp. 71–92.

56. Edward Whitmont, "Individual Transformation and Personal Responsibility," pp. 45–56 See also Sylvia Brinton Perera, *The Scapegoat Complex* (Toronto: Inner City Books, 1986).

57. Charles H. Taylor, "Imagining Apocalypse: Godlike Power and Human Care," pp. 35–44. See also the collection of essays *Facing Apocalypse*, eds. Valerie Andrews, Robert Bosnak, and Karen Walter Goodwin (Dallas: Spring, 1987), including James Hillman's essay "Wars, Arms, Rams, Mars: On the Love of War," pp. 117–36.

58. Demaris S. Wehr, *Jung & Feminism: Liberating Archetypes* (Boston: Beacon Press, 1987), p. 106.

59. Ibid., p. 119.

60. Ibid., p. 126.

61. Mitchell Walker, "The Double: an Archetypal Configuration," *Spring* (1976), pp. 165–75.

62. Ibid., p. 169.

63. Robert H. Hopcke, *Jung, Jungians, and Homosexuality* (Boston: Shambhala, 1989).

64. Ann Belford Ulanov, *The Feminine in Jungian Psychology and Christian Theology* (Evanston, Ill.: Northwestern University Press, 1971), pp. 277–85.

65. Hopcke, p. 143.

66. Ibid., p. 189.

67. Robert Bly, *Iron John: A Book About Men* (New York: Addison-Wesley, 1990), p. 226.

68. Robert Moore and Douglas Gillette, *King Warrior Magician Lover: Rediscovering the Archetypes of the Mature Masculine* (New York: HarperCollins, 1990), p. 5.

69. Clarissa Pinkola Estes, *Women Who Run with the Wolves: Myths and Stories of the Wild Woman Archetype* (New York: Ballantine, 1992), pp. 3–4.

70. Rix Weaver, "The Wilderness," in *A Testament to the Wilderness: Ten Essays on an Address by C.A. Meier* (Zurich: Daimon Verlag; Santa Monica: Lapis Press, 1985), p. 92.

Selected Bibliography

Bibliographical Introduction

The following bibliography is a partial listing of works published by Jungians up to about 1992 that is accessible and useful to the general reader interested in the interface between analytical psychology and the study of mythology. Occasionally, where the title or subtitle does not sufficiently clarify the nature of the content, I have indicated in brackets the particular myths discussed in the text. But I have included many other works that deal with more specific psychotherapeutic topics, with Jung's biography, and with problems of Jungian theory. For a more comprehensive and richly annotated bibliography, the reader can turn with profit to Donald R. Dyer, *Cross-Currents of Jungian Thought* (Boston: Shambhala, 1991), and to Joseph F. Vincie and Margreta Rathbauer-Vincie, *C.G. Jung and Analytical Psychology: A Comprehensive Bibliography* (New York: Garland, 1977). The reader would also benefit from an acquaintance with Jungian journals such as *Quadrant* (of New York's C.G. Jung Foundation for Analytical Psychology), *Psychological Perspectives* (of the Los Angeles Jung Institute), *Harvest* (of London's Analytical Psychological Club), and *The San Francisco Jung Institute Library Journal*. The *Journal o f Analytical Psychology* (London) is of first importance as a professional journal.

It goes without saying that *The Collected Works of C.G. Jung*, published over the years by Princeton University Press (Bollingen Series) in twenty volumes, are the primary source to which every serious reader must have recourse. Volume 20, the *General*

Index, compiled by Barbara Forryan and Janet M. Glover (1979), is of inestimable value for exploring Jung's views on a vast variety of subjects. Volume 19, the *General Bibliography of C.G. Jung's Writings*, compiled by Lisa Ress and William McGuire, originally published in 1979 and now completely revised in 1990, is a checklist of the initial publication, translation into English, and significant new editions, including paperback and periodical publication, of Jung's works. It also gives the interrelation between the Swiss *Gesammelte Werke* and the American edition of the *Complete Works*.

But by no means is all of Jung to be found within the covers of the *Complete Works*. His autobiography, *Memories, Dreams, Reflections*, recorded and edited by Aniela Jaffé and translated by Richard and Clara Winston (New York: Random House, 1963), is rich in insights and perspectives. His correspondence from 1906 to his death in 1961 has been selected and edited by Gerhard Adler, in collaboration with Aniela Jaffé, with translations from the German by R.F.C. Hull; published in two volumes, *C.G. Jung: Letters* (Princeton, N.J.: Princeton University Press/Bollingen, 1973, 1975) has an index at the end of Volume 2. *The Freud/Jung Letters*, edited by William McGuire and translated by Ralph Manheim and R.F.C. Hull (Princeton, N.J.: Princeton University Press/Bollingen, 1974) is a precious resource for understanding the relationship between the two master psychologists. The voluminous transcripts of some of his seminars have also been published recently and are of the highest value as records of Jung's thought evolving spontaneously in front of an audience of professional colleagues, analysands, and friends. The reader should turn especially to *Analytical Psychology: Notes of the Seminar Given in 1925*, edited by William McGuire (Princeton, N.J.: Princeton University Press/ Bollingen, 1989); *Dream Analysis: Notes of the Seminar Given in 1928–1930*, edited by William McGuire (Princeton, N.J.: Princeton University Press/Bollingen, 1984); and the two volumes of *Nietzsche's Zarathustra: Notes of the Seminar Given in 1934–1939*, edited by James L. Jarrett (Princeton, N.J.: Princeton University Press/Bollingen, 1988). Finally, Jung's own essay "Approaching the Unconscious," in *Man and His Symbols* (New

York: Doubleday, 1964; New York: Dell Laurel Edition, 1968), constitutes an excellent popular introduction to his psychology.

Abrams, Jeremiah. *Reclaiming the Inner Child.* Los Angeles: Tarcher, 1990. [a collection of essays, many of them Jungian; the Divine Child]

Anderson, William. *Green Man: The Archetype of Our Oneness with the Earth.* London and San Francisco: HarperCollins, 1990.

Aronson, Alex. *Psyche and Symbol in Shakespeare.* Bloomington: Indiana University Press, 1972.

Aziz, Robert. *C.G. Jung's Psychology of Religion and Synchronicity.* Albany: State University of New York Press, 1990.

Bach, Hans I. "On the Archetypal Complex: His Father's Son— Esau and Dionysos, Satan and Christ—Mythological Aspects and Psychological Implications." *Quadrant* 15 (1973): 4–31.

Baird, James. *Ishmael.* Baltimore: Johns Hopkins University Press, 1956. [puer aeternus and other archetypes in Melville's work]

Bar, Eugen. "Archetypes and Ideas: Jung and Kant." *Philosophy Today* 20 (1976): 114–23.

Barnaby, Karin, and Pellegrino D'Acierno, eds. *C.G. Jung and the Humanities: Towards a Hermeneutics of Culture.* Princeton, N.J.: Princeton University Press, 1990.

Barnes, Hazel. "Neo-Platonism and Analytical Psychology." *Philosophical Review* 54 (1945): 558–77.

Baynes, Helton Godwin. *Mythology of the Soul.* London: Routledge & Kegan Paul, 1955.

Beebe, John. *Integrity in Depth.* Foreword by David H. Rosen. College Station: Texas A&M University Press, 1992. [moral wholeness]

———. "A Jungian Perspective on Interpretation." *Quadrant* 17.2 (1984): 53–59.

———. "The Trickster in the Arts." *The San Francisco Jung Institute Library Journal* 2.2 (1981): 22–54.

Begg, Ean. "Animus: The Unmentionable Archetype." *Choirs of the God: Revisioning Masculinity.* Ed. John Matthews. London: Mandala (HarperCollins), 1991. 151–68.

———. *The Cult of the Black Virgin.* London: Arkana, 1989.

———. *Myth and Today's Consciousness.* London: Coventure, 1984. [Herakles, Sophia, Lilith, Wotan]

———. *On the Trail of Merlin.* London: Aquarian Press, 1991.

Belmonte, Thomas. "The Trickster and the Sacred Clown: Revealing the Logic of the Unspeakable." *C.G. Jung and the Humanities.* Ed. Karin Barnaby and Pellegrino D'Acierno. Princeton, N.J.: Princeton University Press, 1990. 45–66.

Bennet, E.A. *Meetings with Jung: Conversations Recorded During the Years 1946–1961.* Einsiedeln, Switzerland: Daimon, 1985.

———. *What Jung Really Said.* 2nd ed. New York: Schocken Books, 1983.

Bernstein, Jerome S. *Power and Politics: The Psychology of Soviet-American Partnership.* Forewords by Senator Claiborne Pell and Edward C. Whitmont. Boston: Shambhala, 1989.

Berry, Pat. *Echo's Subtle Body.* Dallas: Spring, 1982.

Bickman, Martin. *The Unsounded Center: Jungian Studies in American Romanticism.* Chapel Hill: University of North Carolina Press, 1980.

Birkhauser-Oeri, Sibylle. *The Mother: Archetypal Image in Fairy Tales.* Ed. Marie-Louise von Franz. Trans. Michael Mitchell. Toronto: Inner City, 1988.

Blotner, Joseph L. "Mythic Patterns in *To the Light House.*" *PMLA* 71 (1956): 547–62. [Oedipus, Demeter, and Persephone]

Bly, Robert. "The Hawk, the Horse and the Rider." *Choirs of the God: Revisioning Masculinity.* Ed. John Matthews. London: Mandala (HarperCollins), 1991. 13–28. [male initiation]

———. "I Came Out of the Mother Naked." *Sleepers Joining Hands.* New York: Harper & Row, 1973. [Great Mother, Good Mother, Ecstatic Mother, Teeth Mother]

———. *Iron John: A Book About Men.* Reading, Mass.: Addison-Wesley, 1990. [A symbolic interpretation of a Grimm's fairy tale along the lines established by Marie-Louise von Franz. A Men's Movement classic.]

———. *A Little Book on the Human Shadow*. Ed. William Booth. San Francisco: Harper & Row, 1988.

Bly, Robert, and Bill Moyers. *A Gathering of Men*. Videotape. Public Affairs Television, 1990.

Boa, Fraser. *The Way of the Dream: Dr. Marie-Louise von Franz in Conversation with Fraser Boa*. Toronto: Windrose Films, 1988. [based on the documentary film series]

Bodkin, Maud. *Archetypal Patterns in Poetry: Psychological Studies in Imagination*. London: Oxford University Press, 1934. New York: Knopf, 1958.

Bolen, Jean Shinoda. *Goddesses in Everywoman: A New Psychology of Women*. San Francisco: Harper & Row, 1984.

———. *Gods in Everyman: A New Psychology of Men's Lives and Loves*. San Francisco: Harper & Row, 1989.

———. *The Tao of Psychology: Synchronicity and the Self*. San Francisco: Harper & Row, 1979.

Bosnak, Robert. *Dreaming with an AIDS Patient: An Intimate Look Inside the Dreams of a Gay Man with AIDS by His Analyst*. Boston: Shambhala, 1989.

———. *A Little Course in Dreams: A Basic Handbook of Jungian Dreamwork*. Foreword by Denise Levertov. Boston: Shambhala, 1988.

Bradway, Katherine. "Hestia and Athena in the Analysis of Women." *Inward Light* 91.41 (1978): 28–42.

———. *Villa of Mysteries: Pompeii Initiation Rites of Women*. San Francisco: C.G. Jung Institute of San Francisco, 1982.

Brome, Vincent. *Jung: Man and Myth*. London: Granada, 1978.

Buhrmann, M. Vera. "Archetypal Transference as Observed in the Healing Procedures of Xhosa Indigenous Healers." *Money, Food, Drink, and Fashion in Analytic Training; The Proceedings of the Eighth International Congress for Analytical Psychology*, San Francisco, 1980. Ed. John Beebe. Fellbach, Germany: Bonz, 1983. 249–59.

————. "The Feminine in Witchcraft, Part One." *Journal of Analytical Psychology* 32.2 (1987): 139–56.

————. "The Feminine in Witchcraft, Part Two." *Journal of Analytical Psychology* 32.3 (1987): 257–77.

————. "Intlombe and Xhentsa: A Xhosa Healing Ritual." *Journal of Analytical Psychology* 26.3 (1981): 187–203.

————. *Living in Two Worlds: Communication between a White Healer and Her Black Counterparts.* Wilmette, Ill.: Chiron, 1986.

————. "Nature, Psyche and a Healing Ceremony of the Xhosa." *A Testament to the Wilderness: Essays in Honor of C. Meier.* Santa Monica, Calif.: Lapis Press, 1985. 78–86.

————. "Training of Analytical Psychologists and Xhosa Medicine Men." *Money, Food, Drink, and Fashion in Analytic Training; The Proceedings of the Eighth International Congress for Analytical Psychology,* San Francisco, 1980. Ed. John Beebe. Fellbach, Germany: Bonz, 1983. 237–48.

Burri, Margrit. "Repression, Falsification, and Bedeviling of Germanic Mythology." *Spring* (1978): 88–104.

Campbell, Joseph, ed. *The Portable Jung.* New York: Viking, 1971.

Carlson, Kathie. *In Her Image: The Unhealed Daughter's Search for Her Mother.* Boston: Shambhala, 1989. [Great Mother]

Carotenuto, Aldo. *Eros and Pathos: Shades of Love and Suffering.* Trans. Charles Nopar. Toronto: Inner City, 1989.

————. *A Secret Symmetry: Sabina Spielrein between Jung and Freud.* Trans. Arno Pomerans, John Shepley, and Krishna Winston. Foreword by William McGuire; commentary by Bruno Bettelheim. New York: Pantheon, 1984.

————. *The Vertical Labyrinth: Individuation in Jungian Psychology.* Trans. John Shepley. Toronto: Inner City, 1985.

Carson, Joan. "Visionary Experience in *Wuthering Heights.*" *Psychoanalytic Review* 62.1 (1975): 131–51. [animus/anima, Isis and Osiris]

Champernowne, Irene. *A Memoir of Toni Wolff.* Foreword by Joseph L. Henderson. San Francisco: C.G. Jung Institute of San Francisco, 1980.

Christ, Carol P. *Laughter of Aphrodite: Reflections on a Journey to the Goddess*. San Francisco: Harper & Row, 1987.

————. "Rituals with Aphrodite." *Anima: An Experiential Journal* 12.1 (1985): 25–33.

Claremont de Castillejo, Irene. *Knowing Woman*. New York: Putnam, 1973.

Clarkson, Austin. "Carmen: Bride of Dionysus." *Quadrant* 20.1 (1987): 51–72.

————. "Wagner from Lohengrin to Siegfried: 'Elsa Taught Me to Unearth This Man'" *Quadrant* 22 (1989): 39–52. [Wagner's use of mythology in opera]

Clift, Jean Dalby, and Wallace B. Clift. *Symbols of Transformation in Dreams*. New York: Crossroad, 1984.

Cobb, Noel. *Prospero's Island: The Secret Alchemy at the Heart of the Tempest*. London: Coventure, 1984.

Colman, Arthur, and Libby Colman. *The Father: Mythology and Changing Roles*. 2nd ed. Englewood Cliffs, N.J.: Prentice Hall, 1981. Wilmette, Ill.: Chiron, 1988. [originally published as *Earth Father/Sky Father*]

Colonna, M.T. "Lilith: Or the Black Moon." *Journal of Analytical Psychology* 25.4 (1980): 325–50.

Corneau, Guy. *Absent Fathers, Lost Sons: The Search for Masculine Identity*. Boston: Shambhala, 1990.

Coward, Harold. *Jung and Eastern Thought*. [with contributions by J. Borelli, J.F.T. Jordens, J. Henderson] Albany: State University of New York Press, 1985.

Dallett, Janet O. *When the Spirits Come Back*. Toronto: Inner City, 1988. [Native American (Pacific Northwest) myths and culture, Jungian primitivism]

Desteian, John A. *Coming Together—Coming Apart: The Union of Opposites in Love Relationships*. Boston: Sigo, 1989. [alchemy, individuation]

De Vos, Esther. "Voodoo: Our Link with the Occult." *The Analytic Life: Personal and Professional Aspects of Being a Jungian Analyst*. Boston: Sigo, 1988. 33–50. [Contents of the collective unconscious are experienced as loa by those whose belief system is Voodoo, and as archetypes by those whose belief system is analytical psychology]

Diamond, Stanley. "Jung Contra Freud: What It Means to Be Funny." *C.G. Jung and the Humanities.* Ed. Karin Barnaby and Pellegrino D'Acierno. Princeton, N.J.: Princeton University Press, 1990. 67–75. [the trickster]

Dieckmann, Hans. "The Favorite Fairy Tale from Childhood." *The Analytic Process.* Ed. Joseph Wheelwright. New York: Putnam, 1971. 77–84.

———. *Twice-Told Tales: The Psychological Use of Fairy Tales.* Trans. Boris Matthews. Foreword by Bruno Bettelheim. Wilmette, Ill.: Chiron, 1986.

Douglas, C. *The Woman in the Mirror: Analytical Psychology and the Feminine.* Boston: Sigo, 1990.

Dourley, John P. *The Illness That We Are: A Jungian Critique of Christianity.* Toronto: Inner City, 1984.

———. "Jung's Impact on Religious Studies." *C.G. Jung and the Humanities.* Ed. Karin Barnaby and Pellegrino D'Acierno. Princeton, N.J.: Princeton University Press, 1990. 36–44.

———. *Love, Celibacy and the Inner Marriage.* Toronto: Inner City, 1987.

Downing, Christine. *The Goddess: Mythological Images of the Feminine.* New York: Crossroad, 1984. [Persephone, Ariadne, Hera, Athena, Gaia, Artemis, Aphrodite]

Drake, Carlos C. "Jung and His Critics." *Journal of American Folklore* 80 (1969): 321–33.

———. "Jungian Psychology and Its Uses in Folklore." *Journal of American Folklore* 82 (1969): 122–31.

Dykes, A. "The Medusa Archetype." *In the Wake of Jung.* Ed. M. Tuby. London: Coventure, 1986. 67–86.

Edinger, Edward. *The Bible and the Psyche: Individuation Symbolism in the Old Testament.* Toronto: Inner City, 1986.

———. *The Christian Archetype: A Jungian Commentary on the Life of Christ.* Toronto: Inner City, 1987.

———. *The Creation of Consciousness: Jung's Myth for Modern Man.* Toronto: Inner City, 1984.

———. *Ego and Archetype: Individuation and the Religious Function of the Psyche*. New York: Putnam, 1972. New York: Penguin, 1973.

———. *Encounter with the Self: A Jungian Commentary on William Blake's Illustrations of the Book of Job*. Toronto: Inner City, 1986.

———. *Goethe's Faust: Notes for a Jungian Commentary*. Toronto: Inner City, 1990.

———. *Melville's Moby-Dick: A Jungian Commentary (An American Nekyia)*. New York: New Directions, 1978.

———. "An Outline of Analytical Psychology." *Quadrant* (Spring 1968).

Edwards, Lee R. "The Labors of Psyche: Toward a Theory of Female Heroism." *Critical Inquiry* 6.1 (1979): 33–49. [criticism and extension of Neumann's theories]

Elias-Button, Karen. "Athena and Medusa: A Woman's Myth." *Anima* 5.2 (1979).

———. "Journey into an Archetype: The Dark Mother in Contemporary Women's Poetry." *Anima* 4.2 (1978): 5–11.

Feinstein, David, and Stanley Krippner. *Personal Mythology: Using Ritual, Dreams and Imagination to Discover Your Inner Story*. Los Angeles: Jeremy P. Tarcher, 1988. [includes a section "Tending to the Mythic Vision of Your Community" dealing with collective cultural myths]

Fierz-David, Linda. *The Dream of Poliphilo*. New York: Pantheon, 1950. Dallas: Spring, 1987.

———. *Women's Dionysian Initiation: The Villa of Mysteries in Pompeii*. Trans. Gladys Phelan. With an introduction by M. Esther Harding. Dallas: Spring, 1988.

Fordham, Frieda. *An Introduction to Jung's Psychology*. London: Pelican, 1953.

Fordham, Michael, ed. *Contact with Jung: Essays on the Influence of His Work and Personality*. Philadelphia: Lippincott, 1963.

———. *Jungian Psychotherapy: A Study in Analytical Psychology*. New York: John Wiley, 1978.

————. "Jungian Views of the Body-Mind Relationship." *Spring* (1974): 166–78.

————. *New Developments in Analytical Psychology*. London: Routledge & Kegan Paul, 1957.

————. *The Objective Psyche*. London: Routledge & Kegan Paul, 1958.

Franz, Marie-Louise von. *Alchemical Active Imagination*. Dallas: Spring, 1979.

————. *Alchemy: An Introduction to the Symbolism and the Psychology*. Toronto: Inner City, 1980.

————. *Aurora Consurgens: A Document Attributed to Thomas Aquinas on the Problem of Opposites in Alchemy*. Trans. R.F.C. Hull and A.S.B. Glover. New York: Pantheon, 1966.

————. *C.G. Jung: His Myth in Our Time*. Trans. William H. Kennedy. New York: Putnam, 1975.

————. *Individuation in Fairy Tales*. Rev. ed. Boston: Shambhala, 1990.

————. *An Introduction to the Psychology of Fairy Tales*. Irving, Tex.: Spring, 1973.

————. *Number and Time: Reflections Leading Toward a Unification of Depth Psychology and Physics*. Trans. Andrea Dykes. Evanston, Ill.: Northwestern University Press, 1974.

————. *On Divination and Synchronicity: The Psychology of Meaningful Chance*. Toronto: Inner City, 1980.

————. *On Dreams and Death: A Jungian Interpretation*. Trans. Emmanuel Xipolitas Kennedy and Vernon Brooks. Boston: Shambhala, 1987. [especially Osiris]

————. *The Passion of Perpetua*. Dallas: Spring, 1980.

————. *Patterns of Creativity Mirrored in Creation Myths*. Dallas: Spring, 1972.

————. *Problems of the Feminine in Fairy Tales*. Dallas: Spring, 1972.

————. *Projection and Re-Collection in Jungian Psychology: Reflections of the Soul*. Trans. William H. Kennedy. La Salle, Ill., and London: Open Court, 1980.

————. *A Psychological Interpretation of the Golden Ass of Apuleius.* Dallas: Spring, 1980.

————. *The Psychological Meaning of Redemption Motifs in Fairytales.* Toronto: Inner City, 1980.

————. *Puer Aeternus: A Psychological Study of the Adult Struggle with the Paradise of Childhood.* 2nd ed. Santa Monica: Sigo.

————. *Shadow and Evil in Fairytales.* Dallas: Spring, 1974.

————. *Time: Rhythm and Repose.* New York: Thames & Hudson, 1978.

Franz, Marie-Louise von, and James Hillman. *Lectures on Jung's Typology.* Dallas: Spring, 1979. [Marie-Louise von Franz on the inferior function, James Hillman on the feeling function]

Frey-Rohn, Liliane. *Friedrich Nietzsche: A Psychological Approach to His Life and Work.* Ed. Robert Hinshaw and Lela Fischli. Trans. Gary Massey. Einsiedeln, Switzerland: Daimon, 1988.

————. *From Freud to Jung: A Comparative Study of the Psychology of the Unconscious.* Trans. Fred E. Engreen and Evelyn K. Engreen. New York: Putnam, 1974.

Gad, Irene. "Hephaestus: Model of New Age Masculinity." *Quadrant* 19 (1986): 27–48.

Gallant, Christine. *Blake and the Assimilation of Chaos.* Princeton, N.J.: Princeton University Press, 1978.

Geer, Genevieve. "Through the Prism of America." *Quadrant* 21 (1988): 21–9. [on Henderson's theory of the cultural unconscious]

Giegerich, W. "Ontogeney = Phylogeny? A Fundamental Critique of Erich Neumann's Analytical Psychology." *Spring* (1975): 110–29.

Gilchrist, Cherry. *The Circle of Nine: Understanding the Feminine Psyche.* London: Dryad Press, 1988. [nine female archetypes]

Goldberg, Jonathan J. "Reflections on Oedipus." *Quadrant* 10 (1977): 45–56.

Goldbrunner, Josef. *Individuation: A Study of the Depth Psychology of Carl Gustav Jung*. Notre Dame, Ind.: University of Notre Dame Press, 1964.

Goldenberg, Naomi R. "A Feminist Critique of Jung." *Signs* 2 (1976): 443–9.

———. *Returning Words to Flesh: Feminism, Psychoanalysis, and the Resurrection of the Body*. Boston: Beacon Press, 1990. [Part Two ("Escape from Jung") is a vigorous critique of archetypal psychology and theory.]

Gordon, Rosemary. "Gods and the Deintegrates." *Journal of Analytical Psychology* 8.1 (1963): 25–43. [African religions and mythologies]

Grabenhorst-Randall, Terree. "Jung and Abstract Expressionism." *C.G. Jung and the Humanities*. Ed. Karin Barnaby and Pellegrino D'Acierno. Princeton, N.J.: Princeton University Press, 1990. 185–205.

Greenfield, B. "The Archetypal Masculine: Its Manifestation in Myth and Its Significance for Women." *Journal of Analytical Psychology* 28.1 (1983): 33–50.

Grinnell, Robert. *Alchemy in a Modern Woman: A Study in the Contrasexual Archetype*. Dallas: Spring, 1973.

Groesbeck, C. "The Analyst's Myth: Freud and Jung as Each Other's Analyst." *Quadrant* 13.1 (1980): 28–55.

———. "The Archetypal Image of the Wounded Healer." *Journal of Analytical Psychology* 20.2 (1975): 122–45.

Guggenbühl-Craig, Adolf. *Eros on Crutches: Reflections on Psychopathy and Amorality*. Trans. Gary V. Hartman. Dallas: Spring, 1980.

———. *Marriage—Dead or Alive*. Trans. Murray Stein. Dallas: Spring, 1977.

———. *Power in the Helping Professions*. Trans. Myron Gubitz. Dallas: Spring, 1982.

Gustafson, Fred. *The Black Madonna*. Boston: Sigo, 1989.

Hall, Calvin, and Vernon Nordby. *A Primer of Jungian Psychology*. New York: Mentor, 1973.

Hall, James. *Jungian Dream Interpretation: A Hand-Book of Theory and Practice.* Toronto: Inner City, 1983.

Hall, Nor. *The Moon and the Virgin: Reflections on the Archetypal Feminine.* New York: Harper & Row, 1980.

―――. *Those Women.* Dallas: Spring, 1988. [women's rites of initiation; Villa of Mysteries, Pompeii; Dionysos]

Hannah, Barbara. *Encounters with the Soul: Active Imagination as Developed by C.G. Jung.* Santa Monica: Sigo, 1981.

―――. *Jung: His Life and Work.* New York: Putnam, 1976. [a biographical memoir and a valuable supplement to—and commentary on—Jung's own autobiography]

―――. *Striving Towards Wholeness.* 2nd ed. New York: Putnam, 1971. Boston: Sigo, 1988. [Robert Louis Stevenson, Mary Webb, the Brontës, *Wuthering Heights*]

Harding, M. Esther. "The Cross as Archetypal Symbol." *Quadrant* 11 (1971): 5–14.

―――. "She: A Portrait of the Anima." *Spring* (1947): 59–93. [on Rider Haggard's novel]

―――. *The Way of All Women.* Rev. ed. New York: Putnam, 1970. New York: Harper & Row, 1975. [with an introduction by C.G. Jung]

―――. *Woman's Mysteries: Ancient and Modern.* New York: Bantam, 1973.

Hart, D. "The Evolution of the Feminine in Fairy Tales." *Psychological Perspectives* 1.9 (1978): 46–56.

Haule, John R. *Divine Madness: Archetypes of Romantic Love.* Boston: Shambhala, 1990.

Heisig, James. *Imago Dei: A Study of C.G. Jung's Psychology of Religion.* Lewisburg, Pa.: Bucknell University Press, 1979.

Henderson, Joseph. "Ancient Myths and Modern Man." *Man and His Symbols.* Ed. C.G. Jung. New York: Doubleday, 1964. 104–57.

―――. *Cultural Attitudes in Psychological Perspective.* Toronto: Inner City, 1984.

―――. "The Cultural Unconscious." *Quadrant* 21 (1988): 7–16.

———. "Memories of a Time in Zurich: Origins of a Theory of Cultural Attitudes." *Psychological Perspectives* 16.2 (1985): 210–20.

———. "Stages of Psychological Development Exemplified in the Poetical Works of T.S. Eliot." *Journal of Analytical Psychology* 1.2 (1956): 133–44. [article continued in *Journal of Analytical Psychology* 2.1 (1957): 33–49]

———. *Thresholds of Initiation*. Middletown, Conn.: Wesleyan University Press, 1967.

Henderson, Joseph, and Maud Oakes. *The Wisdom of the Serpent*. New York: George Braziller, 1963.

Herzog, Edgar. *Psyche and Death: Death-Demons in Folklore, Myths and Modern Dreams*. Trans. David Cox and Eugene Rolfe. Dallas: Spring, 1983.

Hillman, James. *Anima: An Anatomy of a Personified Notion*. Dallas: Spring, 1985. [with excerpts from the writings of C.G. Jung]

———. *Archetypal Psychology: A Brief Account*. Dallas: Spring, 1983.

———. "The Bad Mother: An Archetypal Approach." *Spring* (1983): 165–82.

———. *A Blue Fire: Selected Writings by James Hillman*. Ed. Thomas Moore. New York: Harper & Row, 1989.

———. *The Dream and the Underworld*. New York: Harper & Row, 1979.

———. *Healing Fiction*. Barrytown, N.Y.: Station Hill, 1983. [Freud, Jung, Adler]

———. *Insearch*. New York: Scribner, 1967.

———. *Inter Views: Conversations with Laura Pozzo on Psychotherapy, Biography, Love, Soul, Dreams, Work, Imagination, and the State of Culture*. New York: Harper & Row, 1983. [the psychologist interviewed by his anima so to speak]

———. *Loose Ends: Primary Papers in Archetypal Psychology*. Dallas: Spring, 1975.

————. *The Myth of Analysis: Three Essays in Archetypal Psychology.* Evanston, Ill.: Northwestern University Press, 1972. New York: Harper & Row, 1978.

————. "Peaks and Vales: The Soul/Spirit Distinction as Basis for the Differences between Psychotherapy and Spiritual Discipline." *On the Way to Self-Knowledge.* Ed. Jacob Needleman and Dennis Lewis. New York: Knopf, 1976. 114–47.

————. *Re-Visioning Psychology.* New York: Harper & Row, 1975.

————. "Some Early Background to Jung's Ideas: Notes on C.G. Jung's Medium, by Stephanie Zumstead-Preiswerk." *Spring* (1976): 128–36.

————. *Suicide and the Soul.* New York: Harper & Row, 1964.

Hillman, James, ed. *Facing the Gods.* Dallas: Spring, 1980. [essays by various Jungians on Ananke, Athena, the Amazons, Hephaistos, Rhea, Hestia, Hermes, Ariadne, Dionysos]

————, *Puer Papers.* Dallas: Spring, 1979. [Articles by Hillman, Henry A. Murray, Tom Moore, James Baird, Thomas Cowan and Randolph Severson]

Hillman, James, and Wilhelm Roscher. *Pan and the Nightmare.* Dallas: Spring, 1972.

Hoeller, Stephen A. *The Gnostic Jung and the Seven Sermons to the Dead.* Wheaton, Ill.: Theosophical Publishing House, 1982.

Homans, Peter. *Jung in Context: Modernity and the Making of a Psychology.* Chicago and London: University of Chicago Press, 1979.

Hopcke, Robert. "Dorothy and Her Friends: Symbols of Gay Male Individuation in the Wizard of Oz." *Quadrant* 22 (1989): 65–78.

————. *A Guided Tour of the Collected Works of C.G. Jung.* Boston: Shambhala, 1989. [very useful short definitions and bibliographical references to key discussions of concepts and archetypes; does not include the correspondence, interviews, and seminars]

————. *Jung, Jungians and Homosexuality.* Boston: Shambhala, 1990.

Hosmer, M. "Kali: The Black One." Paper presented before the Analytical Psychology Club of New York. Unpublished manuscript, property of the Kristine Mann Library, New York, 1968.

Hudson, Wilson M. "Jung on Myth and the Mythic." *The Sunny Slopes of Long Ago*. Ed. Wilson M. Hudson and Allen Maxwell. Dallas: Southern Methodist University Press, 1966. 181–97.

Jacobi, Jolande. *Complex/Archetype/Symbol in the Psychology of C.G. Jung*. Trans. Ralph Manheim. Princeton, N.J.: Princeton University Press, 1959.

————. *The Psychology of C.G. Jung: An Introduction with Illustrations*. Trans. Ralph Manheim. 8th ed. New Haven: Yale University Press, 1973.

————. *The Way of Individuation*. Trans. R.F.C. Hull. New York: New American Library, 1983.

Jacoby, Mario. *Individuation and Narcissism: The Psychology of the Self in Jung and Kohut*. Trans. Myron Gubitz and Françoise O'Kane. London and New York: Routledge, 1990. [Narcissus]

————. *The Longing for Paradise: Psychological Perspectives on an Archetype*. Trans. Myron B. Gubitz. Boston: Sigo, 1985.

Jaffé, Aniela. *Apparitions: An Archetypal Approach to Death Dreams and Ghosts*. With a foreword by C.G. Jung. New Hyde Park, N.Y.: University Books, 1963. Dallas: Spring, 1979.

————. *From the Life and Work of C.G. Jung*. New York: Harper Colophon, 1971.

————. *Jung's Last Years and Other Essays*. Trans. R. F. C. Hull and Murray Stein. Dallas: Spring, 1984.

————. *The Myth of Meaning: Jung and the Expansion of Consciousness*. Trans. R. F. C. Hull. New York: Putnam, 1971. New York: Penguin, 1975.

————. "Symbolism in the Visual Arts." *Man and His Symbols*. Ed. C.G. Jung. Garden City, N.Y.: Doubleday, 1964.

Jaffé, Aniela, ed. *C.G. Jung: Word and Image*. Princeton, N.J.: Princeton University Press, 1979. [photographs and text]

Jensen, Ferne, ed. *C.G. Jung, Emma Jung and Toni Wolff: A Collection of Remembrances.* San Francisco: The Analytical Psychology Club of San Francisco, 1982.

Johnson, Robert A. *Ecstasy: Understanding the Psychology of Joy.* San Francisco: Harper & Row, 1987. [Dionysos]

———. *He: Understanding Male Psychology.* New York: Harper & Row, 1977. Revised edition 1989. [Parsifal, the Holy Grail]

———. *Inner Work: Using Dreams and Active Imagination for Personal Growth.* San Francisco: Harper & Row, 1986.

———. *Owning Your Own Shadow: Understanding the Dark Side of the Psyche.* San Francisco: Harper & Row, 1991.

———. *She: Understanding Feminine Psychology.* New York: Harper & Row, 1977. [Amor and Psyche]

———. *We: Understanding the Psychology of Romantic Love.* San Francisco: Harper & Row, 1983. [Tristan and Iseult]

Jones, Joyce Meeks. *Jungian Psychology in Literary Analysis: A Demonstration Using T.S. Eliot's Poetry.* Washington, D.C.: University Press of America, 1979.

Jung, C.G., and C. Kerényi. *Essays on a Science of Mythology: The Myth of the Divine Child and the Mysteries of Eleusis.* Trans. R.F C. Hull. Princeton, N.J.: Princeton University Press, 1969.

Jung, Emma. *Animus and Anima.* Trans. Cary F. Baynes and Hildegard Nagel. New York: The Analytical Psychology Club of New York, 1957. Dallas: Spring, 1985.

Jung, Emma, and Marie-Louise von Franz. *The Grail Legend.* Boston: Sigo, 1986.

Kalsched, Donald E. "Fire from the Gods: How Will Prometheus Be Bound?" *Quadrant* 18 (1985): 71–92. [Apocalypse; Hephaestus/Vulcan]

Kaplan-Williams, Strephon. *The Jungian-Senoi Dreamwork Manual: A Step-by-Step Introduction to Working with Dreams.* Rev. ed. Berkeley: Journey Press, 1985–6. [dreamwork methods of the Senoi people of Malaya and the Jungian perspective]

Kast, Verena. *Joy, Inspiration, and Hope*. Trans. Douglas Whitcher. Foreword by David H. Rosen. College Station: Texas A&M University Press, 1992. [Dionysos]

———. *The Nature of Loving: Patterns of Human Relationship*. Trans. Boris Matthews. Wilmette, Ill.: Chiron, 1986. [Shiva and Shakti, Pygmalion, Ishtar and Tammuz, Zeus and Hera, Merlin and Viviane]

Kawai, Hayao. *The Buddhist Priest Myoe: A Life of Dreams*. Trans. Mark Unno. Venice, Calif.: The Lapis Press, 1992. [the life and dreams of a medieval Japanese priest]

Kawai, Hayao. *The Japanese Psyche: Major Motifs in the Fairy Tales of Japan*. Trans. Sachiko Reece. Dallas: Spring, 1988.

Kent, Alice. "The Goddess Mysteries." *The Shaman from Elko*. Ed. Gareth S. Hill. San Francisco: C.G. Jung Institute of San Francisco, 1978. 126–42. [Eleusinian Mysteries]

Kerényi, Carl. *Asklepios, Archetypal Image of the Physician's Existence*. Trans. Ralph Manheim. New York: Pantheon Books, 1959.

———. *Athene: Virgin and Mother*. Trans. Murray Stein. Dallas: Spring, 1988.

———. *Dionysos, Archetypal Image of Indestructible Life*. Trans. Ralph Manheim. Princeton, N.J.: Princeton University Press, 1976.

———. *Eleusis, Archetypal Image of Mother and Daughter*. Trans. Ralph Manheim. New York: Schocken Books, 1977. [Demeter and Persephone]

———. *Goddesses of the Sun and Moon*. Trans. Murray Stein. Dallas: Spring, 1979.

———. *The Gods of the Greeks*. Trans. Norman Cameron. New York: Thames & Hudson, 1979.

———. *Hermes, Guide of Souls: The Mythologem of the Masculine Source of Life*. Trans. Murray Stein. Dallas: Spring, 1976.

Kerényi, Carl, and James Hillman. *Oedipus Variations: Studies in Literature and Psychoanalysis*. Dallas: Spring, 1991.

Kirsch, James. "The Enigma of Moby Dick." *Journal of Analytical Psychology* 3.2 (1958): 131–48. [whales as archetypes, Moby Dick as the image of God]

————. *Shakespeare's Royal Self.* New York: Putnam, 1966.

Kluger, H. Yehezkel. "Archetypal Dreams and 'Everyday' Dreams: A Statistical Investigation into Jung's Theory of the Collective Unconscious." *Israel Annals of Psychiatry and Related Disciplines* 13 (1975): 6–47.

Kluger, R.S. "The Image of the Marriage between God and Israel." *Spring* (1950).

————. *Psyche and the Bible: Three Old Testament Themes.* New York and Zurich: Spring, 1974.

————. *Satan in the Old Testament.* Evanston, Ill.: Northwestern University Press, 1967.

Knapp, Bettina. *A Jungian Approach to Literature.* Carbondale and Edwardsville: Southern Illinois University Press, 1984. [see esp. chapters on the bacchants/Dionysos and on Parzival]

————. *Music, Archetype, and the Writer: A Jungian View.* University Park: Pennsylvania State University Press, 1988.

————. *The Prometheus Syndrome.* Troy, New York: Whitson, 1979.

————. *Theatre and Alchemy.* Detroit: Wayne State University Press, 1980.

Knipe, R. "Pele: Volcano Goddess of Hawaii." *Psychological Perspectives* 13.2 (1982): 114–26.

Koltuv, Barbara Black. *The Book of Lilith.* York Beach, Maine: Nicolas-Hays, 1986.

————. "Hestia/Vesta." *Quadrant* 10.2 (1977).

————. *Weaving Woman: Essays in Feminine Psychology from the Notebooks of a Jungian Analyst.* York Beach, Maine: Nicolas-Hays, 1990. [esp. animus]

Kugler, Paul. "The Unconscious in a Postmodern Depth Psychology." *C.G. Jung and the Humanities.* Ed. Karin Barnaby and Pellegrino D'Acierno. Princeton, N.J.: Princeton University Press, 1990. 307–18.

Laeuchli, Samuel, and Evelyn Rothchild Laeuchli. "Mimesis: The Healing Play of Myth." *Quadrant* 22.2 (1989): 53–64. [re-enacting myth, the myth of Genesis]

Laughlin, Tom. *Jungian Psychology, Volume 2: Jungian Theory and Therapy*. Los Angeles: Panarion Press, 1982. [a critical approach; see esp. chapters 24–30 and the epilogue]

Lauter, Estella. *Women as Mythmakers: Poetry and Visual Art by Twentieth-Century Women*. Bloomington: Indiana University Press, 1984.

Lauter, Estella, and Carol Schreier Rupprecht, eds. *Feminist Archetypal Theory: Interdisciplinary Re-Visions of Jungian Thought*. Knoxville: University of Tennessee Press, 1985.

Layard, John. "Boar Sacrifice." *Journal of Analytical Psychology* 1.1 (1955): 7–13. [Malekulan myth and ritual (New Guinea) and the dreams of a schizophrenic]

———. "Homo-Eroticism in Primitive Society as a Function of the Self." *Journal of Analytical Psychology* 4.2 (1959): 101–16. [male initiation, Malekulan myth concerning origin of sodomy]

———. "The Malekulan Journey of the Dead." *Spiritual Disciplines*. Ed. Joseph Campbell. Princeton, N.J.: Princeton University Press, 1970.

———. "Note on the Autonomous Psyche and the Ambivalence of the Trickster Concept." *Journal of Analytical Psychology* 3 (1958): 21–8. [on Metman's article, see below]

———. *The Virgin Archetype*. Dallas: Spring, 1972.

Leonard, Linda. "Amazon Armors." *Psychological Perspectives* 10.2 (1979): 113–30.

———. *On the Way to the Wedding: Transforming the Love Relationship*. Boston: Shambhala, 1986. [Beauty and the Beast; the hieros gamos/sacred marriage; Wagner's Brunnhilde and Siegfried; the Demon Lover]

———. "The Puella and the Perverted Old Man." *Psychological Perspectives* 10.1 (1979): 7–17.

———. "Puella Patterns." *Psychological Perspectives* 9.2 (1978): 127–43.

————. *Witness to the Fire: Creativity and the Veil of Addiction.* Boston: Shambhala, 1989.

————. *The Wounded Woman: Healing the Father-Daughter Relationship.* Athens, Ohio: Swallow Press, 1982.

Lockhart, Russell. "Cancer in Myth and Dream: An Exploration into the Archetypal Relation Between Dreams and Disease." *Spring* (1977).

Lopez-Pedraza, Rafael. *Hermes and His Children.* New, expanded ed. Dallas: Spring, 1977. Einsiedeln, Switzerland: Daimon, 1989.

————. "The Tale of Dryops and the Birth of Pan: An Archetypal and Psychotherapeutic Approach to Eros between Men." *Spring* (1976): 176–90.

Lowinsky, N. "Why Can't a Man Be More like a Woman?" *San Francisco Jung Library Journal* 5.1 (1984): 20–30.

Luke, Helen. *The Inner Story: Myth and Symbol in the Bible and Literature.* New York: Crossroad, 1982.

————. *Woman, Earth and Spirit.* New York: Crossroad, 1981.

McCully, Robert S. "Archetypal Psychology as a Key for Understanding Prehistoric Art Forms." *History of Childhood Quarterly* 3 (1976): 523–42.

————. "Impressions of a Visit to Lascaux." *Quadrant* (1977): 39–42. [cave art, Great Mother]

McGuire, William, ed. *The Freud/Jung Letters.* Princeton, N.J.: Princeton University Press, 1974.

————. "Jung in America, 1924–1925." *Spring* (1978): 37–53. [more on Jung's contact with the Pueblo Indians]

————. "Jung's Seminars." *Quadrant* 16.1 (1974): 29–38.

McGuire, William, and R.F.C. Hull, eds. *C.G. Jung Speaking: Interviews and Encounters.* Princeton, N.J.: Princeton University Press, 1977.

McNeely, Deldon Anne. *Animus Aeternus: Exploring the Inner Masculine.* Toronto: Inner City, 1991.

Mahdi, Louise Carus, Steven Foster, and Meredith Little, eds. *Betwixt & Between: Patterns of Masculine and Feminine Initiation.* La Salle, Ill.: Open Court, 1987. [an important collection of Jungian—for the most part—essays on the topic]

Maidenbaum, Aryeh, and Stephen A. Martin, eds. *Lingering Shadows: Jungians, Freudians, and Anti-Semites.* Boston: Shambhala, 1991.

Malamud, René. "The Amazon Problem." *Spring* (1971).

Malone, Michael. *Psychetypes: A New Way of Exploring Personality.* New York: Dutton, 1977.

Manchester, John. "Ceremonies, Myths and Stories of the Taos Indians." *Quadrant* 10 (1971): 21–5.

Mattoon, Mary Ann, ed. *The Archetype of Shadow in a Split World: Proceedings of the Tenth International Congress for Analytical Psychology, Berlin, 1986.* Zurich: Daimon, 1987.

———. *Jungian Psychology in Perspective.* New York: Free Press, 1981.

———. *Understanding Dreams.* Dallas: Spring, 1984.

Mattoon, Mary Ann, and Jennette Jones. "Is the Animus Obsolete?" *Quadrant* 20 (1987): 5–22.

Maud, Ralph. "Archetypal Depth Criticism and Melville." *College English* 45.7 (1983): 695–704.

Meador, B. "The Thesmophoria: A Woman's Ritual." *Psychological Perspectives* 17.1 (1986): 25–45.

Meier, C.A. *Healing Dream and Ritual: Ancient Incubation and Modern Psychotherapy.* Rev. ed. Evanston, Ill.: Northwestern University Press, 1967. Einsiedeln, Switzerland: Daimon, 1989. [a "greatly expanded version" of the 1967 book published under the title which has now become the subtitle]

Meier, Fritz. "The Problem of Evil in the Esoteric Monism of Islam." *Eranos Yearbook, Volume 1.* Princeton, N.J.: Princeton University Press, 1954.

———. "The Spiritual Man in the Persian Poet Attar." *Eranos Yearbook, Volume 4.* Princeton, N.J.: Princeton University Press, 1963.

———. "The Transformation of Man in Mystical Islam." *Eranos Yearbook, Volume 5*. Princeton, N.J.: Princeton University Press, 1964.

Metman, Philip. "The Trickster Figure in Schizophrenia." *Journal of Analytical Psychology* 3.1 (1958): 5–20. [parallels with Radin's account of the Winnebago Trickster Cycle]

Miller, David. "Chiliasm: Apocalyptic with a Thousand Faces." *Facing Apocalypse*. Ed. Valerie Andrews, Robert Bosnak, and Karen Walter Goodwin. Dallas: Spring, 1987. 4–24.

———. *The New Polytheism: Rebirth of the Gods and Goddesses*. Prefatory letter by Henry Corbin; appendix by James Hillman. Dallas: Spring, 1981.

Mindell, Arnold. "The Golem: An Image Governing Synchronicity." *Quadrant* 8.2 (1975): 5–16.

Monick, Eugene. *Castration and Male Rage: The Phallic Wound*. Toronto: Inner City, 1991. [a companion to Monick's first book, already a Men's Movement classic]

———. *Phallos: Sacred Image of the Masculine*. Toronto: Inner City, 1987.

Moon, Sheila. *Changing Woman and Her Sisters: Feminine Aspects of Selves and Deities*. San Francisco: Guild for Psychological Studies Publishing House, 1984. [Navajo, Pueblo myths]

———. *Dreams of a Woman: An Analyst's Inner Journey*. Foreword by Liliane Frey-Rohn. Boston: Sigo, 1983.

———. *A Magic Dwells: A Poetic and Psychological Study of the Navaho Emergence Myth*. Middletown, Conn.: Wesleyan University Press, 1970.

Moore, Norah. "Anima-Animus in a Changing World." *The Differing Uses of Symbolic and Clinical Approaches in Practice and Theory: Proceedings of the Ninth International Congress for Analytical Psychology, Jerusalem, 1983*. Ed. Luigi Zoja and Robert Hinshaw. Zurich: Daimon, 1986. 193–214.

Moore, Robert. *Carl Jung and Christian Spirituality*. Philadelphia: Paulist Press, 1988.

————. *King, Warrior, Magician, Lover: Rediscovering the Archetypes of the Mature Masculine.* New York: HarperSanFrancisco, 1990.

Moore, Robert, and Douglas Gillette. *The King Within: Accessing the King in the Male Psyche.* New York: William Morrow, 1992.

Moore, T. *Care of the Soul: A Guide for Cultivating Depth and Sacredness in Everyday Life.* New York: HarperCollins, 1992.

————. "Is the Personal Myth a Myth?" *Rituals of the Imagination.* Dallas: The Pegasus Foundation, 1983. 19–33.

Moreno, Antonio. *Jung, Gods, and Modern Man.* Notre Dame, Ind.: University of Notre Dame Press, 1970.

Murdock, Maureen. *The Heroine's Journey.* Boston: Shambhala, 1990.

Murray, Henry. "In Nomine Diaboli." *New England Quarterly* 24 (1951): 435–62. [Melville]

Myers, Isabel Briggs. *Gifts Differing.* With Peter B. Myers. Palo Alto, California: Consulting Psychologists Press, 1980. [on the use of the Myers-Briggs Type Indicator—MBTI—based on Jung's typology]

Nagy, Marilyn. *Philosophical Issues in the Psychology of C.G. Jung.* Albany: State University of New York Press, 1991.

Neumann, Erich. *Amor and Psyche: The Psychic Development of the Feminine (A Commentary on the Tale by Apuleius)* Trans. Ralph Manheim. Bollingen Series 54. New York: Bollingen Foundation, 1956. Princeton, N.J.: Princeton University Press, 1971. [Aphrodite/Venus]

————. *The Archetypal World of Henry Moore.* New York: Pantheon, 1959. [Great Mother]

————. *Art and the Creative Unconscious: Four Essays.* Trans. Ralph Manheim. Princeton, N.J.: Princeton University Press, 1959.

————. *The Child.* London: H. Karnac Books, 1973.

————. *Creative Man: Five Essays.* Trans. Eugene Rolfe. Princeton, N.J.: Princeton University Press, 1979. [essays on Kafka's

"The Trial," Chagall and the Bible, Georg Trakl, Freud and the father image, and C.G. Jung]

———. *Depth Psychology and a New Ethic.* Trans. Eugene Rolfe. New York: C.G. Jung Foundation for Analytical Psychology, 1969. New York: Harper & Row, 1973.

———. "Fear of the Feminine." *Quadrant* 19 (1986): 7–30.

———. *The Great Mother: An Analysis of the Archetype.* Trans. Ralph Manheim. Princeton, N.J.: Princeton University Press, 1955.

———. "In Honour of the Centenary of Freud's Birth." *Journal of Analytical Psychology* 1.2 (1956): 195–202. [Freud's confrontation with the Jewish Father-God]

———. "The Magic Flute." *Quadrant* 11 (1978): 5–32.

———. "The Moon and Matriarchal Consciousness." *Spring* (1954): 83–100.

———. "The Mythical World and the Individual." *Quadrant* 14 (1981): 5–40.

———. "On the Psychological Meaning of Ritual." *Quadrant* 9 (1976): 5–34.

———. *The Origins and History of Consciousness.* Trans. R.F.C. Hull. Princeton, N.J.: Princeton University Press, 1954.

———. "The Psychological Stages of Feminine Development." *Spring* (1959): 63–97.

———. "The Significance of the Genetic Aspect for Analytical Psychology." *Journal of Analytical Psychology* 4.2 (1959): 125–38.

———. "Stages of Religious Experience and the Path of Depth Psychology." *Quadrant* 21 (1988): 11–34.

Newman, R. D. "The Transformative Quality of the Feminine in the Penelope Episode of *Ulysses*." *Journal of Analytical Psychology* 31.1 (1986): 63–74.

Oakes, Maud. "The Blessing Way Ceremony." *The Shaman from Elko*. Ed. Gareth S. Hill. San Francisco: C.G. Jung Institute of San Francisco, 1978. 59–63. [Navaho]

———. *The Stone Speaks: The Memoir of a Personal Transformation.* Foreword by William McGuire, introduction by Joseph

Henderson. Wilmette, Ill.: Chiron, 1987. [meditations on the stone carved by Jung at his country home in Bollingen]

O'Connor, Peter. *Dreams and the Search for Meaning.* New York: Paulist Press, 1986. [an eclectic approach, partially inspired by Jung and Hillman]

Odajnyk, V. Walter. "The Psychologist as Artist: The Imaginal World of James Hillman." *Quadrant* 17 (1984): 39–48.

———. "Gathering the Light: A Jungian Exploration of the Psychology of Meditation." *Quadrant* 21 (1988): 35–54.

———. *Jung and Politics: The Political and Social Ideas of C.G. Jung.* New York: Harper & Row, 1976.

O'Neill, Timothy R. *The Individuated Hobbit: Jung, Tolkien and the Archetypes of Middle-Earth.* Boston: Houghton Mifflin, 1979.

Paris, Ginette. *Pagan Grace: Feeling the Presence of Hermes, Dionysos, and Mnemosyne in Daily Life.* Dallas: Spring, 1990.

———. *Pagan Meditations: The Worlds of Aphrodite, Artemis, and Hestia.* Trans. Gwendolyn Moore. Dallas: Spring, 1986.

Pearson, Carol S. *Awakening the Heroes Within: Twelve Archetypes to Help Us Find Ourselves and Transform Our World.* San Francisco: HarperSanFrancisco, 1991. [somewhat Jungian in orientation]

———. *The Hero Within: Six Archetypes We Live By.* San Francisco: Harper & Row, 1989. [somewhat Jungian in orientation]

Perera, Sylvia Brinton. *Descent to the Goddess: A Way of Initiation for Women.* Toronto: Inner City, 1981. [Inanna/Ishtar, Ereshkigal, Dumuzi]

———. *The Scapegoat Complex: Toward a Mythology of Shadow and Guilt.* Toronto: Inner City, 1986.

Perry, John Weir. *Lord of the Four Quarters: The Mythology of Kingship.* New York: George Braziller, 1966. New York: Paulist Press, 1991.

———. *Roots of Renewal in Myth and Madness: The Meaning of Psychotic Episodes.* San Francisco: Jossey-Bass, 1976.

Philipson, Morris. *Outline of a Jungian Aesthetics.* Evanston, Illinois: Northwestern University Press, 1963.

Pirani, Alix. *The Absent Father: Crisis and Creativity*. London: Routledge, 1988. London: Arkana, 1989. [Danae and Perseus]

Pops, Martin L. *The Melville Archetype*. Kent, Ohio: Kent State University Press, 1970.

Pratt, Annis. *Archetypal Patterns in Women's Fiction*. [with Barbara White, Andrea Loewenstein, Mary Wyer] Bloomington: Indiana University Press, 1981.

Prochaska, Harry. "Response to 'The Cultural Unconscious'" *Quadrant* 21 (1988): 17–20.

Progoff, Ira. *Jung, Synchronicity and Human Destiny*. New York: Dell, 1973.

Qualls-Corbett, Nancy. *The Sacred Prostitute: Eternal Aspect of the Feminine*. Foreword by Marion Woodman. Toronto: Inner City, 1988.

Radford, F.L., and R.R. Wilson. "Some Phases of the Jungian Moon: Jung's Influence on Modern Literary Studies." *English Studies in Canada* 8.3 (1982): 311–32.

Radin, Paul. *The Trickster: A Study in American Indian Mythology*. With commentaries by Karl Kerényi and C.G. Jung. London: Routledge & Kegan Paul, 1956. [Winnebago Trickster Cycle]

Raine, Kathleen. *The Human Face of God: William Blake and the Book of Job*. London: Thames & Hudson, 1982. [especially the chapter "Blake's Job and Jung's Job"]

Reed, William. "Shamanistic Principles of Initiation and Power." *The Shaman from Elko*. Ed. Gareth S. Hill. San Francisco: C.G. Jung Institute of San Francisco, 1978. 39–53.

Rolfe, Eugene. *Encounter with Jung*. Boston: Sigo, 1989.

Rollins, Wayne. *Jung and the Bible*. Atlanta: John Knox Press, 1983.

Rothenberg, Rose-Emily. "The Orphan Archetype." *Psychological Perspectives* (1983): 181–94.

Rupprecht, Carol. "The Martial Maid and the Challenge of Androgyny (Notes on an Unbefriended Archetype)" *Spring* (1974).

Russack, Neil W. "A Psychological Interpretation of Meyrink's 'The Golem'" *The Shaman from Elko*. Ed. Gareth S. Hill. San Francisco: C.G. Jung Institute of San Francisco, 1978. 157–64.

Saayman, Graham, ed. *Modern South Africa in Search of a Soul: Jungian Perspectives on the Wilderness Within*. Foreword by Sir Laurens van der Post. Boston: Sigo, 1989.

Salman, Sherry L. "The Horned God: Masculine Dynamics of Power and Soul." *Quadrant* 19 (1986): 6–26. [esp. the Celtic god Cernunnos]

Samuels, Andrew. "Beyond the Feminine Principle." *C.G. Jung and the Humanities*. Ed. Karin Barnaby and Pellegrino D'Acierno. Princeton, N.J.: Princeton University Press, 1990. 294–306.

———. "Gender and Psyche: Developments in Analytical Psychology." *Anima* 11.2 (1985): 125–38.

———. *Jung and the Post-Jungians*. London: Routledge & Kegan Paul, 1985.

———. *The Plural Psyche: Personality, Morality, and the Father*. London and New York: Routledge, 1989.

Samuels, Andrew, ed. *The Father: Contemporary Jungian Perspectives*. London: Free Association Books, 1985.

Samuels, Andrew, Bani Shorter, and Fred Plaut. *A Critical Dictionary of Jungian Analysis*. London and New York: Routledge & Kegan Paul, 1986.

Sandner, Donald. "The Navaho Prayer of Blessing." *The Shaman from Elko*. Ed. Gareth S. Hill. San Francisco: C.G. Jung Institute of San Francisco, 1978. 35–8.

———. *Navajo Symbols of Healing*. London and New York: Harcourt Brace Jovanovich, 1979.

———. "The Symbolic Life of Man." *The Differing Uses of Symbolic and Clinical Approaches in Practice and Theory: Proceedings of the Ninth International Congress for Analytical Psychology, Jerusalem, 1983*. Ed. Luigi Zoja and Robert Hinshaw. Zurich: Daimon, 1986. 325–48. [mandala, Bali, Navaho Blessing Way]

Sanford, John A. *Dreams and Healing: A Succinct and Lively Interpretation of Dreams.* New York: Paulist Press, 1978.

———. *Evil, the Shadow Side of Reality.* New York: Crossroad, 1986.

———. *The Invisible Partners: How the Male and Female in Each of Us Affects Our Relationships.* New York: Paulist Press, 1980. [anima/animus]

———. *King Saul, the Tragic Hero: A Study in Individuation.* New York: Paulist Press, 1985.

———. *The Strange Trial of Mr. Hyde.* San Francisco: Harper & Row, 1987. [a fantasy trial of Stevenson's famous shadow character]

Satinover, J. "Jung's Relation to His Mother." *Quadrant* 18 (1985): 9–22.

———. "The Mirror of Doctor Faustus: The Decline of Art in the Pursuit of Eternal Adolescence." *Quadrant* 17 (Spring, 1984), 23–38.

———. *The Mythology of Genius.* The 1975 William James Lecture in Psychology and Religion. Cambridge: Harvard University Press, 1975.

———. "Puer Aeternus: The Narcissistic Relationship to the Self." *Quadrant* 13 (1980): 75–108.

Schapira, Laurie Layton. *The Cassandra Complex: Living with Disbelief (A Modern Perspective on Hysteria).* Toronto: Inner City, 1988.

Schwartz-Salant, Nathan. *Narcissism and Character Transformation: The Psychology of Narcissistic Character Disorders.* Toronto: Inner City, 1982.

Segal, Robert A. "Adonis: An Ancient Peter Pan." *Psychological Perspectives* 24 (1991): 124–32.

———. "Adonis: The Eternal Greek Child." *Myth and the Polis.* Ed. Dora C. Pozzi and John M. Wickersham. Ithaca, N.Y.: Cornell University Press, 1991. 64–85.

———. *Joseph Campbell: An Introduction.* Rev. ed. New York: Mentor (Penguin), 1990.

————. *The Poimandres as Myth: Scholarly Theory and Onastic Meaning*. Berlin: Mouton de Gruyter, 1986. [applies Jungian psychology to a Gnostic myth]

Segal, Robert A., ed. *The Gnostic Jung*. Princeton, N.J.: Princeton University Press, 1992. [introduction by the editor; texts by Jung, Quispel, and others]

Segaller, Stephen, and Merrill Berger. *The Wisdom of the Dream: The World of C.G. Jung*. Boston: Shambhala, 1989. [based on a three-part British television series; also available in videocassette format]

Seifert, Theodor. *Snow White: Life Almost Lost*. Trans. Boris Matthews. Wilmette, Ill.: Chiron, 1986.

Serrano, Miguel. *Jung and Hesse: A Record of Two Friendships*. New York: Schocken, 1968.

Sharp, Daryl. *Jung Lexicon: A Primer of Terms and Concepts*. Toronto: Inner City, 1991.

————. *Personality Types: Jung's Model of Typology*. Toronto: Inner City, 1987.

————. *The Survival Papers: Anatomy of a Midlife Crisis*. Toronto: Inner City, 1988.

Shelburne, Walter A. *Mythos and Logos in the Thought of Carl Jung: The Theory of the Collective Unconscious in Scientific Perspective*. Albany: State University of New York Press, 1988.

Shorter, Bani. *An Image Darkly Forming: Women and Initiation*. London and New York: Routledge & Kegan Paul, 1987.

Sibbald, Luella. *The Footprints of God: The Relationship of Astrology, C.G. Jung and the Gospels*. Boston: Sigo, 1989.

Singer, June. *Androgyny*. Garden City, N.Y.: Doubleday, 1976.

————. *Androgyny: The Opposites Within*. 3rd ed. Boston: Sigo, 1989.

————. *Energies of Love: Sexuality Revisioned*. Garden City, New York: Anchor, 1983.

————. "On William Blake: Reason Versus Imagination." *C.G. Jung and the Humanities*. Ed. Karin Barnaby and Pellegrino

D'Acierno. Princeton, N.J.: Princeton University Press, 1990. 162–73.

———. *The Unholy Bible: A Psychological Interpretation of William Blake*. New York: Putnam, 1970.

Singleton, Mary A. *The City and the Velt: The Fiction of Doris Lessing*. Lewisburg, Pa.: Bucknell University Press, 1977.

Smith, Curtis D. *Jung's Quest for Wholeness: A Religious and Historical Perspective*. Albany: State University of New York Press, 1990. [individuation, Self, alchemy]

Solie, Pierre. "On the Role of the Isis/Osiris Myth and of the Egyptian Book of the Dead in the Treatment of a Vase of Mourning." *The Differing Uses of Symbolic and Clinical Approaches in Practice and Theory: Proceedings of the Ninth International Congress for Analytical Psychology, Jerusalem, 1983*. Ed. Luigi Zoja and Robert Hinshaw. Zurich: Daimon, 1986. 57–66.

Spiegelman, J. Marvin, ed. *Jungian Analysts: Their Visions and Vulnerabilities*. Phoenix: Falcon Press, 1988. [thirteen Jungian analysts reflect on their profession]

Spiegelman, J. Marvin, and Mokusen Miyuki. *Buddhism and Jungian Psychology*. Phoenix: Falcon Press, 1985.

Spiegelman, J. Marvin, and Arwind U. Vasavada. *Hinduism and Jungian Psychology*. Phoenix: Falcon Press, 1987.

Staude, John-Raphael. *The Adult Development of C.G. Jung*. London and New York: Routledge & Kegan Paul, 1981.

Stein, Leopold, and Martha Alexander. *Loathsome Women*. London: Weidenfeld and Nicolson, 1959. [witch figure]

Stein, Murray. "Hera: Bound and Unbound." *Spring* (1977): 105–19.

———. *In MidLife: A Jungian Perspective*. Dallas: Spring, 1983. [Hermes/Mercury]

———. *Jung's Treatment of Christianity: The Psychotherapy of a Religious Tradition*. Wilmette, Ill.: Chiron, 1985.

———. "Narcissus." *Spring* (1976): 32–53.

———. "The Significance of Jung's Father in His Destiny as a Therapist of Christianity." *Quadrant* 18 (1985): 23–34.

Stein, Robert M. "The Animus and Impersonal Sexuality." *Spring* (1970): 126–32.

———. *Incest and Human Love: The Betrayal of the Soul in Psychotherapy*. Dallas: Spring, 1973.

Stevens, Anthony. *Archetypes: A Natural History of the Self*. New York: Morrow, 1982.

———. *The Roots of War: A Jungian Perspective*. New York: Paragon House, 1984.

Storr, Anthony. *Jung*. London: Fontana Press, 1973.

Taylor, Charles H. "Imagining Apocalypse: Godlike Power and Human Care." *Quadrant* 18 (1985): 35–44.

Te Paske, Bradley A. *Rape and Ritual: A Psychological Study*. Toronto: Inner City, 1982.

Ulanov, Ann. *The Feminine in Jungian Psychology and in Christian Theology*. Evanston, Illinois: Northwestern University Press, 1971.

Ulanov, Ann, and Barry Ulanov. *Cinderella and Her Sisters: The Envied and the Envying*. Philadelphia: The Westminster Press, 1983.

———. *The Witch and the Clown: Two Archetypes of Human Sexuality*. Wilmette, Ill.: Chiron, 1987.

van der Post, Sir Laurens. *A Walk with a White Bushman*. In conversation with Jean-Marc Pottiez. London: Penguin, 1988.

van Meurs, Jos. *Jungian Literary Criticism, 1920–1980*. With John Kidd. Metuchen, N.J.: The Scarecrow Press, 1988.

Walker, Barbara G. *The Crone: Woman of Age, Wisdom, and Power*. San Francisco: Harper & Row, 1985.

———. *The Woman's Encyclopedia of Myths and Secrets*. San Francisco: Harper & Row, 1983.

Walker, Steven F. "Landscape as Compensation: Some Multicultural Perspectives." *Studies in the Humanities* 19.2 (1992): 110–25.

———. "Literal Truth and Soul-Making Fiction in R.K. Narayan's Novel *The English Teacher*: Spiritualist Fantasy Versus Jungian Psychology?" *Weber Studies: An*

Interdisciplinary Journal of the Humanities 6.2 (1989): 43–52. [conversations with the anima in a modern Indian novel]

——. "Les mythes dans la tragédie: nouvelles perspectives jungiennnes." *Toward a Theory of Comparative Literature*. Ed. Mario J. Valdés. New York: Peter Lang, 1990. 87–96.

——. *Theocritus*. Boston: Twayne/G.K. Hall, 1980. [The second chapter presents a Jungian perspective on the pastoral idylls.]

Weaver, Rix. *The Old Wise Woman*. Boston: Shambhala, 1991.

Wehr, Demaris S. *Jung and Feminism: Liberating Archetypes*. Boston: Beacon Press, 1987.

Werblowsky, R.J. Zwi. *Lucifer and Prometheus: A Study of Milton's Satan*. Introduction by C.G. Jung. London: Routledge & Kegan Paul, 1952.

Westman, Heinz. *The Structure of Biblical Myths*. Dallas: Spring, 1983.

Wheelwright, Jane Hollister. *For Women Growing Older: The Animus*. Houston: C.G. Jung Educational Center of Houston, 1984.

Wheelwright, Joseph B. *Psychological Types*. San Francisco: C.G. Jung Institute of San Francisco, 1973.

Whitmont, Edward C. *The Return of the Goddess: Femininity, Aggression and the Modern Grail Quest*. New York: Crossroad, 1984.

Woodman, Marion. *Addiction to Perfection: The Still Unravished Bride*. Toronto: Inner City, 1982.

——. *The Owl Was a Baker's Daughter: Anorexia Nervosa and the Repressed Feminine*. Toronto: Inner City, 1980.

——. *The Pregnant Virgin: A Process of Psychological Transformation*. Toronto: Inner City, 1985.

——. *The Ravaged Bridegroom: Masculinity in Women*. Toronto: Inner City, 1990.

Woolger, Jennifer, and Roger Woolger. *The Goddess Within: A Guide to the Eternal Myths That Shape Women's Lives*. New York: Fawcett/Columbine, 1990.

Wyly, James. *The Phallic Quest: Priapus and Masculine Inflation.* Toronto: Inner City, 1989.

Young-Eisendrath, Polly. *Hags and Heroes: A Feminist Approach to Jungian Psychotherapy with Couples.* Toronto: Inner City, 1984.

Zabriskie, Beverley. "Incest and Myrrh: Father-Daughter Sex in Therapy." *Quadrant* 15 (1982): 5–24. [Myrrha, Cinyras, and Adonis]

Zabriskie, Philip T. "Goddesses in Our Midst." *Quadrant* 17 (1974): 34–45.

Zoja, Luigi. *Drugs, Addiction and Initiation: The Modern Search for Ritual.* Foreword by Adolf Guggenbühl-Craig. Boston: Sigo, 1989.